FIRST IMPRESSIONS
AND
STUDIES FROM NATURE
IN
HINDOSTAN

FIRST IMPRESSIONS
AND
STUDIES FROM NATURE
IN
HINDOSTAN

EMBRACING

AN OUTLINE OF THE VOYAGE TO CALCUTTA,
AND
FIVE YEARS' RESIDENCE IN BENGAL AND THE DOAB,
FROM

MDCCCXXXI TO MDCCCXXXVI

BY

THOMAS BACON LIEUT,
OF THE BENGAL HORSE ARTILLERY.

IN TWO VOLUMES

VOL. II

GYAN

Published by

Gyan Publishing House
5, Ansari Road
Daryaganj, New Delhi-110002
Phone: 011-47034999, 9811692060
E-mail: books@gyanbooks.com

Distribution Network
gyanbooks.com
India, USA, Canada, UK, Australia, France

ISBN : 978-81-212-2204-4 (Set)
ISBN : 978-81-212-2206-8 (HB)
First Published, 1837

2nd Impression 2021

Printed at: Gyan Press, Delhi.

First Impressions and Studies from Nature
in
Hindostan Vol. II
Author: Thomas Bacon Lieut

FIRST IMPRESSIONS

AND

STUDIES FROM NATURE

IN

HINDOSTAN;

EMBRACING

AN OUTLINE OF THE VOYAGE TO CALCUTTA,

AND

FIVE YEARS' RESIDENCE IN BENGAL AND THE DOÁB,

FROM

MDCCCXXXI to MDCCCXXXVI.

BY THOMAS BACON, LIEUT.

OF THE BENGAL HORSE ARTILLERY.

IN TWO VOLUMES.

VOL. II.

LONDON:

WM. H. ALLEN AND CO.

LEADENHALL STREET.

1837.

CONTENTS OF VOL. II.

CHAPTER I.

WILD SPORTS.

PAGE

A Second Party.—The Kádir Dhoon.—Daring Exploit of the Shikarri.—An Expedient.—Firing the Jungul.—A Home Charge.—The Elephant Wounded.—Allotment of Sport.—A Wild Elephant.—Attack of the Wild Elephant.—The Charge, Chase, and Death.—Dimensions of the Elephant.—Charms.—The Remains.—Value, Management, and Training of the Elephant.—The Mahawut.—Instances of Extraordinary Sagacity.—A Rescue.—Domestic Habits.—Crossing a Quicksand.—a Narrow Escape.—The Tiger's Leap 1

CHAPTER II.

SIRDHANA.—THE BEGUM SUMROO AND HER COURT.

Titles of the Begum Sumroo.—Amount of the Sirdhana Revenue.—The Palace and Chapel.—Native Christians.—Summers, the Begum's Husband.—The Attack of Patna, and the Massacre.—Capture of Monghir.—Zeb-

PAGE

ul-Nissa.—Murderous Plot.—Suicide of Summers.—A Living Burial.—L'Oiseau.—The Begum's Person.—The Durbar.— Profuse Liberality.— Colonel Dyce.—The Heir-elect. — Officers of the Service. — Bishop Julius Cæsar, the Padri Sahib.—High Mass and Grand Fête at Christmas.—Entertainment of the Visitors —Pride and Precedence.—Homage due to the Emperor of Dehli.—Death of the Begum.—The Funeral Ceremony.—Resumption of the Jaghir.—The Will 32

CHAPTER III.

JOURNEY TO THE HIMÁLA MOUNTAINS.

A Traveller's Choice.—A Start.—Foretastes of Pleasure.—The Roads.—Going down to a Watering Place.—Palki-dák.—Deobund.—Want of Irrigation.—Saharunpore.—School of Monkies.—The Botanical Garden.—Ingenious Method of Constructing Wells.—The Sivalic Ridge.—The Beauties of Khéri Pass.—Dreams and Realities.—Delights of a Dák Trip.—An Unbidden Visitor.—Giving in marriage.—Deyra Dhoon.—Rajhpore.—Foot of the Mountains.—Advice to a Hungry Man.—Ascent of the Mountains. — A Dilemma. — A Venture. — A Perilous Pass, during a Storm.—The Paharri Track.—Bracing Atmosphere.—A Mountain Beauty.—Seven to One.—Easy Divorce.—A Native's Defence of Polygamy 61

CHAPTER IV.

THE HIMÁLA MOUNTAINS.

MUSSOORI AND LANDOUR.

PAGE

Altitudes.—The Sanitarium.—Intended Abolition of the Depôt.—Its Advantages, and Supposed Economy.—The Snowy Range.—Altitudes of the Snowy Peaks.—Compared with the Andes.—The Goitres.—Position of Mussoori.—Panoramic View of the Dhoon.—An Awkward Disclosure.— Portraits.— Family Secrets.— The Joudpore Expedition.—Reports and Rumours.—A Newsmonger.—Opening the Budget.—Phenomena.—Signs of the Times.—Death of Major Blundel by a Fall over the Precipice. — Landour Burial-ground. — Hair Breadth Escapes.—Matter for the Virtuosi 94

CHAPTER V.

THE HIMÁLA MOUNTAINS.

The Bum-bailiff Abroad.—False Alarm.—An Exquisite at Home.—Something Sentimental.—The Common-place-book.—Touching the Society of Merat.—A Review of Public Amusements.—Their Decay.—Mischief-makers. —The Ladies.—A Fracas.—Paternal Affection.—Bear-hunting Expedition.—A Panic among the Koolies.—Flushing the Game.—A Leopard.—Badul Kooli Moun-

PAGE

tain.—The Bear's Track.—Encounter with a Bear.—A Fearful Overthrow.—Cave in the Mountain-side.—Interior of the Den.—The Guides Confounded.—Despoiling the Castle.—Kidnappers.—A Fatal Step.—Conveyances.—The Jaunpaun.—Flights of Romance.—A Restive Pony.—Rapid Dák-travelling.—Return to the Plains 118

CHAPTER VI.

HURDWAR DURING THE FESTIVAL.

The Practice-Season.—Forced Marches.—Travelling Distance of Hurdwar.—The Route.—Languor on the March.—Shooting in the Junguls.—A Ruinous Purchase.—Handsome Equipment.—Late Travelling.—Face to Face with a Tiger.—A Happy Escape.—Entrance to Kunkhul by Moonlight.—Traveller's Fare.—Symptoms of the Mela.—Main Street of Kunkhul.—A Tamasha.—Uproar and Confusion.—Hospitality-hunting.—Hurri-Burree.—An Awkward Mistake.—Grand Season of Pilgrimage.—Derivation of the Name Hurdwar.—Position of the Town.—The Ghát.—Estimate of the Concourse.—The Crush.—Wholesale Destruction of Life.—Female Beauties.—The Ceremony of Ablution.—Appropriation of the Offerings.—The Bazaars.—Sweet-meat Venders.—Tame Fish.—Articles of Trade.—The Cattle-market.—The Gaour.—The Wild Ass.—Native Horse-dealers and Jockies.—Mode of Purchase.—Slave Girls for Sale.—Price of Slaves.—Story of

PAGE

Rahmea, the Slave Girl.—An Elopement.—The Fakhir. —A Treacherous Physician.—The Cheat Unmasked.— Fate of the Beautiful Luchmi.—Excursion into Deyra Dhoon. — Lundhoura. — High Life Below Stairs. — A Counterfeit Rajha.—Imposition Detected.—The Use of a Goat.—Detour through the Junguls.—Tiger Shooting. —A Disastrous Campaign.—A New Enemy.—Malignity of the Terhaie Fever 152

CHAPTER VII.

ANCIENT DEHLI AND SHAHJEHANABAD.

Motives for the Trip.—The Advantage of Display.—A Married Sub.— The Road. — Begumabad. — Singular Instance of Honesty.—A Breakfast by the Way.—Conjugal Felicity.—Trials of Temper.—Fording the Hindon. —A Lady in Distress.—Crossing the Jumna.—Entrance into Dehli.—Arrival at the Begum's Palace.—Distribution of the Garrison.—A New Dilemma.—A Friend in Need.—Inspired with Prophecy.—Courteous Thanks.— The Modern City.—The Population.—The Founder.— Plan of the Fort.—The Gates.—The Chandni Chouk.— Streets and Aqueducts. — Alli Mirdun's Canal. — The Imperial Palace of Akbur Shah.—The Gateways and Courts.—The Dewani Khas and Moti Musjid.—The Palace Gardens, Pavilions, Baths, &c.—The Emperor and his Suite.—Prince Mirza Sulleem.—The Jumma Musjid. — Shah Jehan's Well. — Roshun-ud-Dowla's Mosque.—Massacre of Dehli in 1739 201

CHAPTER VIII.

ANCIENT DEHLI AND SHAHJEHANABAD.

PAGE

Rumours of Death.—Fulfilment of the Prophecy.—Public Apprehensions.—The Nawab Shumsh-ud-deen.—Assassination of Mr. Fraser the Resident.—Investigations.—Impeachment of the Nawab.—His Imprisonment.—Development of the Plot.—The Accomplices.—Apprehension of the Perpetrator.—Disturbances at Jeypore.—Conduct of the British.—Outrage upon Major Alves the Political Agent, with his Party.—The Rani.—Dastardly Murder of Mr. Blake.—The Hindus Defile their Temples with Christian Blood.—Apathy of the British Government.—Sentence of Death passed on Shumsh-ud-deen.—The Eve of Execution.—Interview with the Nawab.—The Last Hour.—Scene from the Ramparts.—Assembled Chiefs.—Prejudice Strong in Death 242

CHAPTER IX.

ANCIENT DEHLI AND SHAHJEHANABAD.

Colonel Skinner, C.B.—His Character and Services.—The Jaghir of Belaspore.—His Sons.—Dehli Church Built by the Colonel.—Native Irregular Cavalry.—Maharajha Hindu Ráo.—His Character.—Invited to a Nauch.—Nauchnis and the Nauch.—Dresses, Ornaments, Songs, Dances, &c.—Alfina, the Catalani of India.—The Nose-

PAGE

Ring.—Punna the Persian Songstress.—The Guf-ta-gu. —Dancing Boys.—Native Refection.—The Scene by Daylight.—Debauchery.—Indraput, Ancient Dehli.—The Ruins.—Mausoleum of Zufdir Junge.—The Gardens. —The Kootab Minar.—The Ascent.—View from the Top of the Tower.—A Stranger.—The Old Man's Fall from the Summit.—Ruins of Toglukabad.—Emperor Hummaione's Tomb.—The Barber's Tomb.—Shrine of Nizam-ud-deen Olea.—Exquisite Sculptures.—The Serai and Bowli.—Jumpers and Divers.—A Frightful Leap — Scrambling for Money. — Jey Singh's Observatory. — The Old Fort.—Feroze Shah's Laht.—Ancient Inscription lately Deciphered.—Attempts of the Jhauts to overthrow the Pillar.—The Madrissa and Serais.—Fatal Issue of a Mock Execution.—Orders to Quit.—Siege of Dehli by Holkar 277

CHAPTER X.

VOYAGE DOWN THE JUMNA.

Leave Merat.—Dehli again.—The Residency.—Native Pomp.—A Visit of Ceremony.—The Procession.—The Durbar.—The Visit returned.—Retinue of the British. —The Rajha's Encampment of Velvet and Gold.—The Rohksut.—Taking Leave.—Terrible Earthquake.—The Jumna.—Delights of a Native Boat.—Fellow Travellers. —A Reduced Train.—Amusements by the Way.—A Christmas Feast.—High and dry on a Sand-bank.—Bindrabund.—The Birth-place of Krishna.—Miracles

PAGE

and Exploits of the God.—Monkies and Mendicants.—Town and Station of Muttra.—Reduction of the Cantonment.—Titles, Compliments, and Invitations 323

CHAPTER XI.

AGRA, FUTTEHPORE-SIKRI, AND SECUNDRA.

The Ancient Village of Agra.—Akburabad founded.—Palaces and Buildings within the Fort.—The great Gun destroyed.—The Marble Pavilion.—Domes of Gold.—The Moti Musjid.—Emperor Akbur the Great.—His Character and early Reign.—Treachery and Rebellion of Bhiram Kahn.—Death of the Minister.—Abul Fazil.—Revenue of the State.—Roads and Aqueducts.—The Kōs Minars.—Futtehpore-Sikri.—Cold Weather.—The Great Gate and Quadrangle.—Shrine of Sheik Selim Tchisti,—The Dewan Aum or Hall of Justice.—Akbur's Durbars.—The Hatti Durwása, and Tower of Tusks.—The Guide.—Bird's-eye View.—The Scene by Moonlight.—Death of Akbur.—Accession of Jehanghir.—Secundra, Akbur's Tomb.—Error regarding the Inscription.—The Gardens.—Jehanghir.—Shah Jehan.—Aurungzebe.—Rebellion of Aurungzebe, who usurps the Empire.—Imprisonment of Shah Jehan.—The City Streets.—The Tajh Mahal.—Carvings and Mosaics.—Plan of the Building.—The Minarets.—The Interior.—Neur Jehan, Shah Jehan's favourite Begum.—Sarcophagus and Screen.—Cost and duration of Erection.—Reverberations.—Incidental Effects.—Grant of the Com-

PAGE

pany for Repairs. — The Gateways, Gardens, &c. — Supposed Design of a similar nature on the opposite Bank, unfounded. — Offer of Purchase at £30,000. — Tomb of Etimaun-ud-dowla.—The Jumma Musjid.— The Tajh Mahal by Moonlight.—A Lounge on Sunday 348

CHAPTER XII.

THE JUMNA FROM AGRA TO ALLAHABAD.

The Ravines, a Harbour for Dukhaits.—Exploits of the Dukhaits.—Mode of Attack.—Ettaia.—Impudence of the Brahmins. — The River Chumbul. — Contrast in Scenery. —The Limestone Bar. —The Goor-Goorri.— Encounter with the Dukhaits.—A Hot Pursuit.—The Prisoners. —A Dukhait's Philosophy. —The Thugs, a Race of Murderers and Banditti.—Their Habitations. —Their Vast Influence.—Means for the Suppressing of Thuggi. —The Blood Drinking Kalli.—Schemes for Inveigling their Victims.—Omens and Ceremonies of the Murderers.—Their Mode of Attack.—Town and Fort of Kalpi.—Temple of Krishna.—Action with the Maharhattas. — Hummiapore. — My Boat on Fire.—A Dangerous Predicament.—Village and Hills of Mháo.— Caverns and Brahminical Remains.—Isolated Rock of Daraol.—Allahabad 385

CHAPTER XIII.

THE GANGES.—DINAPORE.

RETURN TO CALCUTTA.

PAGE

Dinapore.—A Hurricane.—Wreck of my Boat.—Property Saved.—A Dangerous Position.—A Treacherous Leap. —Any Port in a Storm.—Friends in Need.—The Iron Steamers.—"The George Swinton."—Speculations of the Natives.—Steam and Gas Speculations.—A Passing Look upon the Past.—Embarkation.—Return to Old England 422

LIST OF ILLUSTRATIONS.

1. Futtehpore-Sikri .... Frontispiece.
2. The Snowy Range of the Himálas from Landour... *page* 97
3. Mountains east of Mussoori 99
4. The Snowy Range from Mussoori 149
5. Akbur Shah's Palace and Old Fort.—Dehli 229
6. The Jumna Musjid.—Dehli 237
7. Ruins of Toglukabad 305
8. Feroze Shah's Laht.—Dehli 315
9. Serai, near the Ajhmere-gate.—Dehli 318
10. Bindrabund 343
11. Muttra 345
12. Face and Inscription of the Sarcophagus 377
13. Marble Screen in the Tajh Mahal.—Agra 377
14. Butteesa 411
15. Kalpi, on the Jumna 412
16. Isolated Rock of Daraol 419

FIRST IMPRESSIONS,

&c. &c. &c.

CHAPTER I.

WILD SPORTS.—*continued.*

THE following morning, we carried our camp to a village called Maerzapore, higher up on the left bank of the river: we scoured the country for game in our progress, and found it teeming with deer, of which we killed a very large number. Mirchi left us, and set out upon a circuit, to gather information of more tigers: but, in this instance, we stole a march upon him; for, upon our arrival at the village where our camp was to be pitched, several of the *ráiuts* came forth to meet us, with news of a couple of these formidable beasts, who had been dealing destruction among their herds, and breaking through their enclosures.

We instantly remounted our elephants and set forth in pursuit of them; but we had scarcely got beyond the boundaries of our camp, when we espied a strong party of sportsmen, having eight elephants in their train, advancing in the direction of the ground towards which our own intentions were bent. Their object was so evident, that we at once suspected our informants of endeavouring to sell us a bad bargain, having already apprized the other party of the position of the game; no uncommon practice among these rascals, by which they often obtain a double reward: I therefore ordered the spokesman and ostensible leader of them to be taken upon an elephant, in order that he might be punished for his fraud, if our surmises should prove correct: I then mounted my horse and galloped off to the advancing party to ascertain their movements. They turned out to be from Merat; men whom we knew well, and whom Mirchi had quoted as crack shots.

They were now upon the same scent as ourselves, and being before-hand with us, claimed the game, according to the custom in similar cases. I gave them a hint that we should be glad to join them in the chase, but it was not taken, and I, therefore, returned to wreak my displeasure upon our false informant, having confronted him with the other party, and found him guilty of the imposture.

We were too well acquainted with the skill of the other sportsmen to wish to continue anywhere in their neighbourhood, knowing that they would be likely to leave us greenhorns but a scanty share of the choice fruits of the field. Finding moreover that they had ordered their tents to be pitched close to ours, it became necessary that we should enter into some arrangement with them as to the route to be pursued by each, in order that we might not again cross each others' sport.

They returned to camp soon after we had finished our breakfast, but they came empty-handed, for the tigers had quitted their ground, probably in consequence of our firing in the morning, before we heard of them. At dinner, we all sat down together, and came to an understanding that one party should take the left, the other the right of certain villages throughout the *Kádir*;* and having

* The Kádir, or Kádir Dhoōn, is a long tract of country lying within the old bed of the Ganges, forming a valley from one to seven miles in breadth, and extending from Ghurmuktisa as far north as Hurdwar, where it is connected by a narrow pass with the gigantic valley of Deyra Dhoon. The Kádir has apparently been cut away below the level of the surrounding country, by the constant shifting of the river. Its soil is sandy and much impregnated with natron, supporting little vegetation, except the rank jungul grass, and here and there patches of the *jhaint* shrub; it is intersected with deep and unwholesome morasses and quicksands, which afford, in

disposed of this matter to the satisfaction of all parties, we passed the bottle round, and turned the talk upon the merits of the different gun-smiths, and the efficacies of various proportions in charge, weight of ball, &c. ; just as a posse of doctors will invariably be found conferring upon their cases ; a military man discussing appointments and promotions ; the sons of Neptune conversing about clippers, tonnage, cut, &c. ; or parsons comparing souls and salaries. The conversation next ran upon the meritorious exploits of our friend Mirchi, and his admirable qualifications for his office.

"Ah ! he's the keenest sportsman among us after all," said one of the old hands ; "I'll tell you a tale of him which will show his daring ; it occurred while I was out with him, last year. Fred. pass the bottle——Oh ! he's a fine fellow, old Mirchi.—*Koi hi? táza chillaum lao.**—It was at Jácdpore ; we had been for several hours beating about in search of a tiger, which had been playing Tom and Jerry with all the *machaum wallas*† in the neighbourhood, and still avoided

many places, secure retreats to numbers of tigers ; the weight of the elephant rendering it impossible for him to cross to them.

* Who's there? Bring a fresh supply of tobacco for my *hookka.*

† Men set to watch the crops from a sort of a platform raised high in the air upon bamboos, so that they may have a good command of observation.

the search of our scouts, and the track of our elephants. Well, at last Mirchi thought he had got him, and conducted us to a fine promising patch of jungul, which we beat and re-beat, until we, for the first time, thought the old man at fault, and were about to give it up as a bad job; when a tuft of cover, hardly large enough to attract our notice, led Mirchi to exclaim once more, that he was on the right scent, and pushing forward his elephant, he went to reconnoitre the spot. He found it surrounded with a broad *fussun*,* which he thought would hardly be practicable to our elephants; so dismounting, the hardy fellow, with only his usual weapons, waded to the thicket in the centre, and then crawling upon his hands and knees, he thrust his head and shoulders into the very knot of grass where the tiger was supposed to lie. We shouted to dissuade him; we offered him fire-arms; but no, he kept his ground; and two seconds afterwards, we saw him backing out again, as coolly and as cautiously as he had entered, a sure sign that the game lay there. He had seen the tiger, and positively declared that he had stared him in the face within twenty yards. 'Why, Mirchi, you old fool,' said I, 'how could you be such a booby as

* Swamp, and decayed vegetation.

to go and stuff your head into the very jaws of the beast?'—' Have you got any tigers in England, except those that are taken from our junguls?' retorted the old fellow; ' you don't know them so well as I do, sir. Do you think the tiger there would have been as sly as tigers are reported, and as I know them to be, if he had quitted his cover to attack me, and so have exposed himself to you all, whom he knew to be armed to the teeth in search of him. *Wa! Wa! meri buchha*, you must eat some more *chuppatti*, as Kummul Sahib says, before you can teach Mirchi any secrets about the air he breathes.' "

" *Wa! Wa!*" exclaimed old Mirchi, *in propriâ personâ*, as he made his appearance in the tent, interrupting the recital of his own valiant deeds; " ' *Wa! Wa! meri buchha*, Mirchi is sure to hear his own name in your mouth whenever he comes into your presence. Your slave hopes you do not call him as many bad names behind his back as you do to his face. I'm sorry I don't know your honour's language, or I might have heard something worth returning."

" Well, Mirchi, my son, I was only telling the lads of the day at Jáedpore, when you poked your head into the tiger's mouth, and drew it out again before you were quite certain whether the beast was a tiger or buffalo."

"It's true, great sir," replied the old man, with a dry assumption of humility; "Mirchi before now has been compelled to ask your sage opinion in such matters. Perhaps you may deign to remember how that day's sport was concluded."

"Oh! yes, Mirchi, I was just coming to that part of the story when you interrupted me; so now we'll make you tell it for yourself."

"It does not require a very long story, sir, to tell the remainder of that hunt. If I remember right, a few hot-headed young gentlemen wished to urge their elephants through the *fussun* against the will of the sagacious beasts, and the opinion of their old *shikarri*, and would probably have stuck there in the mud for ever, if they had been left to their own counsel. 'Mirchi,' cried one, 'are you sure the *fussun* wont bear us?' 'Mirchi,' said another, 'are you certain we can't go on horseback?' 'Mirchi,' exclaimed a third, 'are you positive we can't go on foot?' 'No, gentlemen,' replied Mirchi; 'man is the lord of the creation, so when it is inconvenient for him to go to the tiger, the tiger must come to him.' 'Nonsense,' says one of the gentlemen, 'we can't drag the place, so how can we drive out the tiger?' 'Why, I'll show you,' said Mirchi, so he borrowed a little fire from the sun, and set the jungul in flames upon the windward side, so that the tiger was driven from his haunt, and took refuge under the muzzles of the gentlemen's guns."

"Bravo, Mirchi!" cried the beginner of the tale; "you shall have a glass of wine in reward for your story."

"*Saláam Sahib,*" said the old man, as he touched his forehead, and suddenly withdrew, on mention of the forbidden spirit.

"I see by the old gentleman's eye," said a happy-looking sportsman, in a ragged shooting-jacket, peeping from under cover of a broad-brimmed green hat, drawn over his forehead to screen his eyes from the light, while he puffed away at his *chillaum,* "I see, by the old gentleman's eye, that he is loaded with news, but he must wait till we've digested our dinners. So, you gents have got Miss Eima out again; I thought she would have been lame for life. That was an awkward shot of yours, friend ——"

"Oh do tell us the upshot of that charge. The *mahawut* gives a very confused account of it, and doesn't know exactly who wounded the elephant after all."

"Why," replied the cozy man in the ragged jacket, "we had the party which you see here, with the exception of yourselves, and one day while using Eima as a beater, because, poor lass, she had been over-worked, we flushed a magnificent tiger, and brought him at once to the charge. He made a home push at Eima, which none of us were able to avert; for the brute was completely within our line before we discovered him, so that we could not pour in the lead, for fear of injuring one another. One battery alone could play upon him in his advance, and that was from our good and jolly companion opposite, who, although he's as sure as a rifle, is, begging his pardon, as slow as a match-lock: and so the tiger effected a lodgement upon poor Eima's head, closing in gallant style, and taking an eye under one paw, and an ear under another, at the same time burrying his fangs deep in the upper part of her trunk with a low gurling noise as of bloodthirsty delight and unslaked vengeance, while he tore and mangled the flesh. Having thus made good his charge, the brute drew up his legs and planted them wide apart over Eima's face, safe from her attempts to crush them by kneeling: thus, in spite of Eima's best efforts, the tiger had, for a while, the fight all his own way, and continued to lacerate her trunk most pitiably. At the moment of the charge, the *mahawut* was fortunately upon the *guddi*,* instead of in his usual seat, or he would probably have fallen a victim to the fury of the beast.

"It was at first quite impossible for any of us to assist Eima with safety to herself, for in her violent endeavours to shake off her antagonist, it was quite as likely that we should hit one as the other. At last our matchlock friend there got his elephant to close quarters with the belligerent parties, and succeeded in getting a shot at the tiger; but, alas! alas!—Oh! give the poor fellow the dish-cover there to hide his head under.—Eima, making a sudden evolution, received his ill drected ball in the off hind-foot. My right-hand neighbour then pushed in, and got a sight of the tiger's head from the opposite side, so that in thus looking down upon him he lessened the chances of wounding the elephant; taking a steady aim, he let fly both barrels in quick succession, and dropt the brute as dead as a stone at Eima's feet. She, poor thing, was so enraged, that she threw herself upon

* Cushion upon the elephant's back.

the carcase, and kneaded it to the semblance of a jelly before her ire was at all quenched. But, come, we had better have in old Mirchi and cut in the *kubbur* (news) for to-morrow."

Mirchi appeared and opened his budget. He had a couple of tigers close in the neighbourhood; and, being here altogether, both parties had an equal claim to the sport, being allowed, according to the established rule, the option of a toss-up for the game, or of forming one expedition in pursuit of it. The latter was agreed upon for the following morning; but seven being, as one of our number remarked, "too big a body altogither intirely, for the rale sport," we determined to dissolve our co-operation immediately after the attack. Mirchi had a tiger for us, he said, at a village called Usseelpore, where the *ráiuts* would readily point him out to us; and for the senior party, he had game within their beat, to which he would conduct them in person.

The next morning, we were upon our ground by sunrise, and having despatched the two tigers with our united forces, we separated, and marched one to the right, and the other to the left of the boundary we had laid down. At Usseelpore we found that Mirchi had not deceived us, for within an hour after our arrival at the place, we had bagged the sport; and hearing of no more tigers, we turned our batteries upon the smaller game. While thus employed in pursuit of wild hog, deer, &c. we came suddenly upon the track of a wild elephant, who, by the recent marks of his depredations, and by the freshness of the boughs which he had broken, we were convinced could be at no great distance from us. We followed his track for at least a couple of miles, but as we saw nothing of him, and did not meet with any natives, I thought the surest plan would be to mount my horse, and gallop into the nearest village for intelligence. This I accordingly did, and found the villagers afraid to venture forth into the junguls on account of the terrible doings of this wild elephant. They said that, within the last few days, he had come down from the Dhoon, whence he had been expelled by the rest of his herd for misconduct; and that in consequence of his disgrace, he had become almost mad with despair, and had in pure mischief and rage been laying waste, and destroying everything which came before him. Several men had fallen victims to his fury; and he had thrown down villages and torn up the fruit-trees. He was now, they said, carrying on his work of destruction in the neighbourhood of Selimpore, only a few miles distant.

Bah! thought I, old Mirchi has played us griffs a slippery trick, because he thought he could not depend upon us. He has sent us to beat up the quarters of a single tiger, and has taken the knowing ones off to Selimpore, for the wild elephant. Moreover, it now occurred to me that, during the whole day, a very heavy fire had been kept up in the direction of Selimpore, much more incessant than would have been the case if the party had only been engaged upon tigers; so that the only conclusion was, that they had encountered this most terrible inhabitant of the junguls. We had measured his footsteps in the morning, and found them nearly half as large again as those of our own elephants, and we therefore sadly regretted not having a hand in the attack of so fine a beast.

I returned with this information to my companions, and, having held a council of war, we determined to infringe for once the terms of our treaty, and march that evening to Selimpore to hear the news, not doubting that a most glorious action had been fought. We started forthwith, and arrived in their camp just in time to hear the engagement fought through again over the dinner-table.

It proved that they had been holding a council of war upon the expediency of sending an envoy to our camp, for the purpose of inviting us to join our forces in the expedition; knowing full well the power and fury of the antagonist with whom they had to deal. But, on the other hand, they feared that any delay in their movements might give the enemy an opportunity of declining the engagement, and of beating a retreat to those wilds where they would be unable to pursue him; after a mature debate therefore they came to the determination of giving him immediate battle, at all hazards.

The wild elephant had taken up his position in a large *tōp*, or garden, of mango-trees, through which ran a road leading from one village to another; and having established his head-quarters here, he suffered no one to approach him; already he had punished with death five or six travellers who had unwittingly intruded upon his solitude.

The attacking party advanced to their work in a close and compact body, armed to the teeth with every barrel in the camp, having the four *háodas* in the front rank, and the four *guddi* elephants bringing up the rear; their object being, not to alarm their adversary more than they could help, by too great a display of their strength, lest he should fly the contest; and at the same time it was necessary that they should take with them a sufficient force, to give them a hope of safety and of victory.

As they drew near the scene of the intended action, they beheld their mighty enemy walking to and fro beneath the trees, and as soon as he perceived them, instead of decamping, which they had feared he would, he walked forth as if to meet them. When he saw the armed men in the *háodas* with appendages which belong not to his kind, and that they continued to advance upon him, he evidently became suspicious of hostility; and with a terrible trumpeting he again withdrew beneath his cover, signifying by every possible means his exceeding wrath and displeasure at the invasion. Still the assailants moved on towards the ground which he had taken up, and although he did not fly, he showed signs of trepidation and uneasiness, which led them to believe that he would if possible avoid the contest; they therefore deemed it expedient to open their batteries upon him at once, being within sixty or seventy yards of him.

The heavy volley thus unexpectedly poured in

upon him, for a moment or two staggered and confounded him, nearly all the bullets having struck him in the head. He speedily recovered from the shock, however, and stirring himself to the very extremity of his fearful rage, he threw his ponderous trunk up over his head, and advancing well his huge tusks, he rushed with terrible fury upon his assailants. Had he succeeded in making good his charge, he would undoubtedly, by his superior power and weight, have overthrown any of the domestic elephants with which he might have come in contact. The *mahawuts* behaved bravely; but, with their most strenuous efforts, they were unable to keep their elephants steady, when their antagonist advanced to the charge; three of them gave way a few paces, leaving the fourth a little in advance, and exposed to the entire shock of the attack.

The sportsmen, however, were too well experienced to suffer a slight confusion among their elephants to annoy them, and when their furious adversary had arrived within about twenty yards, having reserved their fire, they discharged upon him a second equally strong battery, with very steady aim: so well directed were the shots, that nearly every ball took effect in his head, and with more destructive issue than the former, being so much closer. His head was in a measure protected by his trunk, which was raised for the purpose of dealing vengeance, but this delicate member was dreadfully lacerated, and bled profusely. This checked his career, and utterly disconcerted his charge; but he again collected his powers, and returned to the assault.

His attempt was directed more particularly against the elephant who had stood firm in the last charge, and was still in advance of the others; and these two, being only a few paces apart, would certainly have come in dreadful collision, had not the rider, by a most deliberate and well-timed shot, struck the wild elephant in the eye, which deprived him of sight upon that side, causing him to swerve from his direct charge, and apparently inflicting upon him very acute pain.

Another volley from all the batteries completely perplexed him, and finding himself much disabled, and foiled in his repeated charges, he fled the field. Chase was immediately given, and a continued fire was kept up upon him, which brought him again and again to the charge, but without success; for the wary and skilful sportsmen, whenever they observed him to be preparing for the onset, reserved their fire for the moment of attack, and, by their excellent aim, were sure to turn him in his career. It was no easy matter, however, to despatch so enormous an animal, and before he fell he had sustained their united fire more than two hours.

He was ten feet seven inches in height, and of enormous bulk; his head was preserved as a trophy, as were also the hairs from the tip of his tail, which, by-the-bye, the natives believe to be possessed of a most potent charm; being very thick and jet black, they are susceptible of a high polish, and are frequently wrought into bracelets and other ornaments. The syrens of the East esteem a trinket made of these hairs as exceedingly valuable; and when presented by a lover, its magic virtues are precious beyond price, if all they say of it be true.

After hearing the above account from our more fortunate fellow sportsmen, we rode out to the place where he had fallen, for the purpose of viewing his remains. Every species of foul-stomached, carrion-devouring animal, both birds, beasts, and insects, were collected around his carcase, having torn forth the greater part of his intestines. A few discharges of our pieces put them all apparently to flight; but upon our nearer approach, we unhoused several jackals and dogs from his interior, who had been too busily engaged in the satisfaction of their filthy appetites to attend to our warning. The elephant was truly a stupendous beast, and those who shot him, calculated that, from the moment of their first engagement, until he fell, he must have received at least three hundred and fifty bullets.

Before quitting the subject, I may as well mention that, a fortnight afterwards, on my return towards cantonments, I visited the same spot, and found this elephant's hide dried over his ribs, looking like the hood of a waggon, and offering to those who might desire it, a covering from the weather: had we been so disposed, three of us might have dined within. The following year I again sought the spot, and found the bones bleaching in the sun, deprived of every vestige of flesh and sinew. I took one of his vertebræ as a curiosity, and have it to this day.

The next morning we again pursued our routes in two separate directions; but, as the reader has, perhaps, had sufficient of the sport, I will make no apology for digressing, to say a little about the elephants and their habits.

Very exaggerated stories are every-where circulated of the size of elephants found in India, and we hear people talking of this, which was really twenty feet high, and that, which was twenty-four feet. The largest elephant I ever saw was eleven feet seven inches. The commissariat elephants are generally fine animals, and they vary in height from eight to ten feet: they are chiefly from Deyra Dhoon, where they are caught in pitfalls by the natives, the old system of decoying them by the assistance of domestic elephants being exploded. After the animal has fallen into the pit, he is kept there without food or water, until the impatience of confinement gives way to hunger and thirst: he is allowed to starve till too weak to offer any very powerful resistance, and he is then supplied with earth and bundles of jungul grass, which he treads under him, and thus gradually raises himself from his prison. He has then one or two domestic elephants placed over him, to keep him in subjection, and has a scanty supply of food doled out to him as long as he behaves well; but the moment he grows unruly, he is beaten and starved again; so that, under so severe a discipline, he speedily learns to conduct himself with decorum.

Seven or eight months' tuition will generally render an elephant quite fit for any kind of work, and he is commonly sent to market within six months of his capture. The value of a properly-trained elephant in India, sound, and without blemish, varies from 800 to 3,000 rupees, according to their age, size, and acquirements; but the average price is about 1,000 or 1,500, for which latter sum a very good *shikarri* elephant may be purchased.

An elephant's behaviour in action against a tiger depends very much upon the courage and determination of the *mahawut*, who has at all times most complete command over the animal, even to death, when he chooses to exert it. If the driver be resolute and undaunted, the elephant will never disgrace himself; but if, on the contrary, the driver should show signs of fear or indecision, the animal will certainly turn tail and run off: and this, perhaps, is the greatest danger to which the tiger hunter is exposed, barring sun and climate; for when the animal is once fairly off, it is seldom that the *mahawut* can regain command of him, until he has thrust himself under a patch of trees, or some other cover, where the rider will, in all likelihood, be dashed to atoms. These accidents are, however, rare; the *mahawuts* being generally bold fellows, and as alive to the pleasure and excitement of the sport as most of their masters.

The more we see of these noble animals, the more our admiration is excited by them; their docility and sagacity are fully equal to all that has been said of them by historians and others. I could tell many wonderful anecdotes of them, which fell under my own observation; one or two, perhaps, may not be unacceptable to the reader.

Upon one occasion, while shooting upon an elephant called Bansmutti, belonging to the Company's commissariat, at Merat, I had lost the peg which supports the top of the *chatta*, or umbrella, and as we were passing under some trees, I cut off small branches, with the intention of making a new one. The material, however, was found unfit for the purpose, being too green, and I told the *mahawut* to stop and let the servant dismount to find a piece of dry wood. The man replied that there was no occasion for any one to get down, as the elephant would give a piece up. He then struck the animal with the *hankus*, or goad, and told her to find a piece of stick. The elephant immediately gave him in her trunk a handful of dried leaves, which the *mahawut* rejected;

she then took up a quantity of dust, which was also refused by the *mahawut*, who bestowed one or two smart blows, and showers of abuse, upon poor Bansmutti, for her want of intelligence: she then gave up a stick about as thick as a man's wrist, for which she was commended, but told that a smaller stick would do better; and so on, the *mahawut* continued to alter his directions, until a suitable piece of wood was obtained, the elephant moving on at her usual pace all the time, and picking up as she went along whatever she thought the *mahawut* guided her to.

Upon another occasion, I was marching with a friend, who had a vicious turk of a horse, that was always kept muzzled, except while under the immediate care of his own groom; for, with the exception of this one man, no one could go near him with safety. He was always chained by the head and heels, and it was with great difficulty that his own *sáes* could groom him. One evening, my friend and I were sitting outside the tent, watching the man's attempts to get the muzzle on again, after the brute had eaten his corn; when he suddenly broke his pickets, knocked down his groom, and falling upon him, would have torn him to atoms with his teeth, had not one of our elephants stepped forward and driven him from his victim. This is the more extraordinary, as there is a great antipathy to horses among elephants, and they invariably shun them.

Another instance of sagacity, as great perhaps as either of the foregoing, was shewn by the same elephant only a few days afterwards. At a village called Munglour, a little dog belonging to my friend had fallen into a well, without any person having remarked the accident; the elephant, however, must either have seen it, or have heard the cries of the dog, for she went to the well, and there moving from side to side with considerable agitation, continued to cry out, as if for assistance. Her *mahawut* being asleep, no one replied to her repeated cries, believing her to be in want of water. Observing this, the sagacious animal went and aroused her driver from his sleep, and attracted him to examine the well by her movements. Here the dog was discovered and rescued.

It is not, however, the discernment and quick sense of the individual, as exhibited in such instances as the above, which so excites our interest and wonder, as the general sagacity and forethought displayed by the whole race generally, in their habits and in their daily practices. When an elephant returns to camp, after a day of toil and fatigue, if he be ever so hungry or thirsty, he will not taste the food placed before him until he has thoroughly cooled himself. He will stand for half an hour fanning himself with the bough of a tree, and using other methods of cooling himself, but he will not commence his meal until he is quite comfortable. A domestic elephant in India usually receives about twenty pounds of coarse flour daily, made up into large flat cakes; but the greater portion of his food consists in an enormous bundle of fresh boughs, which he himself brings from the forest; his favourite tree is the *nime*, large branches of which he crams in between every fragment of cake. There is no animal so deliberate and so well-behaved at his meals as is the elephant; he listens to every command of his driver, and he never refuses to quit his food, however hungry he may be, provided he sees it put by in a safe place.

It is truly amusing to watch the care and precaution with which an elephant advances into a morass; and if he entertains any suspicion of the soundness of the bottom, he signifies his opinion by a loud trumpeting, and refuses to advance. In such a case, it is very dangerous to urge him against his inclination, as he will seldom turn from any place which is really practicable; and of this his experience has taught him to judge with far greater nicety than his rider can pretend to. If by any chance he should happen to become entangled in a quicksand, his rider stands some chance of being tucked under him as a support; for his ingenuity prompts him to seize for this purpose every thing which comes within his reach, and he would look upon any one of his riders as of equal value with a bundle of grass.

When an elephant has cause to suspect the soundness of the ground over which he is passing, he strikes it at every step with the end of his trunk, and appears in this manner to satisfy himself at once, as he either advances without hesitation, or refuses to go forward altogether.

I was one day returning to camp with my companions, after having been out many hours, shooting over a country where we had a provoking scarcity of tigers; and disgusted with our slow sport, we were nodding with languor in our *háodas,* as our elephants walked patiently along, side by side, when suddenly a flourishing of trunks, and trumpeting from the whole party of elephants made us start to our feet. They broke into a rapid trot, which at first we could not at all account for, but we quickly perceived that the ground all around us was undulating in long waves like those of the sea. The fact was, that we were going over a very large quicksand, and the least hesitation or demur on the part of any of our elephants would instantly have plunged us into it, by breaking the solid crust which had formed over the danger, making the evil doubly perilous. The animals, however, were fully sensible of the extent of their risk, and kept up an easy shuffling sort of trot, gradually diverging from each other, until we again found ourselves on *terra firma*.

It was fortunate that four of our elephants were in the rear, for the surface yielded so much to our weight, that it was apparent very little more would have carried us through; from which, had it occurred, we should have had great difficulty in extricating ourselves: for not only was the quicksand of large extent, but there was, moreover, nothing in the neighbourhood with which we could have supplied our elephants for their support.

Here no elephant individually would have been in any danger, as the ground was more than sufficiently firm for the support of his weight; and we cannot be surprised that the animals should thus have been led into peril. That they should quicken their pace and tread gently over the treacherous ground, is scarcely wonderful; but that they should voluntarily have diverged from each other, so as to separate their weight, instead of huddling together, as is the nature of most animals when alarmed, affords ground, I think, for very great admiration and astonishment.

I could recount numberless stories in illustration of the vast sagacity and exceeding docility of the elephant, but I fear to extend my chapter on field-sports beyond the limits which my book will admit. Any man, who has been six months in the upper provinces of Bengal, will have collected anecdotes of tiger-hunting, &c. sufficient to fill a small library, even if he have never seen the sport. I will only trouble the reader with one more, and that a short one: I introduce it to shew that, though they seldom have the credit of it, black men have sometimes a little presence of mind about them. I know the anecdote to be true, though I cannot authenticate it with names and dates; I can only say, that it was told to me under circumstances which left me no reason to doubt the veracity of the relator.

A sportsman, while firing at a tiger, was thrown

from his *háoda* by à sudden evolution of the elephant, and fell within a few feet of the feline monster, who was excited to the very extremity of his fury by repeated wounds. The man was unable to rise immediately, and the infuriated tiger was upon the point of springing upon him, when the servant in the *kahause*, pulling off his red turban, which was made of very many yards of thin muslin, cast it between the tiger and his intended victim. In his wrath, the brute commenced tearing it to pieces, and thus gave the prostrate man time to recollect himself. In an instant he sprung to his feet and climbed up the elephant's tail into the *háoda*, where, regaining his battery, he quickly despatched the foe, from whom he had escaped by so narrow a chance.

It is, perhaps, worthy of mention, as tending to correct an erroneous idea commonly received, that tigers never, or very seldom, leap upon the object of their attack; I mean that, in their charge, they do not entirely quit the ground. They generally, in all cases which I have seen, raise themselves erect upon the hind legs, when within a few paces of the object they are charging, and taking a step or two in this upright posture, they cast themselves with all their force against it, striking at the same time with their paws. Some few sportsmen have averred, that they have seen the tiger leap upon his prey or upon his foe: now, positive information is certainly better than negative; it is no reason the clock did not strike thirteen because I did not hear it, and I do not mean to say that the tiger never does leap upon his victim, or never has done so.

We know that this animal, like the cat, is formed with peculiar powers for leaping, and that, when pursued, it has been known to spring over brooks, enclosures, and other obstructions, with a wonderful bound: it would be absurd, then, to say that it never does leap in making its charge, or in fixing itself upon an adversary; I merely affirm that it very seldom does so, instinct or experience teaching that the other mode is the more effectual of the two.

A full-grown Bengal tiger will rear himself upright from the ground at least ten feet, and in that posture would easily be able to fix his claws upon the back of an elephant, and in that manner draw himself completely up; so that a superficial observer would be apt to think that he had employed a spring, when such was not the case. This latter is, I believe, a very general notion among those who have not been close observers of the animal, and even among many people in India: the correction here offered is not formed upon the strength of my own remarks merely, but I have the opinions of many true sportsmen to back it.

Having settled this important matter my own way, we will return to cantonments, finding the weather too hot, and the sport too slack, for longer sojourn.

CHAPTER II.

SIRDHANA.—THE BEGUM SUMROO AND HER COURT.

In these days, hot as they were, there was always some gaiety and amusement going forward at Meràt; balls, plays, masquerades, amateur concerts, dinners, routs, &c., and in the cold weather, races, hunting, cricket, rackets, clubs, and the like, rendered the station the goal of every man's wishes, who was unfortunate enough not to be within reach of it. However, as these may be found elsewhere, I will not dwell upon them, but for the better edification of the reader, will pay a visit to the *jaghir* of the notorious old Begum Sumroo, or, to give her titles at full length, Her Highness Furzand Azuzai, Oomdootul Urraikeen, Zeb-ul-Nissa, Begum Sumroo, who resides, and has her court at a small town called Sirdhana, about thirteen miles N.E. from Merat.

The Begum's little territory takes the name of

Sirdhana, from the principal town within its boundaries; it is about twenty miles in length, by twelve in breadth, and is now rich and well-cultivated, yielding a revenue of twenty-five *lahks* annually, or £250,000, leaving her, perhaps, a net income of one-half, having deducted her dues to the British government, and the maintenance of her little army. The old lady enjoys the right of judicature upon her own ground, but, in criminal cases, she is obliged to inform the British government of her intention, before she can bring a man to capital punishment.

The Begum has lately expended a very large sum in building a palace and popish church at her little capital. The former is a handsome and spacious building, though still unfinished: the rooms are very large and well-proportioned, and the furniture costly, though heterogeneous and badly arranged. Like all similar attempts among the natives at an imitation of European style, the whole establishment is a mixture of grandeur and bad taste.

There are a great many paintings about the palace, but most of them are miserable daubs by natives. One or two portraits by Beechey, and a few specimens of Chinnery's landscapes, are valuable; and there are, among a cartload of trash, three or four good likenesses by a native painter, Juan Ram, who has certainly more of the art in him than any other black man with whom I have met: his portraits, as far as features go, are very faithful, servile copies of the flesh; but he falls short, where all his brethren do, in the life and expression, and in figure. He can paint an eye, a nose, a mouth, most accurately resembling the copy; but he cannot breathe life into the canvas, and then he is sure to stick in a cow's leg in a sleeve instead of an arm; and as for composition, or light and shade, I believe he never heard of them.

The church is not an ungraceful building, though its architecture is mixed. It is built entirely for display, however, and will hold a very small congregation in proportion to its external dimensions. Its decorations within are very paltry, and about the altar there is a great deal of tinsel frippery and tasteless ornament, better fitted for a theatre. One slab of white marble there is, which is deservedly admired for the beauty of its mosaic work, being inlaid with precious stones, in the style of the Tajh Mahal at Agra.

The village is populous; it is surrounded by a mud wall, and has a sort of mud citadel within it: but these are not now kept up as military defences. There are about 1,200 native Christians among the inhabitants, who have embraced the popish faith, in accordance with the Begum's religion, for the sake of her charity: these are notoriously an idle vagabond race, by far the worst subjects in the old lady's *jaghir*.

Before noticing her subjects more particularly, it would be but proper to give a slight sketch of the history and person of this extraordinary woman. Her maiden name was Zeb-ul-Nissa (ornament of the sex); she was by birth Cashmerian, but by family Georgian. While quite a child, she was the companion of *Nauchnies*, for which life she was herself educated; but Fate decreed that she should make other people dance instead of being herself obliged to dance for their amusement. In the course of her wanderings, she was seen by Summers, an adventurer, who, being charmed by her personal attractions, more particularly her fair complexion and lustrous eyes, made her his favorite concubine, and subsequently married her.

Summers was a man of obscure origin, a native of the Electorate of Trèves. He entered the French army under the name of Walter Reinhard, from which he deserted, and, in the year 1760 arrived in Bengal, calling himself Walter Summers. In Calcutta he obtained a post as a warrant-officer in a Swiss battalion; from this service, however, he deserted, in hope of something better among the French at Chandernuggur; but here he did not appear to have pleased himself, for he quitted them with as little ceremony as he had hitherto used with others, and pushing his fortunes further westward, he entered as a common trooper the service of Zufdīr Junge, one of the Lucknow princes. Desertion had, however, become habitual with him, and for consistency sake, he again stole away and offered his services to Meer Kassim Alli, the Nawab of a large district in Bengal: this chief, taking an especial fancy to the adventurer, advanced him to some little notice, and raised a corps of infantry especially for his command.

Meer Kassim then held his head-quarters at Patna, and was glad to obtain the assistance of one versed in the European mode of warfare; for he found himself continually at variance with the English, who had a large factory within the place, and who kept a body of troops in the neighbourhood for its protection.

Soon after the arrival of Summers at Patna, Mr. Ellis, the superintendent of this factory, had a dispute with the Nawab, about the passage of some supplies up the river, and the Nawab, rendered insolent by the possession of his new ally, exasperated Mr. Ellis by insults to which English blood would not submit. Collecting his forces, Mr. Ellis made an attack upon the town, and though very far inferior in numbers, he directed his operations with so much skill and spirit, that he quickly drove the black man from the walls, and carried the place by storm. But the advantage which the Europeans had thus gained by their superior warfare and courage, they as quickly lost by their imprudence. No sooner had they taken possession of the place, than they dispersed through it in search of plunder and drink ; so that Meer Kassim, having again collected a sufficient band, had little difficulty in retaking the place, making prisoners of nearly all the Europeans.

Elated with his success, Meer Kassim then marched out to meet Major Adams, who, having heard of the disturbance at Patna, was hastening to Mr. Ellis's assistance. The Nawab's troops were too weak to offer any effectual opposition to Major Adams's force, but they succeeded in deterring them from entering the town: the Major, unable to effect any good here, made an unexpected march during the night upon Monghir, and by a sudden attack, carried this treasured stronghold of the Nawab.

The news of this loss so infuriated Meer Kassim, that he gave immediate orders for the massacre of all the prisoners whom he had taken in Patna, and he pitched upon Summers as a fitting instrument of so horrible a deed, offering him a large reward for the execution of it. This man's avarice and villany were alike disgraceful to him; he entered at once into the project, and the means and manner of the act were utterly revolting to humanity. Meer Kassim, with every profession of sincerity, invited his prisoners to a magnificent feast and *nautch*, which they, quite unsuspicious of his perfidy, gladly attended; and while they were enjoying the entertainment and conversing in all confidence with their host, Summers suddenly entered the apartment with a band of armed men, and cruelly put them all to the sword, while the wine-cup was still at their lips.

Meer Kassim, immediately after this, succeeded in retaking his fort of Monghir, and held it against the English during a siege of nine days; but finding that he should be obliged to surrender the place without capitulation, he fled, with his officer Summers and a few followers. Summers, however, was not the man to adhere to the broken fortunes of a fallen master; he almost immediately deserted, and entered the service of Suja-ud-dowla, son of Zufdir Junge. There, however, he did not long continue, and his restless discontented disposition led him to serve successively with seven or eight different masters; until at last he was taken into considerable favour by Neujif Kahn, for whom he performed many valuable services. Neujif Kahn, in return for these good offices, rewarded him with the present *jaghir* of Sirdhana, the value of which was even then considerable. Although but imperfectly cultivated, it yielded a revenue which enabled the adventurer to live in much state and to amass a large quantity of treasure.

At this time, Zeb-ul-Nissa, whose ambitious and enterprising spirit struck at whatever was within its reach, employed all her arts of fascination to wheedle her master into marriage, offering to embrace the popish religion, which he affected. She was successful in her allurements, and her energetic and nervous mind soon assumed the entire guidance of the territory. Her avarice and love of command, however, were insatiate, and being of a heartless tyrannical disposition, she allowed nothing to stand between her and a desired object. She grew weary of the restraints imposed upon her by her lord and master, and laid a deep scheme for his destruction, hoping to succeed to the sole command and inheritance of the *jaghir*. This she managed with the most consummate craft and policy; for, in the year 1776, she got rid of her husband, and managed to play her cards so skilfully with the British Government, that she was duly instated in possession of the *jaghir*, upon condition of her furnishing for our service three battalions of irregular infantry.

In the present day, at Sirdhana, mention is very seldom made of Summers by any of the Begum's court; and any queries regarding the manner of his death, are answered by her myrmidons with an assurance that he was slain by an emissary from Meer Kassim: at the same time, it is well known that the circumstances of his death were of a nature to demand this mysterious silence or a blind of some sort.

Many inducements combined to render a release from her husband desirable to the Begum. Besides those of ambition and avarice, already mentioned, his low debauched life made him an object of disgust to her eventually. More especially her jealousy was roused by a passion which he had conceived for one of her own slave girls, and this is supposed to have led immediately to the bold project by which she rid herself of him. She entered into a conspiracy with those of her household upon whom she could depend, and concerted a scheme no less remarkable for the cunning and dexterity with which it was executed, than for the revolting barbarity with which it was conceived.

Summers had been engaged in remonstrance with his master, Neujif Kahn, in reference to some supposed encroachments made upon the ground which had been bestowed upon him; and the Begum had little difficulty in persuading him that she had detected a project of Neujif Kahn's, by which he intended to murder them both, and regain possession of the *jaghir*. She therefore urged him to collect without delay all the treasure, jewels, and other valuables, which could be easily transported, and by a rapid flight, to save both their lives and a portion of their riches, for enjoyment in a foreign land.

Summers, at first, listened with incredulity to his wife's tale, conceiving that his behaviour towards his master could hardly have exasperated him so far as to incur risk to his life; but witnesses were brought by the Begum, with a well-varnished tale, and he was at last persuaded, knowing by experience the vacillation of such favour as is bestowed by a native chief, to accede to her importunities, and preparations were forthwith made for a precipitate flight. The Begum did not neglect to represent to her husband, the inevitable consequences of detection, and painted to him the most cruel and excruciating tortures, even to death, which would be inflicted upon them by the enraged Neujif, if he should detect their flight and recover possession of them: she, therefore, extorted from him a vow, to which she also bound herself, that, in case of discovery, they should mutually destroy themselves, and for this purpose each party was provided with a pistol.

Everything being fully arranged, *palkies* were put in readiness, and taking with them all the treasure which they could accumulate, without attracting suspicion among their followers, they quitted their abode late at night, under pretence of paying a visit of ceremony to a neighbouring Rajha. The party were scarcely clear of the boundaries of their *jaghir*, when they were attacked by a strong body of their own soldiers and dependants, well armed and disguised. Resistance and flight were alike hopeless, and in his despair, Summers was reminded of his vow to his wife by the report of a pistol in her *palki*, and immediately afterwards a cry from her attendants. "The Begum has slain herself! Wa! Wa! the Begum has slain herself!" Bloody clothes and portions of his wife's garments were also shown to the unfortunate man, who, in the heat of his remorse and terror, committed suicide with the pistol his wife had given him: the very *ultimum desideratum* of the Begum's plot.

Having been thus successful in her scheme, the Begum was reconducted to her house by her applauding retainers, and here she concluded the tragedy of the day by an act, which will cling with infamy to her character as long as her name shall exist. Within her own tent, she that night buried alive the poor slave girl who had been the object of her husband's passion, and placing her bed over the grave, slept there until morning, lest any one more compassionate than herself should have lent a saving hand to the victim. This deed is said to have preyed heavily upon her conscience in after life, though I do not think that her contrition was shewn in any amelioration of her tyrannical and revengeful disposition.

Four or five years after the above horrible transactions, the Begum attached herself very much to a Frenchman of the name of L'Oiseau, to whom she allied herself by the same loose sort of marriage as that by which she was bound to Summers; but this L'Oiseau appears to have been only a bird of passage, for growing weary of him, as of her former husband, she gave him a handsome amount of cash, and sent him about his business. To him has been erroneously attributed, in more than one instance, the tragic fate which befel Summers; and it is difficult to discover the origin of this mistake, as those about the Begum's court are explicit upon this point.

In person, the Begum is very diminutive, and although aged, and infirm of body, she still retains vestiges of her former beauty. Her features are aquiline, and her complexion, though decayed, and no longer youthful, is fair; she particularly prides herself upon the beauty and wonderful smallness of her hands and feet, which she does not scruple to display when she thinks they may be duly appreciated. Her expression is lively and intelligent, and in her conversation she manages to render herself very amusing and interesting. She appears to exist principally upon tea and the smoke of tobacco, and to keep Death at arm's length more by the energy of her mind than by any remaining strength of the flesh. She has lately had several very serious attacks of illness, and being eighty-eight years of age, according to the nearest calculation, can hardly expect to live much longer. I have frequently been present at her *durbars*,* and have enjoyed the privilege of conversation with her highness, much to my amusement and edification. She usually receives her visitors in a tent pitched outside her palace (except on grand occasions, when she graces the state audience-hall with her presence), and has little display of magnificence or wealth about her person.

Her appearance, at first sight, is mean and insignificant. We find her seated upon a dingy shabby couch, in the cross-legged fashion of a tailor, her little person enveloped in a large yellow cashmere shawl, of exquisite texture, though by no means showy: under this shawl a handsome

* *Durbar*, Levee, Audience of State.

green silk cloak, of European fashion, but embroidered, is generally spread around her, which, as the upper part of her person sinks almost into it, gives her something the appearance of a biffen, or pressed baked apple. On her head she is fond of wearing a turban, after the fashion of men, whom also she apes in other matters; but this head-dress is sometimes with advantage exchanged for a more becoming Mogul cap of dignity, wrought with gold, and jewelled.

She is particularly affable to European ladies, and seldom permits them to quit her presence without bestowing upon them some token of her generosity, according to the native custom, either a cashmere shawl, or a piece of silk, or a jewel, to the value of twenty or thirty guineas. The old lady's generosity, however, is not so apparent in this way as in her donations and benefactions for charitable purposes. She has, during the last few years, given very large sums to the building of churches, the endowment of schools, and the maintenance of christianized natives. A short time since, she sent the Bishop of Calcutta a sum of money amounting to £15,000, to be expended in the promotion of charitable and other religious purposes; and this is not the first gift which she has made in the same liberal manner. She is, as a public character, notoriously generous, when called upon to loosen her purse-strings, distributing freely to the indigent, and in no instance refusing her aid in the construction or benefit of any public institution, in which she can feel an interest, or through which her vanity may be tickled by the attraction of public notice. It is further generally believed that much of this great liberality is practised in expiation of her former misdeeds. In smaller matters, she is not so open-handed, and no fractional expenditure is permitted in her establishment without her own immediate approval; even the common disbursements of her household are inspected and examined by her personally.

It is generally believed that the Begum has had no children, though a report exists that she had a son by Summers. Her affairs were for many years conducted by a half-caste, of the name of Dyce, who married one of her adopted daughters, and acted as her principal both in civil and military matters; but this man was ejected from his office, under pretext of some covert communications with the British Government. The old man, having expended his best years in the service of this woman, is now living in penury in the Sudder Bazaar at Merat, and his son, David Ochterlony Dyce Sombre, Esq., &c. &c. &c., has been instated in his dignities at the head of affairs.

This son was educated at the Dehli college, and is an excellent Persian and English scholar, and although very young, is said to be both active and politic in the discharge of his multifarious duties. The internal economy and the revenue of the *jaghir*, certainly reflect credit upon the government, and I believe Davy Dyce, as he is familiarly called, is entitled to the chief merit in the matter. He is an especial favourite of the Begum's, and the acknowledged heir to all her wealth, which is said to be immense. The *jaghir* itself reverts to government, but there are several handsome houses both at Sirdhana, at Dehli, and at Merat, which are the Begum's own property, and to these also Dyce will succeed. His expectations from her are valued at little less than a million of money: he is a man of enormous bulk, though not more than five-and-twenty years of age, and though his complexion is very dark, he has a fine open countenance, expressive of mildness and intelligence. In disposition he is kind, and as generous as daylight; and he is a very general favourite with all who know him.

There are several officers under Dyce, who have a share in the management of the affairs, civil and military. The oldest of these is an Italian of the name of Ragolini, who has command of the Begum's body-guard, a funny, pinched, unsoldier-like little figure, who has held the same post for many years, and is an invaluable butt to his companions. There is also an officer, formerly of the E. I. Company's service, who quitted his appointment for his present situation, hoping no doubt to reap a more golden harvest than he has yet found practicable. He is a canny, calculating Scot, with whom his own brother would be sorry to drive a bargain; so, although a grumbler, I dare say he has managed to feather his nest pretty well. A more agreeable person is found in another of these officers, an Italian, by name Solaroli, who, though an adventurer from his own country, and probably of low origin, is a man of considerable intelligence and of good manners.

Lastly,—I have saved him as a *bonne bouche*,—"Och! sure he is a patthern of a praist, so he is,"—comes the Begum's father confessor, Bishop of Amatorita, Vicar Apostolic of Sirdhana, Julius Cæsar, commonly called the *Padri Sahib;* the very essence of a papistical priest; the expression of whose handsome countenance is a mixture of sensuality and good-humour; the outward semblance of whose person is an union of coarse cloth, and "bringing forth the fruits of good living;" whose conversation is a mingling of superstition with *double entendre;* whose music is a combination of sacred chant and *chansons à boire;* whose devotion to the fair has obtained for him a just notoriety, and whose soft attentions are ever assiduously paid, with the most feeling discrimination, to the more delicate members of his flock.

As Miss Emma Roberts has very truly remarked, "Bishop Heber seems scarcely to have done justice to this excellent man, in ascribing his popularity to the smoothness of his manners, and his tact in administering to the self-love of his associates." Certainly not, and there is little doubt but the bishop could have given a much more complete idea of the padri's character, had he been inclined to say all he knew. Miss Roberts seems to have heard of Julius Cæsar many years since, when he was at Patna, and where she describes him as "realizing the most beautiful ideas which could be formed of a Christian minister;" doubtless she would imply that he embodies in his own proper person all those amiable qualities which have ever been considered as characteristic of the popish clergy. She says "he is a Franciscan friar, wearing the garb and practising the self-denial enjoined by his order." He certainly does wear the garb of his order before strangers, over both his person and his mind; and as for his self-denial, the practice of that, too, is indisputably the more meritorious when he exercises it, in proportion to his habitual indulgence in the common course of his life.

He has a fine musical voice, well adapted to the chanting of his church service, and I have often heard it at our Merat Beef-steak Club, where he was a frequent guest, pouring forth his favourite song, "The battle of the Nile," in right gallant style, at the top of a roaring chorus. It is this accomplishment, possibly, to which Miss Roberts alludes, when she says "his talents and amiable character render him a welcome and an honoured guest at the houses of the British." Where good wine, good stories, and good songs are to be had, there Bishop Julius Cæsar will undoubtedly be a ready and a welcome visitor.*

The Begum usually gives a grand *fête*, which lasts three days, during Christmas, and to which

* The Reverend gentleman arrived in England in November last, for the purpose of seeing our lions.

nearly all the society of Merat, Delhi, and the surrounding stations is invited. I have by me one of her circulars: "Her Highness the Begum Sumroo requests the honour of ——'s company at Sirdhana, on Christmas Eve, at the celebration of High Mass, and during the two following days, to a nautch and a display of fire-works." Here the burden of the exhibition is distributed pretty equally between our good friend the Bishop, the *Nauchnies,* and the fire-works. Of these spectacles, most who have witnessed them agree that the religious pageantry has the lead, in point of display and finery.

Tents are prepared in the palace-garden for the accommodation of visitors, and every luxury which a profuse outlay can secure is provided for the company; the tables are sumptuously spread, the viands and the wines are alike excellent. Upon these grand occasions, the Begum usually honours the guests by presiding at the table; but she does not herself partake of any food in their presence. Not only are the numerous visitors entertained in this magnificent style, but the whole host of their followers and train are also feasted and fêted, in a manner equally sumptuous in proportion to their condition. When we recollect who the Begum originally was, the diabolical character of her husband, his perpetration of the massacre at Patna, and the many acts of crime and tyranny which she has herself committed, it is strange thus to find an enlightened British community, the victors of the soil, doing homage and seeking favour at her foot-stool, or even condescending to partake of her hospitality.

The dresses of her military officers are the most heterogeneous and varied possible, being worn according to the taste or fancy of each, without regard to uniformity of pattern or colour; but the troops are clad in vests of dark yellow cloth, with some attention to conformity of cut, and they are all armed and appointed alike. They are not very military in appearance, but are said to be good soldiers, both in courage and hardihood.

The Begum has a house at Merat, which she generally visits for a couple of months in the fall of the year, bringing with her the chief of her train. She has also a residence at Dehli, consisting of a splendid mansion and two or three smaller houses, within a very extensive garden; but this she has not frequented for several years past, in consequence of a reprimand which she received from the representative of the British

Government at Dehli, for neglecting to pay him that homage which is his due, in virtue of the dignity with which he is invested; and moreover it is affirmed, as another cause for the aversion with which she now regards this once favourite place, that during the year in which the above-mentioned occurrence took place, her injured consequence and stiff-necked pride gave rise to a misunderstanding between her highness and the old Emperor, Akbur Shah, touching a point of etiquette very galling to the old lady's vanity.

Akbur Shah, being pre-eminent by birth, the pure stock of the ancient Mogul Dynasty, and being upon his own ground in the city of Dehli, insists upon receiving homage from all of an inferior degree who meet him, and even the proud Begum herself is fain to have her elephant kneel down to the Emperor when passing him. This her vanity will not brook, and having more than once been compelled against her will thus to do reverence to a higher prince, she has for several years refrained from visiting Dehli. This arrogant conduct on the part of the Begum appears the more unbecoming, when it is known that she was exalted to her present rank, with the title of Begum, by Shah Ullum, the father of the present Emperor.

While I am still upon this subject, it may be as well that I should anticipate the order of my narrative, for the purpose of mentioning the termination of the Begum's career. Her death occurred at Merat on the 27th of January 1836. The following account was given of the circumstances in the 'Merat Observer:'—

"In our last week's paper, it was our painful task to announce the death of her highness the Begum Sombre, on the 27th, at her residence at Sirdhana.

"Her highness had, some days previously, been attacked by indisposition, from which she had perfectly recovered; when on the night of the 25th, she was suddenly seized with an alarming attack. Dr. Drever had not quitted the house; his patient was then speechless and apparently senseless; the applications resorted to had the effect of relieving her. In the course of the 26th, she lapsed into a state of torpor, and early in the morning of the 27th her spirit fled from its earthly tenement.

"No time was lost in despatching an express to the magistrate at Merat and the agent to the Governor-general at Delhi: the former of these officers reached Sirdhana by noon, and immediately proceeded to the palace, where he was received by Mr. Dyce Sombre, Dr. Drever, and other members of the family. Necessary arrangements were immediately made for the funeral and other ceremonies; and it being announced that Colonel Dyce had repaired to Sirdhana, Mr. Hamilton had an interview with that officer, who shortly after returned to Merat.

"The crowds assembled outside the palace-walls, and on the roads, were immense, and one scene of lamentation and sorrow was apparent; the grief was deep and silent; the clustered groups talked of nothing but the heavy loss they had sustained, and the intensity of their sorrow was pictured in their countenances, nor did they separate during the night. According to the custom of the country, the whole of the dependants observed a strict fast; there was no preparing of meals, no retiring to rest; all were watchful, and every house was a scene of mourning.

"At nine, the whole of the arrangements being completed, the body was carried out, borne by the native Christians of the artillery battalion, under a canopy, supported by the principal officers of her late highness's troops, and the pall by Messrs. Dyce Sombre, Solaroli, Drever, and

Troup, preceded by the whole of her highness's body guards, followed by the Bishop, chaunting portions of the service, aided by the choristers of the cathedral. After them, the magistrate, Mr. Hamilton, and then the chief officers of the household, the whole brought up by a battalion of her late highness's infantry, and a troop of horse. The procession, preceded by four elephants from which alms and cakes were distributed amongst the crowd, passed through a street formed of the troops at Sirdhana, to the door of the cathedral, the entrance to which was kept by a guard of honour from the 30th N.I., under the command of Captain Campbell. The procession passed into the body of the cathedral, in the centre of which the coffin was deposited on tressels. High mass was then performed in excellent style, and with great feeling, by the Bishop. The body was lowered into the vault. Thus terminated the career of one who, for upwards of half-a-century, has held a conspicuous place in the political proceedings of India. In the Begum Sombre the British authorities had an ardent and sincere ally, ever ready, in the spirit of true chivalry, to aid and assist, to the utmost of her means, their fortunes and interests."

"As soon as the family had retired into the palace, the magistrate of Merat proceeded, with the officers of his establishment, to proclaim the annexation of the territories of her late highness to the British Government; proclamation was made throughout the town and vicinity of Sirdhana, by the Government authority, and similar ones at the principal towns, in different parts of the jaghir, according to previous arrangement; so that this valuable territory became almost instantaneously incorporated with Zilla Merat, to which it remains annexed; the introduction of her police and fiscal arrangements having been especially intrusted to Mr. Hamilton, by orders from the Government of India received so far back as August 1834.

"The whole of the landed possessions of her late highness revert to the British, and the personal property, amounting to nearly half-a-crore, devolves by will upon Mr. Dyce Sombre, with the exception of small legacies and charitable bequests."

The personal property proved larger than the sum at which it is here estimated: the mass of it which was bequeathed to Dyce Sombre amounted to eighty lahks, or £800,000, independent of various smaller legacies to her other officers, and to persons about her establishment, and also to charitable institutions. The principal of these were, to her physician, Doctor Drever, twenty thousand rupees; to Mr. Troup, who married one of Dyce Sombre's sisters, fifty thousand; to Mr. Solaroli, who also married a sister of Dyce's, eighty thousand; to many petty officers about her household, various smaller sums; for charitable purposes, a lahk; and to her executor, an old officer of the Company's service, who had been a great favourite of her's while he resided at Merat, seventy-five thousand. Her father confessor, Julius Cæsar, too, was not forgotten, but I am not aware what amount of property was bequeathed to him.

Dyce Sombre, the heir to this rich property, is now about twenty-six years of age; until he is thirty, he will only enjoy the interest of his fortune, but after that period it will fall in to him without tie or control. He told me, just before I quitted India, that he intended to repair to England, as soon as he could be set at liberty, for the purpose of seeing all the wonders of which he has heard so much. His father, the Begum's former governor and generalissimo, whom she deposed, was not mentioned in her will, but he will doubtless be handsomely provided for by his son, who is proverbially kind-hearted and generous. During the life-time of the Begum, he was deterred from rendering his disgraced father any assistance, unless clandestinely, through apprehension of the old lady's wrath; but now he will, I doubt not, acknowledge and befriend him openly.

Such was the end of this extraordinary woman; her age at the time of her death was eighty-nine, though the natives about her had an idea that she was upwards of a hundred.

CHAPTER III.

JOURNEY TO THE HIMÁLA MOUNTAINS.

Not only the snowy ridge, but an inferior range of the Himála mountains, commonly known as the Landour range, is also visible in bright weather from Merat, and it is impossible to behold these stupendous works of nature without a wish to visit them. The travelling distance from Merat to Rajhpore, at the foot of the mountains, is one hundred and twenty-two miles, and this may be run over in a palki within thirty-five hours, if pursued without let or hindrance.

While travelling in the hot weather, it is customary to halt during the heat of the day, and to prosecute the journey in the night, or in the comparative cool of the morning and evening; and for the accommodation of travellers in this respect, bungalows have lately been erected by subscription at Deobund and at Kheri, so as to divide the journey into three stages. These bungalows are open for the reception of all passengers, and are provided with servants and most necessary comforts, which may be made available at a very moderate rate of payment.

It is ten days' march from Merat to Rajhpore, or the distance may be accomplished in twelve hours, by hard riding, upon a dozen good nags. I had my choice of these three methods of transportation to the mountains, whither I was bent upon a visit, and in this, as in all other matters, there was much to be said *pro* and *con* on either side. The palki, or travelling *dák*, as it is called, shakes one most confoundedly; but then it is possible to read a few pages of a novel, or occasionally to take a light nap in passing away the time. Marching is undoubtedly the most comfortable, and enables the invalid to move by easy stages with every convenience about him, but then it takes so long going and returning, that a month's leave of absence is swallowed up in travelling over the road. And the equestrian mode, although the most expeditious, and the most exciting, may prove a little fatiguing to a system enervated by a tropical climate. Twelve hours in the saddle, at ten miles an hour, sounds rather formidable to soft flesh and sharp bones; so I decided on *dáking* it.

I chose the month of October for my excursion, not because the plains are least tolerable during that month, but because the mountains are then most beautiful. To go earlier, that is, in July, August, or September, would be to visit the mountains without seeing them; for, during those months, they are involved to their bases in clouds, which very seldom clear away even for a single day. At the beginning of October, the vapours break up, and then is the opportunity for the artist, or the admirer of nature, to find them fresh from their bath, under all the loveliest effects of accidental light and shadow, and glowing in the warm red hues of autumnal foliage.

In my trip to the Himálas I was accompanied by a brother officer, in quest of what he would find no-where else, if he could not get it in the bracing regions to which we were bound, a new lease of his life; rendered necessary by reason of heavy payments made by his constitution to the climate and free living, whereby his health had become bankrupt, under a congestion of the liver, and his affairs within a nicety of being wound up altogether. As he himself said, his existence felt like a rotten garment hanging to the peg by the last stitch. We determined to make but one halt upon the road, for the better performance of which we sent our *palkis* and *banghis** a couple of stages forward, with the intention of starting ourselves in a buggy at sunset, so as to overtake our *dák* before nightfall.

"Well, Peter," said I, as the vehicle was brought to the door, "as you are sick, jump in upon the near side; I will be Jehu to-day. Are you sure you have forgotten nothing? we shall have no servants to think for us upon the road, you know."

"Yes, thank you, my dear fellow; I have got every thing I believe; drive on."

"Stop, stop, sir," cried a black fellow, rushing out of the house; "here is a bundle of papers which you left upon the table."

"Oh yes, pull up a moment; it's my will. You black son of a donkey, why did you not remind me of it before I got into the buggy? If I had left that behind, I would have broken your stupid black head."

"Well, shall I drive on? you are sure there's nothing more?"

"All right; push along; we are very late; it will

* *Banghi*, a pair of small boxes or baskets, slung one at each end of an elastic bamboo, and carried across the shoulder of a running bearer, who keeps pace with the *palki*, and who takes the name of *banghi-burdar*.

be quite dark before we get to Douralla. Oh! just pull up a moment; I do believe that booby Bhooddoo never reminded me to take my purse. No; just turn round; what a blundering rascal he is! I do believe he would let me go away without my head, unless I thought of it myself."

Well, the purse was brought, and then the watch was missing, and then something else was thought of, so that it was nearly dark before we got a fair start.

There are very few artificial roads in India, out of the immediate vicinity of the principal stations, and the traveller often has to find his way over trackless plains, or through crops and jungul, without any better guide than the sun, or a general notion of the direction in which his destination lies. In this, however, he is more fortunate than when he finds himself compelled by the nature of the ground to follow in the ruts of what the natives call a road. Where the traffic has been limited to one narrow line, be the soil sandy or swampy, the ruts are sure to be knee-deep, and being cut by wheels much closer together than those of our English vehicles, there is no possibility of keeping the carriage upon level ground; first one wheel is sunk to the nave, and then the other; then a bullock *hackeri* is met in a narrow pass with only room for one, and one party or the other must back out.

Darkness quickly overtook us, and being rather uncertain of our ground, we thought it better to go easy, and let our *sáes* precede us. Thus we advanced carefully for some miles, and had arrived within a few furlongs of our destination, when our castle-buildings, and speculations upon the rosy cheeks and improved calves which we were to bring back from the mountains, were, in a moment, dashed to the ground, as were we ourselves also, by a sudden precipitation, horse, buggy, and its contents, down a drop of at least five feet into a pool of stagnant water.

"*Wa! Wa!*" said the *sáes*, as cool as a cucumber, as we saw his figure over our heads in relief against the clear sky; "why you're all in the water."

"I know we are, you fool, and all your fault, for not showing us the hole. You rascal, I'll break every bone in your body if you dare to laugh at me. What do you mean, sir?"

"It's very wrong of your slave to laugh, great sir," replied the man, submissively, "particularly when I believe the Captaun Sahib is killed. See, sir, there are nothing but his legs visible sticking out of the water."

"Ye powers," I cried, "he's certainly killed outright!" and rushing forward up to my waist in the stinking pool, I seized the two objects which had so excited our alarm. 'Twas too late—not to save the life of my friend, but to save my own fingers; for, alas! I had seized two stumps of a prickly-pear bush, which were standing out of the water. The sharp thorns entered my hands and wrists, and the only revenge I could claim was upon the *sáes* for misleading me. My friend was found comfortably stuck in the mud under the inverted buggy, too weak with laughter to extricate himself, and too little hurt to excite my compassion. It was utterly impossible to right the buggy, or to recover our various small articles, which had been buried in the mud; so dragging my friend out of his hiding-place, I assisted him to mount the horse, and leaving the *sáes* in charge of the property, we set forth in search of our palkies. Half an hour's wandering brought us to the village of Kuttowli, where we found them waiting, and having washed and changed our apparel by the way-side, we lighted our torches and made a fresh start, giving orders to our bearers not to separate our palkies during the night, but to travel in company.

I have already hinted that *palki-dák* is anything but that luxurious mode of conveyance which the uninitiated generally suppose it to be; but I have alluded simply to its abstract inconveniences, and have not yet taken into account the heavy contingent miseries which beset the *dák* traveller. As for heat, a man might as well be inclosed in a box-iron; in point of ease, let him prefer a tax-cart over a Devonshire lane; if he would be quiet, let him rather take his passage in the engine-room of a steamer; are his olfactory nerves delicate? he had better travel in a scavenger's cart.

Then there are the chances, no slight ones, of a capsize in a *nulla* (brook); the option of paying an overcharge, or of having a stinking oil-torch crammed into the palki under some humble pretext, the scoundrel knowing that the sudden glare of light thus thrown into the somnolent eyes of the occupant will screen him from chastisement; the continued grunting and grumbling of the bearers, with their cries of "*Aram, Aram, Bhaë,*" as they fall in with others of their class; and the effluvia from the reeking bipeds, as they toil under their burden, together with scanty fare, and an overwhelming power of dust, make up the sum of grievances to be encountered in this method of locomotion.

After quitting Merat, the first place worthy of notice at which we arrived was Deobund, distant about forty-eight miles. It is a large and flourishing native town, built almost entirely of brick, and surrounded with a high wall of the same material. Its inhabitants are chiefly of the Brahmin and Khettri castes, and they are reputed to be very wealthy. The chief trade of the city and the neighbouring district is in sugar, wheat, and tobacco, which are produced in great abundance, and of a fine quality. The soil is exceedingly rich, but labours under a serious evil, in deficient irrigation. There are only two wells in the whole city of Deobund, the loose nature of the soil rendering masonry indispensable in their construction, and the depth of the springs being a bar to more frequent excavations. This information I picked up from an intelligent old *jemmadar*, whom I visited in the *chouki*, while a change of bearers was being effected. We passed through the place at midnight, so that my view was confined to narrow streets of brick buildings, and an occasional gateway standing out in fictitious importance, as seen by the unsteady light of the flambeaus.

We pursued our journey through the night, with little interruption beyond the changing of bearers, being made sensible of our approach to any town by the increased velocity, and the vociferous announcement of our advance, the whole place being made to echo back our titles and dignified qualities, as trumpeted forth by our slaves; "Behold the protector of the poor!" "Make way for the supporter of the universe!" "Stand aside, and see the finger of the firmament go by!" &c.; then bump comes the palki to the ground at the end of the stage, and the whole crew huddle round the doors with the *mussaulchi* (link-boy) at their head, overwhelming the awakened traveller with entreaties for a *buckshis*, or small gratuity: a *chou-anni*, value about fivepence, will send the whole crew away, praying honour and splendour in return for his munificence.

Before eleven o'clock the next morning, we arrived at the civil station of Saharunpore, formerly fortified as a border-fortress to overlook the movements of the Ghoorkas. The defences, which are partly of masonry and partly of mud, were converted into a jail at the termination of the Ghoorka war, and they are still used for that purpose, there being no military retained in the station, with the exception of a small guard over the convicts.

The town has nothing remarkable in it, but about half a mile distant from it there is a large garden and religious establishment belonging to the Gosseins, a class of devotees who dye their hair yellow, and besmear their naked bodies with oil and ashes. The members of this fraternity are reputed to be very wealthy, and to live in great luxury, though practising all the external impositions of rigid abstinence and penance: among them are to be found the most revolting specimens of distortion and deformity, for which their order is notorious.

They have taken under their protection and peculiar fosterage an innumerable swarm of monkies, natives of the place, whom they have tutored into something like discipline. At noon, daily, the officiating Gossein rings a bell, and in an instant all the monkies within hearing assemble before the temple, where they continue walking to and fro, wrangling, chattering, and playing all kinds of antics, until the priest makes his appearance with an earthen pot full of pulse and corn. The excitement now increases; the whole herd, erect upon their hind legs, squeezing, pushing, and jockeying one another, to get closer to the Gossein, are still careful not to venture beyond the limits marked out for them; or if perchance one of them should so far forget himself, he is flogged and sent about his business. The Gossein then scatters the food among them, and a scramble ensues, which baffles all description. The screams and squeaks and growls are changed to blows and bites; every hand is busily employed, between the intervals of fighting, in stuffing the pouches with grain, for no time is given for mastication. In an incredibly short space the whole is gobbled up, and the animals disperse at the sound of the bell, unless it be a holiday or feast, in which case fruit is served out to them. This scene may be witnessed by any passenger; the Gosseins do not here, as is usual among their order, affect any secrecy about the matter.

Not far from the *fakhir's* nest just mentioned, the Company have a botanical garden, on a small scale, for the preservation of such plants as cannot be reared in less temperate latitudes. There is no very great assortment of botanical curiosities, but the gardens are kept in excellent order. Here also may be seen a few zoological wonders, collected by the superintendent of the gardens, whose character, as a shrewd and enterprising naturalist, is well known throughout the country.

We tarried at the house of a friend during the heat of the day, and having re-invigorated our weary bodies with liberal ablutions and refection, we set forth once more upon our journey, as the sun began to dip towards the horizon.

The country all around Saharunpore is highly fertile, though here, as in the vicinity of Deobund, the agriculture is sadly impeded by an insufficient irrigation. I had no intelligent *jemmadar* to furnish me with the precise number of wells, or the speculations of the husbandman, as upon a former occasion; but I had an opportunity of inspecting the method of constructing wells adopted by the natives, which appeared to me an excellent and ingenious plan. The soil, being very loose and sandy, renders abortive all attempts to sink a shaft in the usual way, the excavation being refilled with the falling earth as fast as the labour proceeds. To obviate this impediment, the natives have recourse to an expedient which is thoroughly successful. Upon the intended site of the well, before they commence the process of boring, the workmen build up circular walls of solid masonry, of the dimensions proposed for the work; this is carried to a certain height, in proportion to the breadth and weight of the material, and then the operation of digging commences within the cylinder; the masonry being allowed to sink gradually into the earth as the soil is removed. As the column disappears below the surface, the masons continue to build upon it, great care being taken to preserve the perpendicular, and to keep the superincumbent weight above equal to the increasing resistance.

Upon the north and north-east of Saharunpore, distant not more than sixteen miles, is a range of low mountains, known as the Sivalic Ridge; these form the southern boundary of the valley of Deyra Dhoon, stretching all the way from the countries of Cashmere and the Punjáb, upon the west, to Almora, upon the east. The whole line is rugged and precipitous, but beautifully wooded upon its southern face, while many parts open to a northern aspect are comparatively bare of foliage, or the trees are stunted and ill-favoured.

We came to the foot of these hills at a village called Khéri, and entered them by a pass bearing the same name. It was after nightfall, when our bearers commenced the cautious deliberate step necessary in threading their way through the stormy bed of the mountain-torrent, which here forms the only road. The moon was near the full, and was shining splendidly over the scene, rendering the use of our torches almost superfluous: altogether, I never beheld anything in nature more mystically grand. The abrupt precipices which enclose the pass, looming doubly prominent in a broad flood of solemn light, appeared to stretch their hanging crags and nodding trees towards each other over the thick obscurity of the narrow passage, giving it the effect of a gigantic cavern. At the foot of the nearest projection, a band of wandering *moozaffirs* (peddling merchants) had pitched their little camp, marked by a blazing fire, before which their naked figures were to be seen passing to and fro, like the flitting spirits of a supernatural world.

While still occupied in admiration of this imposing scene, a magic oblivion stole gently over my senses, and carried me more completely away into the regions of enchantment and romance, where the busy imagination, freed from the shackles of the material world, could sport and revel among the wild images of its own creation. I wandered amid the mazes of a dense forest, where

I continued during many pleasant hours, delighting in mild zephyrs and limpid rills; when, suddenly, I was attacked by a terrible tigress, larger than Merat church, and more savage than the Begum Sumroo. A desperate struggle ensued, and I was still panting with the encounter, as my heart thumped loudly against my ribs with terror and excitement, when bump came my palki to the ground, at the end of the stage, just in time to save me from being swallowed alive.

The doors of my palki were open on one side, and I was just about to jump out and stretch myself, when bump came another palki down alongside of mine, and stopped my egress. The doors of this were also open upon the side towards me, the two, as they stood together, forming as it were the interior of a double palki shut up on both sides. As is usual in the hot weather, I was travelling with rather a flimsy costume over my person, and thrusting my body forward into the other palki, I saluted my friend with, "Well, Peter, old fellow, how are you getting on?" To this, however, I received no reply, and fearing that my fellow-traveller might be suffering under a relapse of his illness, I leant close over his face, endeavouring to catch a glimpse of his features.

At that moment, the *mussaulchi* threw open the door of the palki, into which I had now fairly protruded my person; "Oh! Haich—h!" screamed a little, one-eyed, wizen-faced, treble-frilled-night-capped old lady, as the glare of the torch fell upon our faces, nose to nose," "Oh! mercy, mercy! Timothy! Timothy! Stokes! Stokes! here's a man in my palki!"

As may be easily believed, I beat a precipitate retreat, not so much in fear of her Timothy as of the old lady herself; for lo! her countenance struck me as bearing a wonderful resemblance to that of the feline monster of my dream, and her terrible mouth opened so very wide upon the side nearest to me, that I fled in apprehension of the dire peril from which I had so lately awoke.

Slamming together the doors between us, I made my escape on the opposite side, and ordered my palki to be instantly removed from so formidable a vicinity. I effected the exchange of my bearers with all possible despatch, my movements being considerably accelerated by the incessant cries of "Timothy! Timothy! save me! murder!" and the like.

I was on the point of starting, when a third palki turned the corner, and was run up close beside mine.

"My love!" exclaimed a voice from within, in accents of tender enquiry.

"Is that Timothy?" I asked, in an affected feminine voice, returning the soft affectionate intonation of the other.

"Yes, my sweet," replied Timothy.

Then, closing the doors on that side, I put my head out upon the other, and ordered my bearers to hasten on with all possible speed, leaving Timothy and his "sweet" to discuss the mysterious affair.

About an hour afterwards, I was sinking into an oblivious slumber, when I again became conscious of another palki running beside mine; "Hallo! Peter," I cried, forgetting at the moment the occurrence of the late scene.

"Oh! Timothy! Stokes! screamed the old lady, for it was indeed herself; "Oh dear! Oh dear! here's this horrid man with the beard come again. Oh! Timothy! Timothy!"

Ah! thought I, the light was in your face, not in mine, or you would not be calling me a horrid man. Then shouting angrily at the bearers, I asked them how they dared to bring me in contact with a party to which I did not belong?

"Why, sir," said one of the men, "this is

your *Mem Sahib* (wife): do you object to our carrying you near her?"

"You scoundrel, she is not my wife."

"*Wa! Wa! Sahib*," retorted the man with surprise, "why should you deny her? You are travelling from Kurnaul in her company."

"You impudent rascal, what do you mean? I have nothing to do with the woman. I do not come from Kurnaul; I am travelling from Merat."

"Well, sir," said the bearer, "I suppose you know better than the lady; but when you were asleep she desired her palki to be kept quite close to yours, and gave us strict orders not to leave her side."

"No, no, sir, I didn't," cried the lady, "Oh! Timothy! Timothy! I shall be insulted."

I assured the sweet lady she need be under no apprehension; and giving orders to my men to press forward with all expedition, and to keep aloof from all other travellers, I arrived at the foot of the Himálas, just before sunrise, at a pretty little village called Rajhpore.

Here my *dák* terminated, it being impossible to travel up the face of the mountain by such means; but I found ponies waiting for myself and my friend, which had been sent down for us from Mussoori, whither we were destined.

Having outstripped my fellow-traveller upon the road, I had leisure to admire the scenery around me. But, alas! no effort of mine can bestow upon my reader even a remote idea of the picture which I there beheld. The view is of that striking description, which, having been once seen, can never be forgotten, but until then can never be conceived. Ask a man who has not seen the face of the ocean, what it is like? "Oh, it is an immense expanse of salt water," would be a natural reply. Ask a man who has never beheld the snowy range of the Himála Mountains, what idea he has of them? "Oh, they are immense mountains, the largest in the world, covered with snow." Now, the calm smooth surface of a fish-pond would convey to the mind of the former just as adequate a notion of the terrors of the South Atlantic, under the influence of a hurricane, as the second could possibly imbibe touching the stupendous sublimity of the wondrous scene in question, by visiting any of the grandest mountains in Europe. A sense of fear and apprehension mingles with our astonishment in the contemplation of nature upon a scale so vast, so wonderfully magnificent. All the admiration which our puny minds can afford is absorbed at once; ten times the store would be utterly insufficient for a due appreciation of all the grandeur here spread before the sight. Man sinks into nothing in such presence.

Rajhpore is situated upon an elevation sufficient to allow a clear and unobstructed view of the Dhoon, extending east and west within the Sivalic ridge, but it does not stand so high as to detract in any measure from the awe-inspiring altitude of the mountains behind it. Pile rises above pile, vista within vista, in magic variety of form and hue, until the imagination is carried captive into strange regions far far away, alarmed, but still borne on by intense curiosity, among the unfamiliar scenes of a new world. But come, I deal not cleverly in the grandiloquous, and had better descend from my halting Pegasus, and mount the shaggy *ghoont* (hill-pony) awaiting my good pleasure.

My position commanded a long line of the Deyra road, and as I could see nothing of my friend's palki, I determined to ride up to Mussoori without waiting for him. The distance is only seven miles, but when I looked upon the perpendicular track pointed out to me as my route, and then upon the under-sized rat of a pony which was to carry me, I must confess I entertained some dread of the adventure. But stay, what is that dark hurly-burly gathering over the summits of the lower range? While I was yet cogitating upon this inquiry, the fleecy vapours, which at first had hung around the steeps, were rapidly transformed into dense masses of sooty clouds, which descended half way down the face of the mountains; here they were terminated in a cut line, as straight as the edge of a ruler shutting out from view the heights above, and leaving the lower half involved in deep shadow. The low country of the plains was still laughing in the sunshine, but I augured a storm in the highlands; and this the natives confirmed, assuring me that it would be very violent, and recommending me to defer my journey until it had passed over. "But," said I, "I am positively starving; is there any gentleman's house in the neighbourhood where I may put up?"

"No, sir," replied an old *havildar* of the Ghoorka guard; "but you need not wait long, the storm will have passed away in two or three hours, and then you can go and look after your breakfast."

"Two or three hours! and you expect me to wait calmly all that time for my meal, when I tell you I have not tasted food since two o'clock yesterday?" I put spurs to my pony's sides, and away I went up the ascent. The first mile or two of the road I got over pretty well; but after this I found myself in the region of the clouds, with hardly light enough to see the narrow pathway over which my pony was scrambling.

A division of the road into two diverging tracks brought me to a stand-still; there was little choice; one way appeared to me as good, or rather as bad, as the other. My directions were, follow your nose and you can't go wrong, there is only one road; now here were two roads, therefore it was plain that I had already gone wrong; and unwilling to get involved in the mazes of so wild and terrific a country, I determined to wait by the way-side and rest my pony, hoping that ere long some passenger might be forthcoming, who would put me in the right way. I dismounted, therefore, and allowed the animal to graze over the bank whereon I sat. Full half an hour I remained lost in contemplation of the vast scene before me; a few large drops of rain, and the cravings of an importunate stomach recalled my roving thoughts;

the shadows of bread and butter, slices of ham, omelets, eggs, and cups of smoking tea, passed in review before my hungry fancy, and inspired me with new energy.

"Right or wrong," said I, "here goes." I jumped upon the pony, gave him his head, and away I went up the narrow path-way, leaving the little animal to select his own road; he will smell the corn-bin, thought I, as he took the road to the left, so I urged him into a better pace, although it struck me at the time that the other road looked most like a thoroughfare: "*kooch pur warni,*" (never mind), said I aloud, as the bracing air into which I was now rapidly ascending caused a proportionate rise in the barometer of my spirits; "if I go wrong, I go wrong; and if I go right, why so much the better; so shove along, good pony;" and another application of "Latchford and Crowther" touched him along at a real good pace up the perpendicular way.

Gradually the path became narrower and still narrower where it was cut out of the face of the straight-up-and-down cliff; in places the surface was intersected with water-courses, and my progress was so much impeded with loose stones and roots of trees, that more than once I involuntarily cast my eyes from my narrow footing, no longer a road, to the unfathomable abyss over which it hung. Truly, it was nervous work; every moment it grew darker, and as my apprehension awoke, I paused to consider seriously what I was about. I stood in the very densest volume of the clouds, unable to see three yards in any direction; suddenly, a vivid flash of lightning almost blinded me, and the next moment, a crash of rattling thunder rent the clouds in circling eddies all around me; then a rushing wind came sweeping down the mountain, and nearly carried both me and my pony over the precipice. A word to the wise, thought I, as I forthwith dismounted, having no ambition for so ethereal a flight.

"Bah! botheration!" I could not help exclaiming aloud; "what a consummate fool I must have been to have allowed a little senseless brute like this to bring me into such a perilous situation! any body but a booby would have known that this could never be the road to Mussoori; why it's no broader than the Mussulman's bridge into heaven; no human being, or four-footed beast, in its senses, would have attempted such a cruel bad steep; the other was of course the road; I thought so at the time, but this vile rascally pony would insist upon bringing me into this horrible Pandemonium: I can hear a boiling Phlegethon below, and a whirlwind of shrieking demons above me. A plague upon my folly, in suffering myself to be duped into such a miserable predicament by a stupid, insensible, brainless beast like this!"

I thought of descending again to Rajhpore, but the rain fell in such torrents as to render the pathway, over slippery greasy mud and rolling stones, quite impracticable to the most cautious descent. Neither was I at all in the humour for prosecuting my journey upwards: I was undoubtedly upon the wrong road, and should be getting involved deeper and deeper in the wilds of the mountains, from which I might not be able to extricate myself. My only alternative then was to remain where I was till the storm passed over; an arrangement which I hardly felt to be an enviable one, starving as I was with hunger, and wet through to the bones, as a Frenchman would say.

Again and again I vented my ire upon the obnoxious pony; upbraiding him as the cause of all my misfortunes, and half inclined to thrust him over the precipice. Poor beast! he endured the whole weight of my gall without a murmur: there he stood, emitting clouds of steam, with his hind legs firmly stretched out to keep him from slipping backward; his head drooping to the ground; his tail tucked tightly in between his legs; the water streaming down his shaggy coat in all directions, and the breath evolving from his nostrils, like the smoke from a fish-fag's backy-pipe. Presently, he drew up his head, pricked his ears, and uttered a short whinny of pleasure, which it was not difficult to construe. Immediately afterwards, I heard the scrambling paces of another pony coming up the path below, and unwilling that any person should find me thus irresolutely sticking *inter utrumque tenens*, I mounted at once, and again urged on my pony.

I was quickly overtaken by a gentleman upon a powerful *ghoont*, a perfect resemblance of a cart-horse in miniature. I turned in my saddle, and looking the stranger in the face, said, "If I offer to let you pass, I fear there will scarcely be room for you to do so."

"Don't mention it," said he, "but you had better keep an eye to your nag's head, or you may chance to be out of my way quicker than you calculate. A hundred yards further on, you will find a niche, where I shall be obliged by your going aside, so that I may take the lead. I wonder you should attempt this track upon such a sorry brute as that you ride."

I explained my ignorance of the country, and requested information as to the way to Mussoori. In reply, I had the satisfaction of hearing that I was not exactly upon the wrong road, but simply that I had chosen the most difficult, and one which was called the *Paharri** track, because seldom used except by the natives on foot, or by those who were well mounted and accustomed to the difficulties of the passes. My fellow-traveller went speedily a-head, but my pony having so good an example before him, would not suffer himself to be far outstripped, and we soon got into fine weather again, leaving the clouds and the tempest below us.

So refreshing is the bracing air upon the mountains to the calcined constitution, and so exhilarating to the dried-up spirits of a *koi hi* from the plains, that the new flood of energy and delight almost carries off the reason of the traveller, as he ascends into these celestial realms; the fancy takes its flight beyond all power of control; and the spirits imbibe excitement even to intoxication. The most unmusical of men may be heard trying

* *Paharri*, a mountaineer, from the word *Pahar*, a mountain.

his voice in song, or striving to break-in his lips to a whistle: he who never before loved poetry shall be heard to spout for once,

> "Under the greenwood tree,
> Who loves to lie with me,
> And tune his merry note,
> Unto the sweet bird's throat,
> Come hither, come hither, come hither."

When about a couple of miles from Mussoori, I overtook a young *Paharri* damsel, driving cows; my attention was caught by her graceful figure, and her highly picturesque costume. Her hair was gathered into a knot upon the crown of her head, and thence fell in the fashion of a horse's tail down her back; across her shoulders a bright red scarf was loosely thrown, and from her waist a short grey petticoat descended to her knees; below which a finely rounded leg and well-turned ankle gave a finish to the figure, and formed by no means its least attraction. As I passed, the girl, instead of screening her face from observation, as do the modest females of the plains, looked innocently up in my face, exclaiming, "Do not drive my cows, I pray you, sir, for they may scramble off the road, and then I shall have much labour in collecting them again."

I was surprised at the freedom and simplicity

of the damsel's address, and more so at her comely countenance and sparkling eye, the *Paharris* being characterised by the broad cheek-bones and small twinkling eye of the Chinese.

"Well then, my pretty lass," I replied, "you must let me amuse myself by talking to you as far as our journies may lie upon the same road."

"Very well, sir; but what can a *Feringhi Sahib* have to say to a poor girl of the mountains?"

"Why, you see, I am a stranger in these parts, and wish to pick up information respecting your beautiful country. Young and artless as you appear to be, you will be able to tell me much of which, though a traveller through many countries, I am yet in ignorance."

"Alas! sir," replied she, "is it for the infant to instruct its parent? or for the young kid to direct the steps of the goat? I am but a child in knowledge, and do you bid me show you what our wise men call their own? Shall I tell you of my cows, or of the butterflies which sport over the flowers, or of the eagles sailing aloft yonder?"

"Yes, even there you could tell me much which I do not know. But have you no family or home to talk to me about? there I cannot enter, and can only learn by hear-say. Are you married?"

"Married! certainly, I am married, and have seven handsome husbands, the finest men in the village; but I cannot say they are such tall straight fellows as the servants who follow you gentlemen from the plains."

"Seven husbands, did you say? what, all your own? or did I misunderstand you?"

"Ay! truly, seven husbands; what else should I say? we are not like the unfortunate women in the plains, who, it is said, have but one man, good or bad, belonging to them. But I am wrong to say seven; I have only six now; one of them I discharged yesterday; he was an idle useless fellow, with only one eye, and a crooked back."

"What, do you send them away if they have any defects, or if you do not love them?"

"Certainly; or if a man should be idle or poor, a woman could not be expected to keep him, when she might have fifty better. Go your way, sir; my cows go up this turning to the right."

"But tell me before you go, my pretty girl, if all the women in your villages are as fortunate as yourself in the number of their husbands; and if it be usual with them to turn their good men off with as little ceremony as you appear to have done?"

"Why," said the woman, "all my sisters are not considered so handsome as I am; but some have two husbands; some have three or four; few are so poor as to have only one."

"And would you have more than seven, if you could find them to please you?"

"No; if I have more than seven, it is impossible that they should be all good. Seven is a happy number."

"Then, I suppose you will get another to supply the place of the seventh whom you discharged yesterday?"

"When I find one whom I can love."

"But do not your husbands quarrel? are they not given to jealousy one towards the other?"

"No; why should they? are they not treated according to their deserts?"

"Have you any children?"

The girl drew her red scarf over her face, and turning abruptly away, followed her cows.

A discussion upon the subject of polygamy, which appeared a short time since in the Calcutta papers, elicited from a native the following very pertinent rejoinder in its defence:—

"Sir,—You English gentlemen are very fond of complaining against the natives of this country, because they marry many wives. If your religion and the customs of your country don't allow you to have more than one woman as wife, why should we be guided by you, who are of another nation and religion? It is a true thing, which every body acquainted with Asia knows, but how it happens nobody knows, that there are more women than men in this country, whether because more females are born, or because you Englishmen kill the males in battle, magician only can tell. Then, in this case, giving one woman to every man, what is to become of the remaining many women? They must have somebody to love them. The plain truth is, we are destined by nature to have many wives and much happiness—it is our good fate to have many wives—it has been so from the beginning of the world. Don't then, I pray, interfere with the decree of nature."*

* This letter is a correct copy of the writer's composition, and not a translation. The author was educated at the Mussulman college in Calcutta.

CHAPTER IV.

THE HIMÁLA MOUNTAINS.

MUSSOORI AND LANDOUR.

MUSSOORI stands 7,500 feet above the level of the sea; the place is an extensive collection of gentlemen's residences, situated on the southern face of the ridge, called the Landour range, which forms the first step towards the eternal regions of congelation, in the gigantic pinnacles commonly called the Snowy Range. The climate during the greater part of the year is so exquisitely pure and bracing, that one is tempted to declare it the finest in the world.

About a mile from the eastern extremity of Mussoori, overlooking the village of Landour, the Company have established a sanitarium for the benefit of their European soldiers, where any man, whose health is considered to be irrecoverable in the plains, may be sent for resuscitation in this invigorating climate. The barracks are roomy and comfortable, as are also the bungalows for the reception of the officers on duty. Such an institution does honour to the government which maintains it, showing as it does a regard for the comfort and well-being of its servants, which commands our admiration and praise.

So wonderfully salubrious is the climate in all common cases of a disorganized system, that I have known instances without number, wherein men have arrived from the plains apparently upon the very brink of the grave, almost without signs of animation, life being reduced to its last flicker in the belief of all, and of the unfortunate himself, who suffers himself to be carried up the mountain, under a full conviction that his days have come to their close, beyond the aid of medical skill or of the most healthful of climates; and at the end of the season, or in a very few months, I have seen these men walking or riding about, in all the enjoyment of comparative health and vigour.

During the cuttings and clippings of our late Governor-general Lord William Bentinck, a rumour was very generally circulated, that it was his lordship's intention to abolish the sanitarium, as a measure of economy; but, fortunately, the matter terminated in discussion, and there stands the dépôt to this day. For the credit of our government, let it not be supposed that so paltry a consideration would weigh with them against the lives, to say nothing of the comforts and happiness, of their service-worn soldiers. But it is reasonable to suppose, though I have no very exact data to go upon, that this invalid dépôt is a saving rather than an expense to the government; and doubtless Lord William discovered this, or judging by analogy, he would hardly have withheld his retrenching fingers from it.

Let it be remembered, that by the time a recruit is landed in India, he will have cost the government at least £100; and in order to keep up the efficiency of the regiments, the place of every man who is swept off by disease must be filled up by a recruit. If a man, therefore, be suffered to die in the plains, there is a clear loss to the government of £100; whereas, if the life be saved—but we know the old saw, "a penny saved is a penny got;" barring in this case the expense incurred in the saving, which at most will be but a small fraction of £100. But then, as I said before, what have we to do with pounds, shillings, and pence, when lives are in the balance?

From the western side of Landour, a most im-

posing view of the Himála Peaks, the snowy range, is obtained; more particularly from the point called Lall Tebor: those who have travelled towards these gigantic pinnacles affirm that no where are they to be viewed to greater advantage than from this spot: when closer to them their mystery is in a measure lost in tangible reality, and when farther away the effect of their altitude is diminished. From Lall Tebor their distance is about thirty miles, and the elevation is sufficient to give the beholder a clear uninterrupted view of them, over the swelling sea of mountains which fills the middle-distance. Owing to the exceeding purity and brilliancy of the atmosphere, a startling ocular delusion takes place, when these snowy mountains are lit by the slanting rays of the sun; especially in the early morning, when the floating mists below cut off from the eye any gradual approach through the intervening scenery: so very close do these distant mountains appear, that the beholder considers them almost within his grasp, and would, if he fired a gun in that direction, expect to see his bullet perforate the snow.

The highest of these peaks is Dhewallaghiri (the white mountain), in which the river Ghunduk has its rise. The exact height of this has not yet been determined, but those accounts which are considered most authentic state it to be about 27,400 feet above the level of the sea: thus exhibiting a difference of nearly 6,000 feet between this and Chimborazo of the Andes, the height of which is fixed at 21,470 feet. But this is not the only peak of the Himálas which greatly exceeds those of the Andes; twenty of them have been ascertained to rise above the altitude of the latter. Jumnoutri, in which are the sources of the Jumna, has been laid down as 25,500 feet: this mountain rises in three peaks, the centre one of which is the highest, and the other two points are said to be the wives of the superior. Gungoutri, upon which the Ganges takes its rise, is said to be 25,250 feet, and here, upon the apex, some castes of the Hindus affirm that Mahadeo has erected his throne; others consider that the mountain is itself the god of destruction. No villages have been found at a greater altitude than 14,000 feet, and even here the natives are squalid and unhealthy. Cultivation has been carried as high as 14,500 feet, and vegetation as far up as 16,000. The *goitres* are prevalent among the *paharries* in every part throughout these mountains, but they do not seem to regard the disease as a deformity.

HILLS, EAST OF MUSSOORIE

The houses at Mussoori, though small, are very commodious, and are built something in the style of English cottages. They are stuck about the sides of the mountains, like gulls' nests on a cliff, there being scarcely ten square yards of level ground to be found in the place, except such as has been carved out of the rocky steeps. The position of the place is exquisitely romantic, and the view from it grand beyond description. A verbal outline of the most formal kind is all I dare attempt.

Upon the left, that is, eastward of the place, lies that magnificent extent of mountains through which the sacred Ganges forces a broken and disturbed course, fading, as they recede from the eye, in all the endless tints of mountain-scenery, from the rich autumnal browns, in the foreground and middle-distance, to the palest azure and aerial grey; along the foot of these, a narrow stream of water is seen, creeping in beautiful contortions over the surface of the level country, until it is lost in the distance, where the earth and sky are blended into one. This last expression will hardly be intelligible to those who have not witnessed what the words are intended to convey. To the beholder thus exalted above the level of the plains, no positive horizon is visible, the landscape, as it recedes in distance, being gradually obscured until it vanishes entirely from the sight, mingling imperceptibly with the sky, as the intervening body of atmosphere increases. Thus, when the sun's rays happen to be strongly reflected from any distant stream of water, so as to catch the eye of a person stationed on the mountains, the course of the river may be distinctly traced, like a silver thread running into the sky, beyond the distance at which all the rest of the landscape vanished; a phenomenon which, though easily explained, is at first sight startling, as it is strange to those living in the level country.

The centre of the picture is an expanse of distant lands well-nigh endless, embracing many towns and villages, rich in stupendous forests, and intersected with patches of cultivation, through which streams and roads are seen winding in all directions. Upon the right, far, far in the distance, the Jumna runs meandering through a succession of undulating lands, thickly studded with trees, in a serpentine and fantastic course, the nearest extremity of which is shut out by the abrupt and precipitous outline of mountains in the neighbourhood of Budrajh. When the day is tolerably clear, the Sivalic ridge of hills is seen stretching itself directly across the champaign country, from the Ganges to the Jumna. At times, over the summits of these hills, a fresh extent of plain is again visible, mingling with the sky. It has been stated to me by those upon whose word I can depend, that during the month of November, when the atmosphere is clearest, the white houses at Moozaffirnuggur have been distinctly seen, with the assistance of strong glasses: this is a distance of eighty-two miles.

A day or two after our arrival at Mussoori, I went with my friend Peter to pay a visit to a brother officer; we found he had visitors in the house, and the whole party were just sitting down to tiffin.

"Allow me," said the host, "to introduce you to Major and Mrs. Stokes." An innocent bow from Peter assured me that he had no recollection of the name.

"Timothy, my love," said Mrs. S., "put your napkin about your neck, or you'll be making a mess of yourself."

A nearer view of my heroine rather improved the picture which I had formed of her, in my hasty glimpse by torch-light. My impression had then been, that she lacked an eye; but by more narrow scrutiny, I discovered a second, situated in the lower regions of the cheek, in a line between the corner of the mouth and the lobe of the ear; but the lips, taking fright at so near a proximity to this invading luminary, had shied off at a tangent to the opposite side of her face, leaving the teeth in their original position, as a guard against any further intrusion. Her Timothy had undoubtedly been a good specimen of a man in his younger days; but, unfortunately, his beauty had been spoiled by a kick from a horse, which had closed his starboard port, and laid his nose upon its beam-ends over to larboard; however, poor man, it was not his fault: the pair were both of them good creatures, and as amiable as doves.

When the business of the table grew slack, and there was time for conversation, my friend Peter began to amuse the company with a ludicrous recital of my rencontre with the old lady in Khéri Pass; I kicked his legs under the table, but he withdrew them and continued his tale, giving the scene rather a warmer colouring than was borne out by the account which I had rendered him. Mrs. Stokes listened with marked interest, until it came to a description of the night-cap, &c., when thinking it high time to put a stop to all further particulars, she turned to me and exclaimed ; "So! was it you, my dear Sir, who so kindly escorted us through the pass? Oh! we were so much obliged to you, for indeed we were seriously alarmed at the thieves and tigers ; and if anything had happened, you know Timothy would have been of no use at all, poor man, he's so dreadfully afflicted with the tic-douloureux. Indeed, we were highly indebted to you for your company."

Peter now used all his efforts to smooth the old lady down. "Really," said he, "these rencontres in *dák* travelling are sometimes most awkward. I myself was coming up the same night, and had a bit of an adventure not unlike your own. I had dozed off for an hour or two, and when I awoke, I found a palki beside mine, which I concluded was that of my friend here. I called out to him to know how he was getting on, but receiving no answer, I naturally supposed he was asleep; so lighting my cheroot, I fell into a train of happy musings. Presently, I was aroused by a sweet soft voice from the next palki, exclaiming 'James! James! my love!'

"I did not answer; and the lady ordered her palki to be brought closer. 'James,' she repeated, 'James, my love!' raising her voice, 'how provoking you are! Do you choose to answer me?' Still, I did not reply, and the lady continued, 'You need not pretend to be asleep; I can see your cheroot, and I insist upon your throwing it away immediately; making a chimney of your mouth; I declare I will never kiss you again if you don't give up that vile practice; so you need not expect it: I have told you so a hundred times; and now I'll keep my word, you see if I don't.' —— 'James! you obstinate brute!' she again burst forth, after a considerable pause. Her patience was fairly worn out, and she thrust her head and arm into my palki with an energy which made me involuntarily guard my head.

"'My name is Peter, Madam,' said I; 'can I be happy enough to make myself useful to you?' An immediate recognition took place. Who do you think it was? Pretty little Mrs. T——. Alas! poor little thing, her fright was so excessive I feared she would go into fits."

"Ah! poor girl," said Mrs. Stokes, "and enough to frighten any young person, I'm sure. You gentlemen do wear such monstrous beards now-a-days. Timothy, I'm so glad you never had beard; ai'nt you?"

It was during this month, October 1834, that a

large army was assembled by order of Lord William Bentinck, with the avowed object of an expedition against Joudpore, the capital of the province of that name, in consequence of disturbances fostered by Rajha Maun Singh, one of the most powerful of independent native princes in India. The alleged cause of this hostility was stated at head-quarters to be the protection afforded by the Rajha to those murdering depredators, the Thugs, and to certain of his subjects, who had obstructed the navigation of the Indus; but it was well known that Maun Singh was not merely a shield to the perpetrators of the latter evil, but the instigator and origin of it.

The force under orders for action was very large: such an army had not been seen in India since the siege of Bhurtpore; and from the circumstance of its being large enough to bring famine upon the inhabitants of Joudpore, by its ordinary consumption, it as generally adjudged by all wiseacres, that the head of our government had a sinister and more weighty matter in view than the suppression of the Joudpore disturbances. This, however, proved to be unfounded: no sooner was the army put in motion towards the Rajha's dominions, than, anticipating nothing short of utter annihilation, he succumbed at once to the terms imposed by our government; the greater number of the regiments were then remanded to their quarters, and the remainder were ordered to take the field against a set of plundering vagabonds in the country of Sheikáwut, who, under cover of their little independent forts, had been long carrying on a system of robbery and depredation, both among themselves and upon travellers, whenever they could do so with impunity.

But I am anticipating matters; during the month of my visit to the mountains, the Joudpore army being as yet in preparation for the general move, the whole country was afloat with rumours and reports the most ludicrous and unfounded: insurrections, invasions, massacres, rebellions, assassinations, conspiracies, rapine, and every sort of outrage, were flying all over the face of the country in the letter-bags. Such incessant correspondence was kept up at this time between friends in every corner of India, that the *dák* revenue must have assisted materially in defraying the expenses of the expedition.

The current news was daily brought to me by an eccentric little old man, who was apparently the butt of his corps, and of all his acquaintance.

His whole life was spent in search of news, and he certainly had enough upon his hands at all times: he believed everything which he heard, and his correspondents found no little amusement in stuffing him with all sorts of humbug. Little Fogg might be seen hurrying post-haste round to the houses of all his acquaintance, to deliver himself of his budget before it had become stale. Wet or fine, the weather made no difference to him, further than that at one time his little cotton umbrella was stuck over his head, and at another time under his arm, as he bustled along with a face as full of importance as his pocket was full of letters.

"Well, have you heard the news? have you heard the news? haven't got a moment to stay—only, couldn't help coming in to mention that Lord William has been carried off by a fit of apoplexy; and Sir Charles, having assumed the reins of government, has countermanded two-thirds of the Joudpore force, and ——"

"But I say, Fogg, haven't you made a mistake? are you sure it was not perplexity?"

"The very best authority, my dear fellow; had a letter from my friend, Colonel Twig, this morning; here, I will leave it for you to read—haven't got time to stop now—not mentioned in the public prints from political motives; but it's perfectly correct, sir, take my word for it; good-bye. Oh! you've not heard, perhaps, that the princess Victoria has been shot by some miscreant about the court—shot through the head with one of his Majesty's waistcoat-buttons; and I'm positively assured by the Colonel, who has many friends about the royal household, that her Majesty has been brought to public trial—signs of the times, sir,—charges not stated—most barbarous murder—capital thing for the poor half-batta subs—Lord Mulgrave's the man, sir; a certain staff-appointment to me—but I must really be off. Well, sir, another correspondent states—there, I can leave you that letter too—that the Joudpore Rajha has refused to negociate, and has applied for advice and subsidy to the court of Russia, so that there's not a doubt we shall be involved in a war with that nation; and then, from the rotten state of our council-board, and from the decay of our commissariat, depend upon it we shall go to the wall, sir,—not a doubt of it. By-the-bye, I forgot to mention that old Runjeet Singh is dead; foolish enough to risk another attempt, abortive of course, to subdue Cashmere: he lost his ninth life by a poisoned arrow, which pierced his brain through his only eye. Good morning to ye—shall I leave this bundle of papers? the latest from Europe, but no news in them—perhaps you would prefer some of these letters—there, you shall have half a dozen of them; pray take care of them; the information is valuable—not to be had in the public journals. The Duke of Wellington has been stoned to death by the populace, and the Lord Mayor of London has been burnt upon the top of the monument—horrible, atrocious thing—you'll see—letters No. 4, 6, and 7;" and away little Fogg would trudge to the next house, with the same tidings of death and destruction.

Ten minutes afterwards, in he would come again, "Ah! more news for you, sir,—more news—stirring times these.—Seven corps of native infantry have mutinied at Nusseerabad, on Monday last, and murdered all their officers; they then went over to the Joudpore Rajha, but receiving intelligence of Lord William's death, they returned to their duty, and have given themselves over for trial;—they say every thing is going wrong at head-quarters—so there's a devil of a rumpus in Leadenhall-street when the news gets home. By-the-bye, is not the beautiful Mrs. B——, who was up here last season, a great friend of yours?—latest intelligence, my dear sir,—she has been carried off from her husband's residence by the brother of Maun Singh, with whom she is now living as his sultana; and although the Rajha has been frightened into an offer to restore her, the little vixen refuses to go back;—horrible, eh? good morning—I'll call again if I hear any more news." In ten minutes time, the little man would be sure to find his way back again, with a fresh store of absurdities, which his friends found it easy to foist upon him.

One evening I was pacing my virandah for exercise, wrapt in admiration of the most brilliant sunset I had ever looked upon, when Fogg joined me, with his usual burden of news. While my little friend was running on with his usual volubility, he suddenly stopped short.—"By the powers! sir, more signs of the times;—did ever you see such a thing? Well, I've seen solar rainbows, and lunar rainbows too, but I never before saw or heard of a rainbow, when both the sun and the moon were out of the way. Why, the sun has been set at least ten minutes, and the moon won't rise till thirteen minutes after nine. Ah! something terrible is going to happen, I see."

That which now absorbed all poor Fogg's apprehensions was certainly a strange phenomenon, and difficult of solution at first sight. Over the mountains, to the eastward, we beheld a perfect, unbroken arch, of a most beautiful rose-colour, forming at least three-parts of a circle; no other hue mingled in its colouring, but the centre of the arc was the least brilliant. "As plain as a voice from heaven, sir," continued my companion; "don't you observe? one foot of the arch rests upon 'The Priory,' and the other upon 'The curse of God.' Ah! the papists, the papists, sir; not a doubt of it—shall make a memorandum of the date in my event book, we shall hear of something very horrible; mark my words."

"Pooh! pooh! Fogg, don't you see the cause of it? though the sun has set, there is a flood of golden light upon that towering cloud fully sufficient to account for this extraordinary bow. Why, it's as bright as an English sun."

"Fudge, sir, fudge! who ever heard of a blood-red rainbow made by a cloud? All stuff and nonsense, sir; you'll not talk such trash when you've got my experience;" and away bustled the old gentleman, in a huff, to look out for a more docile disciple.

On the 12th of the month, as I was returning from a morning ramble over the mountains, I was startled by a piercing shriek, and then a rushing noise, as of a heavy body dashing down the *khud** below me. On second thoughts I attributed the noise to the fall of some detached mass of rock, probably launched over the precipice by mischievous or idle hands; but I was quickly undeceived, and attracted to the spot by the vociferous lamentations of a native servant, in the road beneath me. I hastened down to the place, and met several of the European soldiers from the barracks, also hurrying thither, for they had witnessed both the cause and issue of what had occurred.

An officer, Major Blundel, of H.M. 11th dragoons, was returning home upon his *ghoont* from the house of a brother-officer, and, as he rode leisurely along the road, having observed a snake upon the bank, he gave orders to his *sáes*, who walked behind him, to destroy it. The man was unable to find the reptile, and the Major with the intention of assisting in the search, turned his pony round, but injudiciously, with its head towards the bank, instead of facing the precipice. The road was very narrow, but there would have been no difficulty in turning, had the latter mode been observed. As it was, the pony, unmindful of the danger

* *Khud;* precipitous valley; such only as we find among mountains.

which lay behind him, made rather too wide an evolution, and his hind feet slipped over the brink of the precipice, which overhung a yawning abyss at least seven hundred feet in perpendicular height.

His imminent peril for a moment paralysed the old gentleman; but the pony, with immediate sense of its danger, made the most strenuous efforts to regain its footing, clinging with wonderful tenacity by his fore-legs, and catching at the roots and vegetation with his teeth to save himself; and in this he might perchance have succeeded, had not the Major made an attempt to dismount, thereby throwing the pony off his balance. Down, down, they went—a long shrill scream rending the air before them, as they dashed headlong through it, in their fearful career. Down, down, the awful gulf, full seven hundred feet without obstruction, were they hurled; and then their further course was broken, though not stayed, by jutting crags and splintered stumps of trees; onward they rolled, tumbling from point to point, followed in their downward flight by detached fragments of rocks and loose stones, upset from the mountain side, until at last they reached the torrent-bed, at the bottom of the wild descent, and here their mangled bodies lay jammed in the narrow channel.

With great difficulty a few of us succeeded in reaching the place where the corpse of the old Major lay. A sickening spectacle here presented itself. The whole of the back part of the head was wanting, and the features were completely obliterated; the figure was horribly lacerated, and was scarcely to be recognized as a human form: the bones of the right fore-arm were driven clean through the body, the flesh and muscles being torn away, from the elbow to the wrist, leaving the hand protruding from the side below the ribs. By passing a native's *kummurbund* (waist-cloth) carefully round the body, we at last managed, though with great labour, to get it up to the road, and then it was carried to a small vacant bungalow on Colonel Young's estate, where a military court of inquest was immediately assembled, to investigate the circumstances of the case. A few days afterwards, I followed the body to its grave in the beautiful little burial-ground at Landour.

It struck me as a remarkable circumstance, that among the hundreds of tomb-stones accumulated there, not one bore record of a similar fate, or of death by accident. This seems strange indeed, in a place surrounded as Landour is with unfenced precipices, and local dangers of all sorts, where a single step to the right or left may plunge the traveller into destruction; and, referring again to the many hair-breadth escapes which I have myself seen or undergone, cannot but excite our astonishment. Not a single instance of the kind had occurred within the memory of the residents, except in the cases of a few natives. Major Blundel was an universal favourite; so cheerful and so generous was he, that the sad catastrophe just told, threw a check upon all our gaieties; which, in an idle community like that of Landour and Mussoori, may be accepted as the sincerest testimony of sorrow and esteem.

The above accident appeared to affect the nerves too, as well as the sympathies, of our society; for though very few were known to walk before, scarcely a soul was seen to ride afterwards, except, by-the-bye, those dauntless and most perfect horsewomen, Mrs. P—— and Mrs. Y——. *Ghoonts* and ponies, turned out to grass, were staring over every bank and paling in the place, and "the sweetest pet of a creature" might be had for a compliment.

My own beast was near sharing the same fate, or a worse. Only a few days after the Major's death, I was galloping home from my evening round of visits, and overtook a lady walking, with whom I stopped to converse. My pony was impatient, and insisted upon walking a little a-head of her, so that I was obliged to turn round in my saddle when addressing her. Suddenly, she became deadly pale, and sinking back against the cliff-side, covered her eyes with her hands, exclaiming, in a voice faint and broken with terror, "Oh, for heaven's sake, Mr. B——!" I was hastening to her assistance, but in turning to dismount I discovered the cause of her alarm;—my heart sprung to my throat as I beheld my terrible peril. The edge of the road, or rather path-way, for it was not more than four feet wide, had been built up with large loose stones, and my pony, abandoned to his own guidance, was stepping from stone to stone upon the extreme brink of a frightful *khud*. Had one stone given way, had the animal made a false step, how La Ruse would have bewailed my exit by the precipice-slip! In cases where any particular difficulty is to be passed, it is invariably the better plan to give the pony his head, and allow him to select his own footing; he will then carry his rider over places apparently impracticable: but where the road is easy, let the rider keep an eye to his beast, lest from over-security he should step into hidden danger.

There are some very beautiful cataracts in the vicinity of Landour and Mussoori, but none of them are of any great volume; and as foaming boiling water-falls are to be found in most journals, tours, excursions, sketches, &c., the reader, I am sure, will gladly dispense with a description. There is also vast matter for literary labour, and technical lore in the animal creation, particularly in the branches of ornithology and entomology; but upon subjects such as these, I am fain to admit my utter ignorance: volumes have already been written, and volumes will yet be written, concerning them; but, alas! I am unable to offer a single page. I can admire the variety and beautiful plumage of the pheasants; I can shoot them and eat them; but I can go no further, unless perchance I should prescribe a sauce for them.

CHAPTER V.

THE HIMÁLA MOUNTAINS.

It was during this month, that the whole debtor community of the Upper Provinces was "thrown into the most dreadful state of alarm and confusion," by the sudden appearance of one Mr. Stagg, a bailiff, bearing innumerable warrants, rendered most formidable by that small word *capias*, from the Sheriff of Calcutta, for the apprehension of the persons of Messrs. Dobbs, Fibs, Thomson, Johnson, Jackson, and very many others. This respectable limb of the law had visited Merat, with his pocket full of writs, ready for execution; but here his reception was colder than he quite relished, for some sporting lads, who loved a spree better than they loved justice, ducked him with little mercy in the black waters of the Kalli Nuddi; in consequence of which it was understood, that he had taken his departure for Mussoori. Throughout the place, a servant might have been seen squatting at almost every door, to scrutinise the persons of all visitors; and not a few handy bludgeons might be found in the corners of most bachelors' quarters.

One very wet and gusty day, being obliged by business to go forth and brave the driving storm, I wrapt myself in a large blanket great coat, and embellished my head with an oil-skin hat, my legs with a pair of jack-boots; in which very suspicious costume, had I given it a thought, I might have expected to be pitched over the precipice, in mistake for the dreaded bum-bailiff. My respectability was certainly questionable, and it was little marvel that the servants stationed at the entrance of the houses should shut up the doors and disappear with a caution to their masters, as I galloped through the place.

It was about eight o'clock when I presented myself at the house to which I was bound: the door was banged in my face, and away went the man to give warning of a stranger's approach. Dismounting, I entered without ceremony, and meeting the servant in the passage, I demanded to be informed if his master were at home.

"No, sir," replied the servant; "my master went to Budrajh last Monday, and will not be home for a week;" and then sticking himself in the middle of the passage, with the air of a bull-dog guarding a bone, he added, "my master will be angry if I allow you to enter his house while he is absent, therefore you had better go away."

"False slave!" said I; "I hear your master's voice within; make way; there is no ceremony between him and me; but you are a new servant, and do not know me;" and thrusting the man aside, I abruptly entered my friend's chamber.

"Open the window! open the window!" cried he to another man, as he went hopping and spinning about the room on one leg, unable from confusion to get the second limb into his trowsers—for he had just bounced out of bed, in an agony of apprehension;—then, seeing me close upon him, he caught up the still unmanageable half of his garment, and rushed from the window into the wet grass, under a pelting shower of rain. Never shall I forget the pitiable expression of his countenance as he turned to see if I gave chase: still undeceived, away he ran, as swiftly as his legs would carry him, into the next house, for protection against the supposed bailiff. A few words upon a slip of paper, despatched by the hands of a slave, soon brought him back, laughing most heartily at his mistake.

"Well, Sackville," said I, "how do you like the mountains after all?"

"Why, my dear fellow, it's rather an unfortunate day to put such a question; but, generally speaking, there is no place in the world to be compared to them; the atmosphere is so pure and exhilirating; one says so many good things; and then the people make the place agreeable; and the appetite is so good; what a pity it is we can't have our Beef-steak Clubs up here instead of at Merat! I spent yesterday at the Leicesters'; quite delightful, upon my honour; such a bright and lovely morning too, it made one quite poetical; there were so many witty things said, and so many good things to be eaten, that—yes—under the influence of so rarified an atmosphere, one can do these things creditably. Upon my veracity, my dear fellow, it is my firm opinion that if the most consummate dolt that ever suffered strap at a day-school, could only obtain a bottle of air from Jumnoutri or Gungoutri, he might at pleasure out-wit the leading boy of his class, so bracing, so invigorating are the effects of the climate, not only to the constitution and the spirits, but to the wits also. Why, never before in all my life did I coin such a vast assortment of brilliant things as yesterday fell upon the ear of the beautiful Mrs. Leicester; you shall hear a few of them some day; I'm making up a book to take on furlough with me; by Jove, sir, I wouldn't despair of the first fortune and the first beauty in England—just such things as fairies and angels would love to talk about—so brilliant, so enchanting, yet so light and delicate."

"But the Leicesters are rather slow, are they not? I hear Mrs. L. is very romantic and vastly conceited: I have not seen her."

"Not seen her, my dear fellow! I'll take you the first fine day—she's quite a pet of mine. Such an eye, such hands and feet, such a figure—and then her voice—quite impossible to do the agreeable to any one else when she's present—her wit's decidedly above par too, I can tell you—such ready repartee, such happy hits;—and then you know, her eyes do say so many brilliant things. I took a stroll with her in the garden yesterday, and, unaccountably, except by sympathy, our walk extended into a ramble down the *khud*; and there we found ourselves beside a dashing torrent, which by a natural process caused the stream of our felicitous sayings to flow afresh. The birds were warbling all around us—'twas quite entrancing. 'Really,' said Mrs. Leicester, 'this is very sweet! couldn't you wish always to live in such a lovely bower as this? See, our harmonious voices have set those saucy birds tuning their tiny throats to echo back our melody. But I don't chuse to be outdone by them; I've heard them long enough, and now they shall listen to me, if they have as much taste as they have music in their composition.' She rested herself upon a projecting point of rock, and poured forth in most exquisite style that touching thing, 'The Misletoe Bough.' When she ceased, her last notes seemed to hang suspended in the air, as if loth to melt away. The greatest compliment she received, was a pause in the music among the branches; as for myself, I was so much overcome that, upon my faith, I couldn't grant a single word of admiration. Oh! it would have been a cruel sacrilege to have said a syllable after such a flood of moving melody. I could but drop a tear; but I couldn't have said a good thing—no, not for a staff-appointment."

"Well, Sackville, that's all uncommonly good; very descriptive of the state of things, no doubt;

but I've come with rather a weighty matter on my hands——"

"Ah! a message from Pepperdale, I suppose," said Sackville, turning over the leaves of his common-place book,—common-place indeed—"well, I'll listen to it immediately, only take your coffee while it's hot, and in the interim I'll read you a page or two from this, as you've urged it."

"Friday the 11th.—Called on the Leicesters, and was introduced to the beautiful Mrs. Summersdown—'Mr. Sackville,' said Mrs. Leicester, 'you have just had the honour of being introduced to the beauty of Merat, known among her friends here as the Mountain Rose. Juliana, dear, this is Mr. Sackville, the new Romeo, who has joined the *corps dramatique* since you left Merat.'—'Mrs. Leicester will not be offended,' was my reply, 'if I venture to intimate that she too might take an appropriate name from the world of flowers. The Lily of the Valley would receive a higher compliment than has ever yet been paid to it by poets, if you would permit me to call you after it.'—'You are too late, my dear sir,' replied Mrs. Leicester; 'I have enjoyed that flattering title for the last two years, and am now sadly afraid that I am going out of season at last.'"

"Ah! ha! not so bad, was it?"

"Oh! excellent; but come, my good fellow, I really wish to have a little chat with you."

"Ah! certainly, yes—I will but read you a paper I have written for the Merat Mag., that's forthcoming. I think you'll like it, upon my word; Merat is decaying so very fast—but you shall hear—dated the first of the month; headed 'Touching Merat,'—not a bad heading, is it? Well now, just listen. 'Merat was once the gayest station in India, and is still supposed to be so; but alas! how changed is Merat!' 'Of course, you are going to the races to-morrow, Mrs. Slender?'—'Why, really, Mr. Fairfax, they are not worth going to; one never sees any body there; besides I can't get up so early.'—'Mrs. Ransom, I hope you mean to make me one of your party to the play to-morrow night: you've seen the bills?'—'I should be quite proud of your escort, my dear Mr. Fairfax, but we don't go. I'm so much afraid of catching cold in that draughty house. Besides, four rupees is really more than we can afford to pay for a ticket, every month.—'Oh! indeed you must go; you didn't see The Hunchback performed last week; 'pon my honour, 'twas the best got-up thing that I ever witnessed. The amateurs expect a bumper house after so successful a piece; there are two performers new to the station, and a very promising first appearance.'

"Doors open at eight o'clock—half-past eight, two men in the pit—nine o'clock seven people in the house. 'I say, Mr. Manager,' cries one actor, 'are we to play to this beggarly account of empty benches?'—'Oh! certainly, my dear fellow; the play should be performed if there were only two in the house, or people would make it an excuse for staying away in future. There's the gun—prompter, stand by to ring up—first bell at the pause in the overture—clear stage, gentlemen, if you please.' Tingle-tingle-ting--up goes the curtain, and on struts a hundred rupees' worth of tinsel on one side, and twice that value of silks and satins upon the other, for the entertainment of thirty rupees' worth of tickets in the house. Oh! fie upon ye, fair ladies, to whose bright charms and sparkling eyes the compliment of a free-gratis-for-nothing admittance is given. Let the scenery and wardrobe go to the hammer, and let the house be rented to the Temperance Society, as a brewery for ginger-tea!

"'Well, Fothergill, my friend, will you go as my guest to the Beef-steak Club next Tuesday? I know you've a good song when you like; but somehow you've laid by your pipes lately. We expect a gayer party than usual; the General has promised to come!'—'No, thank ye, my good fellow, I have adopted early hours lately, and moreover, am too hoarse to sing!'—Yes, 'tis a true bill; Merat, thou art literally gone to the dogs, since the station pack was established! Ask young Foxbrush if he's going to Lady Tulip's ball to-night? 'Why, no, my dear Fairfax, I can't; the dogs throw off at Saini to-morrow morning; so I must be early to bed if possible.'

"'We once had a court crowded with right scientific racket-players;—now a match can't be had, except by taking in the spoons. Scroggins is busily engaged in firing Hecate's back sinew, and Muggins is off to the kennel, to give Harmony a few grains of calomel, and Music a dose of castor oil. The pack is a good pack, I allow, a very pretty pack, and will some day, I hope, be a still better pack: but what is the use of the dogs? there is no country for them. You might just as well hunt a drag along the King's highway, as follow the dogs across Merat plains. Merat! again I say it, thou art gone to the dogs! But how? why? what's the reason? the cause of all this change? Why, thus it is. The mountains are so charming—ay, there's the rub—the mountains are so charming, that the moment the hot season sets in, away fly the fair dames to the regions of snow, in order to save their health and complexions. Simla and Mussoori swarm with petticoats and cripples, like an English watering-place; with this difference only, that in the former the proportion of petticoats to the has-been bloods is as fifty to one. Well, these sweet ladies, having no men to amuse them, and nothing in the world to do with themselves, are induced to skirmish for want of other occupation. Most ladies in India drop all their little accomplishments from sheer indolence, and then when left to themselves, their tongues are their only resource. Then again, the men at Merat, during the absence of the ladies, get attached to their stables and their kennels, play billiards and double-dummy, never dress except for mess, and never call except on duty. The consequence is, that when the ladies return in the cold weather, they are all at logger-heads among themselves; and the men, being disinclined to join parties, visit no one. So there is a stagnation of society, without one halfpenny-worth of cordiality or good-fellowship.

"Ride down the mall, once so gay and cheerful, and you will see the same, same faces every evening, looking as sour as yesterday's butter-milk, and as long as a kitchen poker. If a ball should be proposed, oh! Mrs. Green won't go because Mrs. Fairbright is to be there, of whom it is said, that she was divorced by, or did divorce, her former husband. Mrs. Sourlips can't go because the Countess Kissitoff is to be present, who is reported to have committed a *faux pas* on board ship, coming out. Bah! If this woman be pretty, or that fascinating, as sure as fate, some evil-tongued old harridan will spit a blemish upon her fair name. —— 'On the very best authority, she was seen walking in the garden by moonlight with young Griffin;' or, 'she allowed Captain Whiskerandos to tie her sandal; besides, she really goes on in such a way, galloping up and down the course with young Fairhead.'

"Alas! alas! those days, ever the shortest, are gone, when all was life and glee, all harmony and good-will: when every shoulder was put cheerfully to the wheel, and every hand lent a lift. How many days have I spent in painting scenes for our Drury, and chalking Cupids and garlands for our ball-rooms! The walls of our mess used once to re-echo to the measured tread of the young, the gay, and the beautiful; music and laughter rang around; lustres sparkled, glasses shone, plate glittered, eyes emitted fire—all was gay, glorious, fascinating. Now, nothing is heard within those halls, but the heavy step of the armed heel; or, if people do meet, 'tis only for the purpose of abusing one another.—How was it at the last ball? 'La! Mr. A. do look at Mrs. B., she's quite indecent; really, I must quit the room.'—'Goodness me! Mr. C., do look at Mrs. D., what a fright the poor thing has made of herself! I suppose she means to be called sweet Anne Page; never saw such a thing in my life.'—Then a shrug of the shoulders from one lady; eyes cast up to heaven by another; 'do look!' from a third, sends one home to bed, disgusted with the ill-humours of the women, instead of charmed and kilt by their pretty, prattling, nonsensical nothings. What says Byron somewhere in Don Juan?

"'The women much divided, as is usual
  Among the sex, in little things or great;
Think not, fair creatures, that I mean to abuse you all,
  I have always liked you better than I state:
Since I've grown moral, still I must accuse you all
  Of being apt to talk at a great rate.'"

"There, now;" continued Sackville, "what do you think of that? rather racy, eh?"

" All very true, Sackville, every word of it ; but come, now, to business ; I'm in a hurry."

" Ah ! certainly, I'd quite forgotten,—if there be any thing about which I'm conceited, it's the use of my pen—that, and my shooting. By-the-bye, some bears have been seen at The Hermitage; have you a mind to go out ? we shall have fine weather in a day or two."

A bear-shooting excursion was soon set on foot, and it was agreed that we should push our operations three or four marches into the interior, in the direction of the large conical mountain called Taien. We procured small hill-tents, which could be carried by our *paharries*, there being no other method of conveyance practicable, whither we were going ; and having made all necessary preparations, we set out upon our expedition a few days after the above dialogue.

As we rode side by side along the narrow path, I could not help remarking that the gay Sackville was not in his usual spirits.

" Am I not ?" said he, " I'm a great ass then. It's only a little *fracas* with the Leicesters. The fool has denied me the house, and forbid me the lady's acquaintance. Did you not hear of it ? We were out yesterday morning—no damage.

By-the-bye, you've heard me talk of my old governor: here's a characteristic epistle I got from him yesterday; it arrived just as I was going to meet Leicester, and it very much set my conscience at rest with regard to my friends at home; listen.

"'Dear Septimus, Nov. 3d, 1833.

"'Received your's dated March 10th, about six months since, and were glad to hear of your good health; hope you still enjoy it. Thank God, most of us are pretty well; though none of your sisters are married. By-the-bye, if you think you could manage to support her till she gets a husband, I'll send out one of the girls to you. Georgy's the prettiest, but Bella's better taught and more showy, your mother says. Let me know which you would like to have. I suppose you don't recollect much of them. They send their love to you.

"'Your's ever,

"'GEORGE SACKVILLE.'"

This specimen of parental affection it was, and not "the little *fracas*" with the Leicesters, which weighed upon his spirits, for, puppy as he was in many things, he was not without strong feelings, and a warm heart. He continued ;—"It was many months since I had last heard from home, and when I saw my father's hand-writing, I broke the seal with a trembling hand and a kindling anxiety. 'Thank God,' I exclaimed, 'here is news of them at last.' Tush! here was a specimen of a father's love!"

Three short marches brought us to Taien, the proposed field of our action. We had ridden on before our servants and the *koolies* who were carrying our baggage; and Sackville, who had recovered his spirits, was playing all sorts of pranks for my amusement. Among other accomplishments, upon which he prided himself, was the art of imitating various birds and beasts; and while waiting for the arrival of our tents and camp-equipage, he proposed to waylay and frighten our followers. Secreting ourselves, therefore, in a patch of underwood, overlooking the track up which we had ridden, we lay in ambush, perfectly silent, until the first man made his appearance, under a load that would have better fitted the back of an elephant. Sackville uttered a terrible roar—"*Urra! Urra!—Wa! Wa!*" screamed the man, as he dropt his burden and ran off, as fast as terror could drive him, to the village for protection.

Two minutes afterwards, a second appeared "*Wa! Wa!*" said he, soliloquising aloud, "Ram Chundur has grown weary of his *bojh*, or some prowling tiger has taken a fancy to his ugly person. Well, so much the better; he won't want me." A thundering bellow from Sackville made him too drop his load, and thus he stood for a moment petrified with fright, trembling from head to foot, with his eye fixed upon the thicket where we lay; then, taking a bound over the edge of the road, away he went scrambling and tumbling down the *khud*, at the imminent risk of his neck.

The whole body of our retinue now came upon the ground, and great indeed was their amazement to find the burdens of their companions abandoned in the road. "God has taken them," said one. "They have fallen over the precipice," said a second. "Bears have carried them off," said another. Here a roar more fearful than either of the former struck terror into the whole company. Down went every man's pack, and each fled with precipitation, excepting only two old servants, who having, the one a double-barrelled gun and the other a matchlock, thought it beneath their dignity to fly. Dabi Singh, my *kullassi*, who had been much with me upon sporting excursions, and who was himself a tolerable shot, cocked and presented his piece in an instant; and so good was his judgment, and so correct his aim, that the ball whistled between us, cutting off the twigs of the bush behind which we lay concealed.

"Enough! Enough!" cried Sackville, and as he spoke, a second bullet, still nearer to the mark than the first, passed clean through the crown of his large straw-hat. "Hold, you rascals," we shouted simultaneously, as we rushed forth and found the other man blowing his match in preparation for a shot. "*Wa! Wa!*" said Dabi Singh, "Suckbill Sahib is so like a bear, he will be shot some day, if he lives till he is old enough."

Our first day's hunting was a blank, and although we saw the foot-prints and other vestiges of those we sought, we were unable to discover their haunts. In the night, however, we received an unexpected visitor in our camp, and his reception was possibly warmer than he had anticipated.

It was past midnight, when I was aroused from my sleep, by the report of a gun close to the tent: then followed a yell of agony, which must have moved the heart of the marksman to pity, and then the gurgling groans of ebbing life, as from some dying monster. I sprung from my bed to ascertain the cause, and was met at the tent-door by my friend Septimus Sackville, in his night robes; he had a gun in his hand, and his features were glowing with excitement and success.

"Come and see him, my boy," cried he in triumph; "as pretty a leopard as you might wish to see. I've stole a march upon you this time. The *Tchokedar* came in and gave me notice of it, while you were asleep, and being anxious to have him all to myself, I took your gun, and crept out, under cover of the outer *kurnaut* (wall of the tent). I caught the rascal in the very act of seizing one of your goats, within twenty paces, and in the open moonlight. Oh! such a sweet shot I had, and you will find the ball between his eyes." This proved to be the case, much to the delight of my friend, who anticipated sending a trumpeting article of all his gallant deeds to the Sporting Magazine, immediately upon our return to Mussoori.

The next morning, some *paharris* from the village offered to conduct us to a spot where two bears had established their winter-quarters, and where they considered it likely that a whole family might be found. We set out immediately after an early breakfast, and walked about four miles through a winding valley, which runs to the eastward of Taien; and at last, taking our course up the bed of a small mountain torrent, we again worked our way into the high lands, and up the steep face of the mountain, called Badul Kooli. This, our guides informed us, was the termination of our journey, and that a large cavern, overlooking the precipice, was the spot where they expected we should find the bears. We had been wandering for more than a mile without a road or pathway, and were therefore somewhat surprised when the men directed us to move forward upon a little beaten track, leading along the very edge of a rising cliff.

"Why, my friend," said I, "after passing through so much wilderness without seeing a single bear, is it probable that we shall find them in a frequented path like this?"

"Certainly, sir," replied the man; "is it not this which we have been seeking? Do you not remark that this track is beaten by the feet of bears only? Does a human being leave such a foot-mark as that behind him? You had better prepare your guns, for we shall not go far without falling in with one."

There was only room for one upon the narrow

path, and it was matter of dispute for some time as to who should have precedence. At last, Sackville ceded me the honour, in consideration of his good fortune the previous night. We moved on in silence about half a mile, and I was already suspicious of our guides' veracity, when a sudden turn in our course brought us in sight of a large cavern in the side of the mountain, the entrance to which was apparently closed with thick underwood. Just opposite to this cave, in the middle of the path up which we were advancing, lay an enormous bear, basking in the sun.

Immediately upon perceiving our hostile line advancing upon him, he reared himself upon his hind legs to his extreme height, stretching his arms wide apart, as if meditating an attack; but suddenly altering his determination, or his valour, like that of Bob Handy, oozing out at his finger-ends, he again took to all four legs, and commenced a growling retreat. We were about forty yards from the beast, and before I could get a steady shot at him, Sackville hastily fired past me, and hit him in the loose skin about the neck. This did him little damage, but it brought him at once to the charge. We were standing upon the very edge of the precipice, and had the animal been allowed to make good his attack, we should inevitably have been hurled into the giddy gulf below us.

"Keep your second barrel, Sackville," I cried, "don't fire till I have fired;" and fixing myself steadily, with a leg in advance, and with my gun presented, I awaited Bruin's charge. He hurried on, spreading his arms wide apart in anticipation of a delicious hug, and growling most awfully. On, on he came, till, within a dozen paces of me, he trod the very brink of the precipice; then letting drive both bullets in succession at his broad chest, I dealt him his death-blow, and he went rolling head-over-heels to the very bottom of the *khud* below. "*Khoob luggis! khoob luggis! Wa! Wa!*" screamed our followers; "this is fine sport indeed. Oaks will be plentiful:"—alluding to the acorns, which are food to these animals.

We fully expected to find Bruin's mate in the vicinity, and beat the ground all around the cavern; but our search being unsuccessful, Sackville proposed that we should explore the interior of the cave, which the *paharris* assured us was Bruin's mansion. I hesitated a moment before I assented to this proposition; for, thought I, if Sackville does not care for his father, I do for mine. I certainly should not have proposed it myself, but being thus invited, I could hardly say "Nay, I am afraid," so I said, "yes, most willingly!"

We reloaded and carefully examined our pieces, and I also slung a little pea-rifle over my shoulder, and stuck a pistol in my waist-belt. Sackville had his double-barrel and a pistol, and with this formidable battery, we had little to fear, provided we took all chances coolly, and adhered to our arrangement of firing alternately. Neither our guides nor any of our servants would follow us, in this adventure; so we had an additional argument for going. Side by side we advanced into the den, proceeding till it became too dark for us to see our footing.

"There, don't you hear something?" asked Sackville in a whisper.

"Whereabouts?"

"Whereabouts! why, a-head there! I'm sure I heard a noise, and a low growl."

"I hear the trickling of water," said I; "but nought else.

"But we can't see our way."

"Thank ye for the information, but I have had other warnings already. I got a most confounded crack over the shins just now, and stepped into some mud up to my ankle."

"Did you? don't you think we could get on better with a light?"

"Undoubtedly; but where, in the name of Fortune, are we to get one?"

"Hush! there's the bear; stand by. No, it s only the wind, I believe. But there's no saying what horrible place we may be getting into here. Eh? Don't you think its rather mad?"

"Well, come," said I, "we'll back and get a light; there is a village hard by, the men said: we shall be able to buy some oil there; and then we will make a *mussaul* (torch) in five minutes."

So we returned from the bowels of the earth, neither of us at all sorry to see daylight again, or to taste pure air, though we were both equally unwilling to express any apprehension of danger.

Having procured oil, a torch was quickly constructed, and we returned to our adventure followed by the two guides, one of whom carried the light and the other a short spear. On our first essay, we had probably advanced within a few paces of the extremity of the cave; for when lighted it proved of no very great depth, perhaps not more than thirty or forty paces. Its termination was formed in an angular or wedge-like recess, down the centre of which a little rill of water had excavated a deep fissure. Nothing was to be found within, and we were about to return to the open air, when one of the guides proposed that we should eat our tiffin in the cave, and some little delay occurred in persuading the man that the situation was not a delectable one: while we were yet discussing the matter, he suddenly exclaimed "Mercy! mercy! Shaitan! Shaitan!" (the devil! the devil!) and dropping his spear, he was about to fly, when I seized him by the arm; and he with the torch making a similar attempt was detained by Sackville.

"Where? where?" said I to my prisoner; "what do you see up there?"

"Let go! let go!" roared the alarmed *paharris*, "the devil, it is the devil; we shall all be devoured."

"Tut! tut! my son," said Sackville;" you are quite safe in our company, the devil won't come near us with these bright barrels. Where is this thing? I can see nothing."

"Alas! sir, I am a wicked man to have treated my wife so ill. I see his eyes looking down upon me, and nothing but the devil could get up there."

"Up where? It's impossible."

"Indeed, indeed! sir, I saw both his eyes, each as large as a cooking-pot, glaring upon me; he had a face like a lion, and two tusks larger than an elephant's."

We advanced the torch in the direction pointed out by the man, and there, in a small recess excavated in the side of the chasm, up to which the water-course formed a flight of steps, we beheld the grinning snarling face of a monstrous bear. This, as we found by the nursery, was Mrs. Bruin, Mr. B. having been unfortunately knocked over the *khud*, by a couple of ruffians, about half an hour before. A long low rumbling growl informed us, that the lady was not in the humour to receive visitors; but rudely disregardful of her wishes, we presented ourselves before her, with the muzzles of our pieces thrust within five yards of her face: she rose with an air of wrathful indignation, and with a savage growl which echoed through the cavern like thunder, and should have made us tremble; but less penetrable than herself, we returned her compliment with a warm salute, louder than her own, which brought her to our feet without further parley. A few death struggles, and poor Mrs. B. was no more; she closed her "cooking pots," and fled to join her loving lord, or to the frame of her next metempsychosis.

Her dwelling was now plundered, and two fine promising babes were kidnapped from their paternal roof. These interesting little creatures were despatched in a *banghi*, one to the tender care of the "Mountain Rose," and the other to Maha-rajha Hindu Ráo, the deposed chief of Gwalior, then residing at Dehli. I have since visited them both, and it was admirable to behold with what facility they were educated to eat plum-cake, or squeeze a cat to death. May they grow up to be as distinguished characters as their parents!

A few blank days wearied us of bear-shooting, for the season not being sufficiently far advanced, we were unable to find the sport we were in search of; pheasants and *chikore* were sufficiently plentiful, but they ill repaid the toil and danger of pursuit: We then turned our attack upon the deer, which offer the most exciting sport possible, to the sportsman who is practised in the art; but we, being more efficient in the *háoda* than on foot, abandoned it in despair, when we came to compare notes with a brother sportsman, whom we met in our rambles: this was G. C—— the most skilful and indefatigable deer-stalker who ever strode through the Himálas; he it was whom Mirchi, our old *shikarri* in the Kadur, had established as his idol, under the name of "Judge Kummul Sahib."

We returned towards Mussoori, having slain only one bear in addition to those already mentioned. Upon the road, at a place called Budrajh, Sackville had nearly been dashed to atoms, through a circumstance which, however tragic the termination might have been, was in itself so ludicrous that it became quite impossible to refrain from laughter; and even Sackville, as soon as he found himself safe, could not help joining in my merriment.

His *ghoont*, which was a remarkably quiet animal, and a very sleepy one, used to do so many odd things, that it at last became a joke between us that the animal was subject to absence of mind and reverie. We had nearly reached our journey's end, when turning to speak to Sackville, I beheld him sitting back in his saddle, with a rein in each hand, sawing away at the pony's mouth with no very gentle hand, and abusing him with no very gentle speech. The animal's head was cast aloft, and his eye was fixed upon a red cloth which lay upon the bank above him; onward he walked, sideling towards the precipice, in spite of all Sackville's most strenuous efforts to check or turn him. The rider grew pale with fear, as he saw the inevitable result, and he re-doubled his blows about the poor beast's head, but still without effect. He was about to throw himself off, when the *ghoont*, still unmindful of his danger, stepped beyond the brink, and away he went head over heels into the *khud* below, rolling down the side of the mountain at least five hundred feet, where he was found with his neck broken. As for Sackville, with his usual good luck, he, to his utter amazement, discovered himself sitting in a most comfortable niche, and supported by the trunk of a tree, without scratch or bruise. His escape was almost miraculous, and his first words were, " Lucky dog !"—His *sáes's* exclamation (the man was a Mussulman) was much nearer to the mark: "*Khodá-ki khoosi hi*" (this is God's pleasure).

The steeps about Mussoori are so very perpendicular in many places, that a person of the strongest nerve would scarcely be able to look over the edge of the narrow footpath into the *khud*, without a shudder of instinctive dread. The roads, as may be supposed, are quite inaccessible to all wheeled vehicles, but ladies, who have not sufficient courage, or are otherwise disinclined to ride, have a conveyance which is denominated a *jaun-paun,* or by corruption a jump'em: this a modification of the *ton-jaun,* or garden-chair, used in the plains, which is again a variety of the palki, being carried upon the shoulders in the same fashion. The former of these is a seat something like a chair, but of more substantial build, and supplied with a foot-board; it is swung by a pivot upon two lateral poles, so that it may always retain a perpendicular position, without which, upon such precipitous ground, a lady would be liable to be thrown from her seat; four *paharris* carry this vehicle, and it is really wonderful with what security they transport it over the most broken and difficult ground.

It is considered by most people dangerous to ride any other animal, among the mountains, than the *ghoont* or a mule; but during my stay at Mussoori, I continued to ride, without any inconvenience, a little Katawar pony, which I had sent up from Merat; and, strange it is that, although in the level country he had been so intractable and vicious as almost to induce me to shoot him, from the time of his arrival in the mountains he became perfectly manageable: once only did he play me a trick—but of this in its place. The change in the beast's temper was probably attributable to fear, lest in the giddy mountain passes any unruly behaviour might be the cause of a headlong flight down the *khud:* as a precaution against this possibility, I invariably rode him in a Hindostani *chahjama,* or padded saddle, without stirrups, so that I could throw myself off at a moment's notice.

At the end of the month it became time that I should again return to my military duties in the plains; and it was with a heavy heart, or, as the Indian metaphor expresses it, a "small liver,"* that I found myself compelled to quit the exquisite fairy land in which I had met with so much real pleasure and hospitality. Putting climate, scenery, and adventure, all out of the question, there was much, very much, still to be regretted in leaving Mussoori. Sackville also was returning

* This expression is very common among the natives of the Upper Provinces. "*Oos-ki kulleji bahoot burri ho-jaga;*" "his liver will become very large,"—meaning, he will be very much delighted. The first time I heard it, was upon the occasion of a compliment paid by a servant to one of my brother officers, who was about to be married; placing his hands before him with becoming humility, he said, "*Gurreebpurwan, golam-ne sumjha ki ap shaddi kurroge: Ap-ki kulleji kaisa burri ho-jaga. Khodú rukho ki beebi-ka kulleji bhee itni burri hoga.*" "Protector-of-the-poor, your slave understands that your honour is going to be married. How large your honour's liver will become! God grant that your wife's may also be as large!"

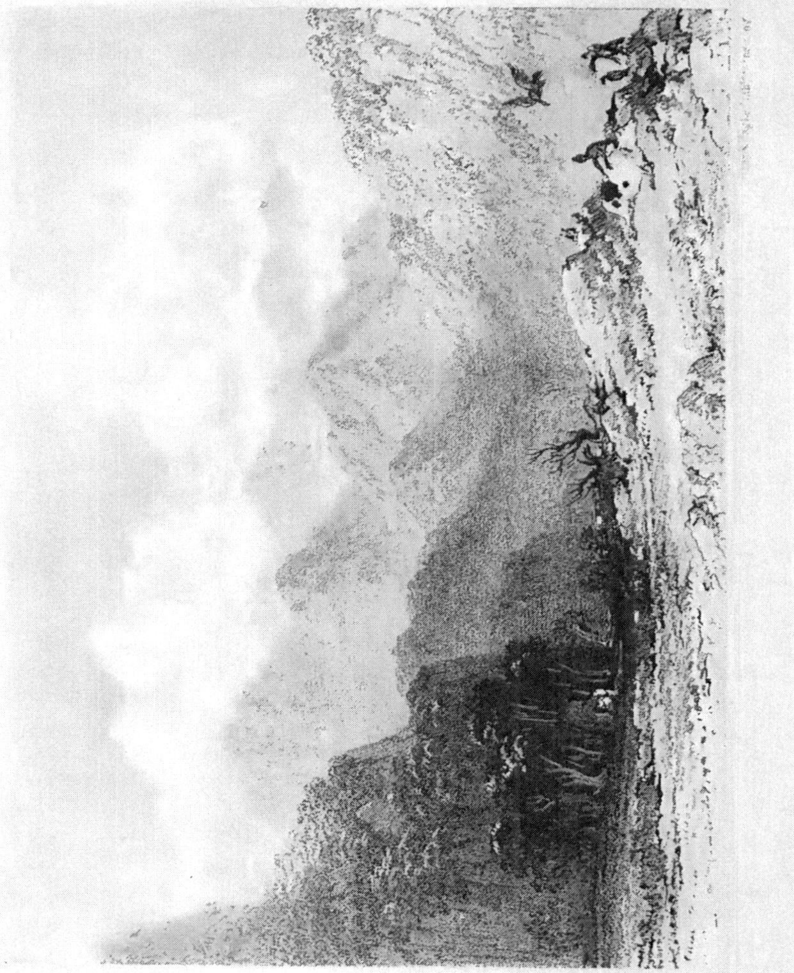

to Merat, and I could not help expressing myself to this effect, as we rode down towards Rajhpore together.

"Ah! my dear fellow," said he, "men are scarce here, and the ladies make much of us young fellows, when they can get us. Society is on a more cordial, more English-country-life-like footing here, than it can possibly be in a large military station; there is such a liberty, such a freedom of life, and such an absence of humbug; and then the climate, and the scenery—Oh! those lovely snowy peaks! and then the delicious butter!"

"Eh? what's that, Sackville? butter? delicious butter? snowy peaks? climate? scenery?"

"Aye, the climate, scenery, and delicious butter, I say, are so many additional sources of grief in quitting these sweet mountains. Did Mrs. Leicester never tell you, I'm passionately fond of good butter?"

Here our romantic conversation was interrupted by my pony refusing to proceed, he having taken a vast antipathy to a large white stone upon the road-side; and I was sadly afraid that Sackville would have his revenge, in a laugh at my expense. Persuasion and force were alike unavailing; he was obstinate, and I was determined; and thus we continued at cross purposes at least a quarter of an hour, until patience gave way on both sides; and at last, a few desperate plunges bringing me within a few inches of the brink, I jumped off with the intention of sending so dangerous a brute out of the way of further mischief: seizing him by the head, while he was yet rearing to strike at me with his fore-feet, I thrust him backwards over the precipice,—a barbarous act truly, but no sooner was it done than it was repented of. The poor beast rolled about twenty or thirty yards, and there most fortunately obtained a footing; three yards further, and he would have found a perpendicular fall of, at least, three hundred feet. When I had fully relented me, I gave earnest of my restored humanity, by going to the animal's assistance: with very great difficulty I managed to get him once more upon the road, where he stood trembling with excessive fear; for many minutes, he was scarcely able to keep his legs.

Having arrived at Rajhpore, we got into our palkis, and set off for a race all the way to Merat, believing that we had barely sufficient time for the accomplishment of our journey, before the expiration of our leave. Our apprehensions, however, were groundless, for, by offering small rewards to the bearers at each stage, we reached our destination in twenty-eight hours from the time of our quitting Rajhpore; the distance is one hundred and twenty-two miles, and this I believe to be the shortest time in which the run has ever been accomplished.

CHAPTER VI.

HURDWAR, DURING THE FESTIVAL.

The practice-season, as the winter is usually styled in India, commences in November, and terminates in March; and this being the only time of the year in which the military can undergo their full drills and discipline, both officers and men are kept up to their work, and leave is seldom granted to either, except in very urgent cases. As, therefore, it is hardly probable that the reader should desire a diary of cantonment life, after the slight specimens which have been already given, I will make no apology for passing at once to the conclusion of this period.

The burden of our military duties having been removed immediately after the reviews, with which the practice-season closes, my friend Sackville proposed that we should pay a visit to the celebrated Hindu city Hurdwar, during the *mela,* or grand festival, which was then approaching. We had short notice for preparation, and in order to reach the place while the fair was at its height, it became necessary that we should make forced marches.

Having made our arrangements in a very hasty manner, with more regard to expedition than comfort, we started from Merat on the 5th of April, hoping to reach our destination upon the 10th; having been informed that the fair would commence on that day and that there would be nothing worth seeing after the 12th. The travelling distance from Merat is ninety-seven miles; so that, in order to accomplish our object, it became necessary that we should march nearly twenty miles daily, an undertaking to which we feared our cattle would not be equal.

Our route lay through Dowralla, Kuttowli, and Moozaffirnuggur, in the road over which I had travelled to the Himálas, from whence it branched off to the eastward, through Poor, Munglour, &c. At this last-mentioned place, we arrived on the fourth day's march, and here, the evil which we had half anticipated displayed itself: our cattle, more particularly the camels, having had to wade through heavy marshes, arrived at the encamping ground so thoroughly jaded, that we were obliged to give them a day's rest. I endeavoured to prevail upon my companion to prosecute the remainder of the journey with me, upon one of the elephants; but he too was subdued by lassitude, for that morning we had been mischievously led astray upon the road, and, after many hours' wandering, arrived in camp, almost as much fatigued as the unfortunate horses which carried us. It was here that the elephant Bansmutti rescued the dog from the well, as stated in a former page.

Idleness in camp is, if possible, more intolerable than the same evil elsewhere; and as my best arguments failed to allure Sackville from his couch, when the sun began to decline, I took my gun and went in search of sport. The game I found abundant, and I was led on by success, farther and farther from camp, notwithstanding the repeated suggestions of my servants, who thought it was high time to retrace our steps. At last, the increasing dusk compelled me to desist from the pursuit, and it was only as I gave up my gun to my servant to carry, that I discovered how thoroughly fatigued I really was. To walk all the way back to the tents was quite out of the question, and I had serious thoughts of making each of the *koolies* in turn carry me home pick-a-pack, when in the neighbourhood of a small village, I espied a most ill-favoured starvling of an animal, scarcely deserving to be called a pony, the very prototype of Cruikshank's lean kine. This beast, however unpromising in appearance, I determined to avail myself of, and entering the village, I demanded to be informed who the fortunate owner of this steed might be.

The wonder and alarm, at first occasioned by my appearance, prevented my immediately gaining the desired information ; and in reply to further inquiries, I elicited that white men were scarce in those parts, and many of the younger inhabitants of the village had never before seen such a thing. The old fellow who acted as spokesman informed me, that about four years previously, the collector of the district had visited them (his wife, 'the beauty of the world,' was with him), making settlements of their boundaries and revenue assessments.

Ultimately, a bargain was concluded for the purchase, and the sum of one rupee, about one shilling and ninepence, was disbursed from my treasury as the price of the steed; the seller assuring me that the animal was of excellent pedigree, and, though a little out of condition, could travel with ease fifty miles daily. "Yes," said my bearer, making use of a pleasantry, the parallel of which is familiar in England, "if you put him into a cart, he would certainly do so, whether dead or alive."

Having thrown a cloth over the sharp back of my unwilling, but still unresisting nag, I mounted and set forth, amid the acclamations of a crowd of young children who flocked after me, shouting every term of honour and admiration. The elder part of the population were exceedingly respectful, and anxious to be of service, more especially he who had made himself rich by the sale of his pony. I had certainly no right to be annoyed by the impertinent interest thus taken in my person; for had I made my appearance in such trim in any village in old England, I should undoubtedly have attracted as much notice among the urchins of the place, so *outré* was my costume and equipment.

Thus, we proceeded on our return to camp, which was then about four miles distant; and being uncertain of the exact direction in which we should go, I preferred continuing with my servants to going a-head, for the greater facility of making inquiries about the way; indeed, had I been willing to quicken my rate of travelling, I suspect my pony would not have understood any other pace than a walk, as it is probable he had never practised any other. I led the van, having my bearer beside me carrying my gun over his shoulder; the rear was brought up by a straggling line of *koolies,* who had been employed in beating up the game. Our way lay through a narrow winding path, in many places scarcely passable, on account of the swamps and morasses with which the country was intersected; for we were in the upper extremity of the Kadir. On either side of the track, a wall of jungul grass rose above our heads, cutting off all prospect, except the limited one before us. The night was closing upon us fast, and our situation would have been not only uncomfortable, but probably dangerous, had we been altogether without light; but most happily we had a brilliant moon above, which lighted us upon our journey quite as effectually as the daylight.

Suddenly, every foot, every eye, every tongue, was stayed; and, if I may judge of others by myself, every heart beat quick with fearful apprehension. Immediately in advance of our party, at a distance of not more than twenty yards, the jungul parted, and a huge tiger stood before us in all the terror of unsubdued majesty. I made an effort to seize my gun from the hand of the servant; but, at that instant, the brute upon which I was mounted reared with fright, and fell backwards with me to the ground. Fortunately, I escaped without serious injury, and when I recovered my feet, the tiger had disappeared; having walked off though the opposite side of the jungul, as unconcernedly as he had broken in upon our quiet march. My charger had fled, and so had all the *koolies,* the only man who stood by me being my own personal attendant; but, although the former had not carried me very far upon my road, he had done me a service which more than recompensed me for the high price which I had paid for him: he prevented me from obtaining possession of the gun, and this in all probability saved my life; for, had I shot at the tiger and wounded him, he would assuredly have come down upon me, and the consequences would have been most likely fatal, both to myself and the bearer; for I had only one ball in my gun, the second barrel being loaded with small shot.

I did not reach the camp until after eight o'clock; and I then found that my friend Sackville, having become alarmed about me, had taken a strong force of our followers, with a couple of elephants, and had gone forth to the different villages to make inquiry about me. I instantly despatched messengers to recal him; but this was not very readily accomplished, and it was past ten o'clock ere we sat down to our dinners. The meal was seasoned by a long lecture from Sackville upon the impropriety of my having allowed myself to be led beyond the bounds of discretion in pursuit of sport, however enticing it might have been rendered by success. I am very sorry, for the reader's sake, that I am unable to recollect more than the bare subject of my friend's discourse; or I might be tempted to take to myself the credit of some of his ingenious sentiments.

Having determined to ride the next day's march on horseback, during the cool hours of the evening, we sent our tents, and the greater part of our camp establishment, forward to Hurdwar, early in the morning. I also gave orders for an elephant to be in waiting for us at Kunkhul, a town about two miles nearer than our destination; for, knowing by experience what mad scenes are enacted at all Indian *tamáshas* (fun, amusement, riot), whether religious or accidental, I anticipated that we should be unable to get safely through the crowd on horseback. The precaution proved not unnecessary.

We arrived at Kunkhul at ten o'clock at night, having a most brilliant moon to light us on our way; a circumstance most favourable for our inspection of the place, together with the native ceremonies and processions. We found our elephant in readiness for us at the entrance to the town; but the *mahawut* informed us that the baggage cattle, having been over-worked, were far in the rear, and he thought they would hardly reach Hurdwar during the night. Truly this was pleasant news to weary travellers, intimating that they must keep a severe fast, and a sleepless night, having no chance either of dinner or bed. By great good fortune, we had in the *kahause* a bottle of beer and a few biscuits, which, although the former had been boiled, and the latter re-baked, by a noon-day sun, were speedily discussed with hearty appetite.

With the exception of some handsome temples and *ghats* by the river side, together with the *serais*, or places of accommodation for the pilgrims, Kunkhul consists almost entirely of one broad street; forming a succession of gateways and edifices, built after the Hindu style of architecture, for show rather than convenience of habitation: indeed, they are seldom tenanted except by a single poor family, placed there for the purpose of sweeping and keeping the place in order: a few of the upper stories are occupied by aged Brahmins, who are permitted to reside there by the benevolence of the proprietor. As seen by moonlight, the effect of this street was particularly grand; all the tawdry paintings, and tinsel decorations, with which the buildings are covered, taking the appearance of richly sculptured mouldings and basso-relievo carvings. The street is perfectly even in its breadth throughout, extending in a right line nearly three-quarters of a mile, rendering the perspective of the buildings very picturesque, as the jutting towers and balconies stand out one beyond the other, in all the endless variety of form and design of which Hindu architecture is susceptible. On either side of the way is a raised embankment, upon which are erected temporary huts for the accommodation of peddling merchants and shop-keepers; in the manner of our booths at a country fair.

As we advanced, we found the way so densely crowded, that our elephant could with difficulty find room to plant his feet; and so intent were the multitude upon their own affairs, that they paid not the least attention to the shouting of our *mahawut*, who unceasingly employed his lungs most vigorously in endeavouring to clear the road before us. Finding the man's voice of no avail, I made trial of another expedient, and found the application of a hunting-whip, which I carried in my hand, a much more efficient instrument. However, the elephant managed very well for himself, taking by the shoulder, and putting aside all those who impeded his progress: this he effected with his trunk.

There seemed to be but one common object in the mass of human beings moving below us, that of endeavouring to excel one another in creating an uproar. Processions were moving in all directions, with flying flags and paltry pageantry displayed with wonderful conceit, as the mob rolled to and fro, shouting, singing, screaming, and playing upon all sorts of unmusical instruments: since the scattering of the generations of Noah at the destruction of the tower of Babel, never was there such a confusion of languages heard. Here were gathered together men of every Oriental nation, from the countries upon the north, south, east, and west, and habited in every variety of costume. It was a spectacle worth witnessing, even at the penalty of the offence wherewith our olfactory nerves were abused; the steam and effluvia arising from so dense a throng of human beings being insufferably noxious. Our encamping ground lay about half-way between this place and Hurdwar, a distance of about two miles.

Having arrived at our destination, we were totally at a loss how to dispose of ourselves until our camp-equipage should arrive; and I proposed to Sackville that we should enter any one of the numerous tents around us, and throw ourselves upon the hospitality of the occupant, rather than remain in the open air without food, or covering from the night dews. To this, however, my friend wisely objected, thinking that we should receive but cold entertainment and little civility from any persons whom we should happen to disturb from their sleep. I therefore took a stroll round the collection of tents, hoping to find some one, later than the rest, still moving; but being disappointed, I at last began to question the *tchokedars* as to the names of their masters, and very quickly found out a friend, whose good services I could depend upon. It was with great difficulty that I at last persuaded the man to awaken his master, but having gained my point, my friend in need came forth, and having ascertained the nature of my demands, forthwith entered most cheerfully into arrangements for supplying us with a sufficient meal. A grilled fowl, some cold beef, and a bottle of beer quickly restored our strength and good humour; and the hospitality of our host we repaid, by recounting our adventures upon the road, as soon as we could find leisure for the tale; that is, when we lighted our cigars and filled our tumblers with *brandy-pani*.

We were about to make our beds upon the ground, within our friend's tent, having been supplied with mats, cloaks, &c., when part of our baggage arrived, just sufficient for our accommodation; our *charpáhis*,* and a small pall—the smallest sized tent—which had been used as a cooking-tent. These we ordered to be hastily put in order for our reception, and right gladly did we lay our wearied bodies down to rest. Fagged as we were, however, it was long ere we could com-

* *Charpahi*, a Hindostani bed of the lightest kind; consisting simply of a narrow frame-work of wood, upon which is stretched a reticulation of broad tape, and this is raised upon four slight legs; so that the whole affair may easily be lifted by one hand, or carried from place to place upon the back. These beds are just such as we may believe to have been in use, at the time of our Saviour's sojourn upon earth, as is to be inferred from many expressions made use of in the New Testament: for instance, in the case of the cure wrought upon the impotent man, wherein he is bidden to take up his bed and walk; the miraculous obedience to which command, I remember to have been doubly imposing to me when a child, as my imagination reverted immediately to the heavy four-post bedstead, with all its furniture and hangings, in which I had been accustomed to sleep.

pose ourselves to sleep, so incessant was the hubbub and confused tumult without. We were situated close to the horse and cattle market, and were surrounded on all sides by the tents of other visitors, consequently we were in the very midst of the uproar, or *hurri-burree*, as it is expressively termed in Hindostani.

Our camp was crowded in all directions with elephants, camels, dogs, old women, horses, ducks, bullocks, crows, young women, buffaloes, pigs, donkies, children, goats, geese, sweetmeat-venders, grass-hoppers, drunkards, bull-frogs, exhibiters of fireworks, sheep, cats, men, vultures, and every kind of pest, trumpeting, roaring, growling, screaming, bellowing, neighing, howling, shrieking, crying, lowing, shouting, cackling, squeaking, braying, swearing, grunting, whistling, squalling, croaking, singing, groaning, snoring, laughing, moaning, &c. &c., incessantly throughout the night.

I had possibly been asleep half an hour, when I was aroused by my servant, in compliance with the instructions I had given him over-night, for we intended visiting the *ghát* with the early dawn. When I opened my eyes, I found the *purda* (screen, in this case the curtain of the tent) upon the side next to the road had been opened by the servants to admit light; and thus Sackville and myself, snugly stowed into a little hole where we had just room for our beds, were exposed to the curious eyes of all passengers. I was reprimanding my servants for not opening the tent upon the other side, when suddenly a gay party of officers, with ladies in their company, went by upon elephants, enjoying an excellent command of observation over our defenceless position: I instantly recognised the party, and as ill-luck would have it, some of them also recognised me before I could get my head under the bed-clothes.

The period for the ceremonial ablutions is fixed by Hindu astronomers and pundits, for the day on which the sun enters Aries, which is computed by them to be the one-and-twentieth day after the vernal equinox. Every twelfth year, when Jupiter is in Aquarius at the time that the sun enters Aries, the ablution is considered to be very much more efficacious in cleansing from iniquity; at this period, therefore, the influx of pilgrims is greatly increased. This year was unfortunately not the duodecimal festival, but we were assured that we should see quite sufficient of confusion and concourse to give us a very correct idea of the same. If additional noise and tumult be all that we were to have gained by being present upon a grander occasion, I cannot but agree with my friend Sackville, that we were fortunate in having escaped it.

The derivation of the name Hurdwar is ambiguous: during my short stay at the place, I had at least half-a-dozen different *pundits* from the city at my tent, to each of whom I paid a trifle for an opinion upon the subject. One told me that the name was derived from *Hari*, one of the titles of Vishnu, and *dwara*, by corruption *war*, a gate, or narrow pass; another said that it was not Hari, or Vishnu, the preserving deity, but *Hara*, or Mahadeo, the destroyer, who gave the name to the place; so that between the two, I was at a loss how to determine the point, more especially as the temples, in the town and its vicinity, are pretty equally dedicated to one and the other. One circumstance seems to point out the latter derivation as being probably correct: Gunga, the Ganges, is represented in Hindu mythology as the daughter of Mahadeo, its stream issuing from the body of Gungoutri, which, it has been previously mentioned, is considered by many the proper personification of this deity; I think we may therefore assume that the town took its name from Hara, not from Hari, particularly as no mention is made of the latter deity in connection with the source or stream of the sacred river, until it is traced further to the eastward. The word *dwara* applies to the escape of the river from the mountains, through the narrow bed which is here cut in the Sivalic range; after which it has an uninterrupted course, until it reaches the ocean; a direct distance of nearly nine hundred miles, and about sixteen hundred miles following the windings of the stream; the travelling distance of Hurdwar from Calcutta is eleven hundred and twenty miles.

Those least sensible of the picturesque could hardly visit Hurdwar, without being struck by its exceeding beauty, and the wildness of its position. The mountain, at the foot of which the town stands, is a high conical point, of abrupt bold outline, partially clad with foliage intermixed with splintered trunks of trees, fractured by the storms from the higher lands beyond the Dhoon. Upon the opposite side of the river is the sacred mountain, the Hara or (if the reader should prefer it) the Hari-ki Pahar (the mountain of Hara or Hari); in a line with the jutting foot of which, the great *ghát* has been erected, as the most holy spot which could be selected. The infant Ganges is here fordable, except during the monsoon.

Although mounted on our elephant, it was with very great difficulty that we pursued our way to the new *ghát*, at which the ceremony of ablution is performed. On the road before and behind us, as far as the eye could reach, was a continued flood of human beings, rolling on towards the Ganges, into which it disgorged itself. Every avenue was crammed, every inch of ground appeared occupied, and even the house-tops and balconies were crowded to excess. At a snail's-pace our elephant moved onward with the tide, without losing his temper or injuring a single individual, although the natives were squeezing between his legs and under his body, in their anxiety to get to the *ghát* before the day advanced. The uproar and the effluvia were even more intolerable than they had been the preceding night at Kunkhul; and this, independent of the disgusting spectacles which are frequently exhibited, both at the *gháts* and by the way-side, I should have thought sufficient to deter any ladies from visiting such a scene. Several, however, were present on this occasion, though, in all probability, ignorant of what they were to witness, until they found themselves in the very midst of it: in which case, the reproach should fall upon those, their chaperons, who had the bad taste to conduct them thither. The number of pilgrims is generally in excess of 300,000, though this year it did not amount to 200,000. The throng of a London mob would give no sufficient idea of the continuous rolling stream of men and women to be seen at the *ghát*, forcing their way in conflicting courses. Dreadful scenes of strife and contention frequently occur, and the incessant groans and screams testify how severely the weak suffer.

For the prevention of violence, Government have stationed a guard of *sipahis* at the head of the *ghát*, and sentries along the narrow passages which lead to it; but this measure is not always effectual. In 1819, when the influx of pilgrims was computed at two millions, a dreadful scene of destruction took place. The infatuated multitude, in their anxiety to be among the first in the stream as the sun rose, made such a rush towards the *ghát*, that those upon the head of the steps were impelled forward over those below, with a force quite irresistible; and which, once put in motion, could not be stayed, until the way was clogged with the bodies of the victims, who were squeezed and trampled to death. The number of lives lost in this tumult amounted to four hundred and thirty-six, among whom were eleven of the Government *sipáhis*, who were borne away by the violence of the mob, and perished in their brave attempts to restore order.

This catastrophe was in a measure attributable to the confined size of the old *ghát*, there being only room for about five or six to descend a-breast; orders were, therefore, given for the construction of a new one upon a grander scale; and now, under direction of Government, a noble flight of steps, seventy-five feet in breadth at the bottom, leads down to the water's edge, and the danger which before existed is greatly diminished. The erection of this *ghát* induced many affluent Brahmins to undertake the construction of new temples and buildings by the water-side, some of which were still in progress during my visit. This has added greatly to the beauty of the town, as seen from the island immediately opposite. The towering pyramids and accumulating domes exceed in magnitude, though they do not rival in number, those of Benares.

Among the myriads of women, who here exposed their persons without regard to decency, I did not remark more than four or five who had any just claims to beauty; but this is, perhaps, owing to women of high caste, who are usually the handsomest, concealing themselves, so that we had only the lower orders to look at. Those of rank are carried into the water in litters, attended by two officiating Brahmins, who repeat prayers during the immersion, and thus they are screened from vulgar eyes: others, with some sense of modesty, go into the water with their clothes about them, although this is of little utility; for, the moment the thin muslin drapery is saturated, it clings tightly to the form. I have said, that very few of the women were beautiful; I spoke exclusively of the countenance, for nearly all who were young, were of elegant and finely rounded figure, and some few might have been selected as models of symmetry. Their complexions were of every variety of shade, from the positive black of the Bengallis to the beautiful transparent and comparatively fair skins of the Circassians, Georgians, Cashmerians, &c.

Every pilgrim entering the stream is under the necessity of sacrificing to the god a small piece of gold, which is dropt into the water with certain forms of prayer, without which the ablution cannot be efficacious. Those of high birth and affluence frequently devote a whole handful, or more, of the precious metal at each immersion; but the poverty-stricken, among those who seek purification, cannot be expected to display such profuse liberality in their offerings, and a piece of gold of no greater value than four annas, about sixpence, is considered quite as effectual as the rich man's wealth, if it be afforded in proportion to the means of the individual.

After the ceremonies are concluded, the gold thus sacrificed to the river-god affords a rich harvest to the priests, who may be seen up to their waists in the water, fishing about in all directions for the treasure. Some, trusting to their quick sight, prefer diving, or rather squatting below the surface, turning over the pebbles and sifting the sand; others make use of a small circular net, like an angler's landing-net, and by these means a man not unfrequently collects, in a single day, more than a poor subaltern receives for a month's pay. The *jogies* and *gosseins* manage to secure this privilege to themselves, not in virtue of any just claim, but by threats of anathema and perdition to all those who should dare to invade their preserves.

From the *ghát* we proceeded to the bazaar, where we beheld merchandize from every quarter of Asia. I had been told that I might here procure anything and everything of Eastern produce or manufacture; and I certainly could not but believe this true, as I turned from side to side of the principal street. That, however, which is exposed publicly to view is chiefly showy rather than valuable, and where mock pearls and tinsel ornaments are displayed in the low dirty shop-windows, real gems and jewels may frequently be purchased within, at the value of a prince's fortune. The show on the exterior is made up chiefly of articles of apparel, native ornaments, arms, horse's trappings, elephant's gear, toys, and the like, which, being familiar in all cities throughout India, can be of little interest to the European visitor who seeks novelty. All these are to be seen in the principal street, a nasty, ill-smelling, narrow lane, between two rows of stone houses, which, as the elephant moved along, I could almost touch on either side.

Another of the streets, still less wholesome than

that just mentioned, running parallel with the course of the river, is devoted to the exclusive manufacture and sale of sweet-meats, than which nothing in the world can be less tempting to an English appetite; though, by-the-bye, I was commissioned by a lady at Merat to purchase her a large quantity of these *metais* from one Bindrabund Gopemohun, the Angel of Hurdwar, who has his shop at the corner of the Chowdri's Chouki.

At the little *ghát*, which terminates this street, may be seen hundreds of fish, many of them as large as salmon, swimming to and fro perfectly tame; so much so, that they will feed from the hand. The Brahmins, and other religious devotees, are in the habit of feeding them daily with flour and other favourite food, and they may be seen playing around the person of the man while he is bathing, and jostling one another for the prize.

According to the authorities of Raper, Hardwicke, Colebrooke, Rennel, &c., the principal trade consists in tobacco, antimony, asafœtida, dried fruits, such as apricots, figs, prunes, raisins, almonds, pistachio-nuts, and pomegranates, from Kabul, Candahar, Moultan, and the Punjáb; shawls, *dhotics*, and *puttoos* (blankets made of the shawl wool), from Cashmere and Amritsir; spotted turbans, looking-glasses, toys, with various manufactures in brass and ivory, from Jeypore; arms and shields from Rohilcund, Lucknow, and Silhet; bows and arrows from Moultan and the Doáb; rock-salt and precious stones from Lahore; *buftas* and piece-goods from Rahn, Loudiana, and the banks of the Sutlege. The Marwa country supplies a great many camels, and a species of rough flannel called *loui;* from the Company's territories are brought coarse cotton cloths of every kind, muslins, sarsnets, cocoa-nuts, and various woollen cloths. These form the chief articles of commerce, and for the disposal of them, almost as many foreigners visit Hurdwar, as do pilgrims for the religious festival.

Being glad to escape from the dirt and riot of the narrow streets, we hastened through them, and proceeded to the cattle-market, which is held upon the high road between Kunkhul and Hurdwar, and this we found of all things in the place by far the best worth seeing. The Persian and Kabul horses were the finest, there being no very high caste Arabs at the fair: *zummeendari* (country bred) cattle were very abundant, but of no great value: there were, however, some excellent specimens of Kutch and Katawar galloways, and also *ghoonts.*

The most valuable horse in the market might possibly have been purchased for fifteen hundred rupees, about £150, and the prices ran as low as forty and fifty rupees.

Elephants, camels, and bullocks of every kind, and of all prices, were there for the inspection of the curious. The value of the former has been already noticed as varying from three thousand to eight hundred rupees. Camels, or more properly dromedaries, for they have but one hump on the back, fetch a medium price of sixty or eighty rupees, but a high caste *sawarri*, for the saddle, cannot be procured for less than a hundred and fifty rupees, and they are frequently sold much higher.

The attention which we might at any other time have bestowed upon these animals was very much absorbed in admiration of two beautiful creatures, not often to be seen even at Hurdwar. These were, a wild ass from Lukput Bundur, in Kutch, and a gaour, a species of the bison, from the deep forests in the province of Gundwana. The latter of these, from his superior stature and handsome though fierce appearance, demands precedence. He was sixteen hands two inches in height, being a little taller than any horse in the fair; his form closely resembled that of the buffalo in many respects, but his legs were shorter, straighter, and more powerful, and his head was broader and more like that of the ox, as were also his horns. Upon his withers he had a hump, very like those of the common Indian bullock, and his coat was a fine glossy dark brown, almost black, having evidently been well oiled and groomed by his owner, who expected a very handsome sum for him, not for the sake of any useful purpose to which he could be put, but as a curiosity simply. These animals are very scarce, as was apparent from the excitement exhibited among all classes of natives, and their exertions to get sight of this specimen. He had been taken in a noose but a short time previously, and, being full grown, was exceedingly fierce and intractable, and must have cost the possessor great pains to transport him to Hurdwar. Among my sporting acquaintances, I have never met with one who had shot a specimen of this animal, and I therefore conclude it to be very rare, or to inhabit solely the province from which this was brought.

The ass had been caught in a pit-fall, by mere accident, and had also been conveyed to this general mart for the same purpose as the gaour; for his indomitable vice and ferocity rendered him utterly useless as an animal of carriage or draught; indeed, it is said that they have never yet been domesticated. They are gregarious animals, generally found upon the salt deserts, and among the brackish lakes along the banks of the Rhun: the one in question, having been solitary, is conjectured to have wandered from his herd, or, perhaps, in consequence of his vice, to have been expelled by his kind, as elephants are known to drive from their society any individual who may misbehave, or disturb the general tranquillity. The specimen which I had here an opportunity of inspecting was much above the size of the domestic ass, being upwards of twelve hands high, and stout-built in proportion; his colour was darker than that of the common ass, and his form approached more nearly to that of the horse; but he still retained the unerring distinctive marks of his genus, the long ears and the dark line down the back and across the shoulders. The brute was so indocile, that none but his own attendants could approach him, and they only by alternate intimidation and the offer of his favourite food; his voice was, perhaps, the most curious and peculiar distinction between him and the despised drudges of his species: it neither resembled the bray of the latter, nor was it the neigh of the horse, but was a snorting impatient sort of cry, accompanied with a soft fretful whining, of a most pitiful kind. His food was much saturated with salt-water, otherwise he rejected it, and he had a large lump of rock-salt, to which he was continually applying his tongue. I had heard it frequently stated in India, that the flesh of the wild ass was highly esteemed by the natives, and I put the question to the owner of the beast in question; his response was decisive: "Do Moslems love the flesh of pigs?"

Of all the innumerable rascals and impostors to be met with at Hurdwar, the cattle-dealers, perhaps, take precedence. Their tricks and manœuvres for passing off damaged and vicious cattle, are far more ingenious and more numerous, than can be boasted by our Newmarket jockies, or London stable-keepers. They understand all the arts of drugging, dyeing, &c., to perfection, and will score teeth or put on a tail, in a style well worthy of admiration. They never deal openly, but the bargain is struck by signs carried on out of sight of bystanders: it is thus performed. A cloth is thrown over the back of a horse, and under cover of this, the buyer and seller communicate the amount of price and offer, by touching the joints of the fingers; thus avoiding the possibility of those around gaining any information of the terms of purchase. This, it is to be understood, is practised between natives only; if an European wished to deal, he would do so within his own tent, or elsewhere in private.

Upon our return to our tents, we found there a man waiting our arrival with a very different sort of merchandise to any we had hitherto seen. He had with him two young girls, whom he had brought down from the Punjáb, and these he was anxious to dispose off as slaves; offering the eldest, who was the least comely of the two, and about sixteen years of age, for one hundred and fifty rupees; and the other, who had really some pretensions to beauty, and was younger by about four years, for two hundred. The poor little things, putting their hands before them, in an attitude of supplication, begged earnestly that we would purchase them, declaring that otherwise they should starve, and vowing to be faithful and obedient to us. Finding that we were not inclined to become purchasers, the man took them away, and the same proffer was made at every tent: they were ultimately purchased by a native gentleman, residing in the neigbourhood of Dehli, for about half the sums above-mentioned. This traffic in slaves is considered to have been long since abolished, but it is still surreptitiously practised throughout the upper provinces, and at any of these fairs, girls may be purchased: they are generally from Georgia, Cashmere, Kabul, the Punjáb, or Moultan.

One of my servants, a Mussulman, had a slave-girl, whom he had purchased for the sum of twenty-four rupees, about £2. Her history, as far as she was herself acquainted with it, is a very romantic one, and the reader will perhaps excuse my giving a slight sketch of it, which may be condensed in very few pages.

The name of the girl was Rahmea; she was handsome, not more than seventeen or eighteen years of age, a native of Almora; her parents were not Ghoorkas, as might thence be naturally inferred, but settlers from some large town upon the banks of the Chináb, in the district of Kishtáwar; the girl herself was ignorant of the name of the town. Her mother had been exceedingly beautiful, and, though poor by birth, had been exalted to great honour and dignity, as the wife, or favourite concubine, of a petty Rajha, who, by virtue of his comparative wealth, was looked upon as the principal man of the town; but he was a dissipated, debauched character, according to his wife's account, and she, therefore, thought it no sin to decamp from his bed and board, and furnish herself with a more sober, though less consequential, lord and master; and being in fear of vengeance from him, upon whom she had turned her back, she quitted the neighbourhood and fled with her new spouse to Almora. Here they continued to live in peace and happiness for several years, having a bond of unity in the existence of a little daughter, who was considered the beauty of the place.

When the daughter had arrived at the age of ten years, she was one day playing, with others of her acquaintance, in the neighbourhood of the temples, when she was accosted by an old man, in the guise of a *fakhir*, who asked her many questions about her father and mother, their names and history; the child unhesitatingly gave the religious man all the information in her possession, and further told him that her father lay at home sick of an ague, which no medicine would cure. Upon this, the holy professor tendered his services, and was gladly conducted by the little girl to the habitation of her parents, who, unsuspicious of evil, thankfully received the advice and remedies which he proffered them.

The drugs having been administered, the symptoms of the patient grew more and more alarming; but the loving pair were comforted by the *fakhir's* assurances, that all would be well, and that a very few hours would suffice to free the sufferer from his malady. In company with the beautiful matron,—who, contrary to the general rule among eastern women, was still fascinating even though she had been ten years a mother, and twice a wife—the disinterested old priest sat and watched the sick man, giving him from time to time fresh draughts to quench his thirst; until at last, as midnight approached, the patient declared his conviction that life was fast ebbing, and would no longer credit the assurances of his physician. The old stranger was still arguing the point with him, when suddenly the poor man's features became dreadfully convulsed, and after lingering about an hour in the most exquisite torment, he expired, affirming with his last breath that the *fakhir* had poisoned him.

"Even so," said the disguised Rajha, for it was he, the lady's former lord; "even so; I have poisoned you: would that your pangs had been doubly, ay, ten-fold more excruciating! And, now, Luchmi," said he, turning to his *quondam* love, "what better fate do you expect from your injured master? Your nose is my first demand, and your matchless daughter is the next;" and then, at his command, the hut was immediately filled with armed men.

The beautiful Luchmi was gagged, and bound; and her ruthless captor, with his own hand, severed her nose from her face; she was then placed on horse-back, under the charge of one of the Rajha's followers, and was conveyed away, the daughter knew not whither; certainly with no very happy purpose, for nothing of love or tenderness was seen in the tyrant's bearing. There can be little doubt that, if suffered to live, she must have been confined for life, her only lot protracted misery; but there is better reason to believe that the ruffian would have destroyed her, when the heat of his reproaches and abuse had in a measure evaporated.

As for the poor child, Rahmea, she was carried to the Rajha's zenána, and continued for a few months an unwilling concubine of the murderer of her father; but having made more than a few attempts at self-destruction, she was ultimately cast adrift upon the wide world, with no fortune but her native comeliness. This gave her value in the eyes of one of the Rajha's dependants, who obtained permission to take her into his house; and business soon after carrying him to Dehli, he disposed of her to my servant, Secundur Kahn, for the trifle above-mentioned, being wearied of the poor girl's unbending indifference.

At the time that Secundur Kahn related this tale to me, the girl had become greatly attached to her master, having been with him about six years, and being the mother of three fine children: I expressed a wish to see her, and my servant instantly complied. She was quite as handsome as he had described her; but I could elicit from her no intelligible replies to my inquiries, touching her history, or that of her mother. This apparently did not arise from shyness or stupidity, but from a disinclination to converse upon the subject with a stranger, and therefore I forebore to probe her further.

I must be excused for anticipating the regularity of my narrative, for the purpose of mentioning that the pair are now living in comparative affluence; Secundur Kahn having succeeded to a small patrimony in the neighbourhood of Lucknow, only a few months previously to my quitting India.

We remained at Hurdwar, visiting the *ghâts*, bazaars, &c. daily, until the fourteenth, when the splendour of the festival having faded away, we were not sorry to quit the noise, dirt, flies, and evil odours of this holy place. After the twelfth of the month, very little business was carried on in the market; and, owing to some mismanagement on the part of the collector of customs, large quantities of merchandise, which had arrived at the place, were deterred from being brought into the town in time for sale, in consequence of a delay in granting the *rowanas*, or duty-permits.

Having heard most extraordinary accounts of the picturesque beauties of the road through Deyra Dhoon, leading from Hurdwar towards the Himálas, I determined to explore it for a few miles, for the sake of the scenery; but being unable to prevail upon my travelling companion to go with me, I sent out a small tent or pall, to the distance of twenty-five miles, and rode thither during the cool of the morning. Here I remained through the heat of the day; and having made a few sketches by the way-side, I rode back again to Hurdwar by moonlight the same night. Most amply rewarded was I for the exertion, for never could imagination have conceived anything one-half so grand, so exquisitely rich, as the scenery all along the road over which I passed, especially as I saw it by moonlight on my return. It was, however, much in the same style as the scenery which has been already described as characterizing the whole country in the neighbourhood of the Himálas. I will not, therefore, weary the reader by further detail.

After leaving Hurdwar, we returned leisurely towards Merat, halting wherever we were tempted to do so, by the beauty of the scenery, or where game happened to be more than usually abundant. For both these very good reasons, we remained two days at a village called Lundhoura, seventeen miles distant from Hurdwar.

Within half a mile of the village, is a handsome house and garden, formerly the favourite residence of Ram Dial Singh, and still belonging to the family. The importance of the place attracted our attention, and curiosity induced us to seek admission. At first, we were told that, the Rajha being absent, we could not be permitted to enter, and we were about to try the effect of reward, when the gates were thrown open, and in the Rajha's name we were bid welcome to his castle. We were then informed that the chief would be pleased to see us, and would shortly hold a *durbar*, or audience, for our presentation: in the interim, we were requested to walk round and view the estate. This was more honour than we had anticipated, and more than we were fit for, being clad in sporting suits, soiled and bedraggled by a long day's shooting through briars and swampy ground. I therefore sent a polite message to the Rajha, begging to be excused the honour of attending him, unless he would condescend to overlook our unworthy apparel. This point having been conceded by the great man, we were shortly afterwards ushered to the presence-chamber.

We found the Rajha, a very fine handsome young man, clothed in an ordinary suit of raiment, squatting upon a low *charpáhi*, without any of the insignia of his rank, or any display beyond a small guard of armed attendants: these stood round the apartment, and two young slaves, handsomely appointed, stood behind him, the one with a hand-*punka* (fan), the other with a *chowri*, to keep off the flies. Our dignity was not a little mortified that, contrary to the custom of men of his rank, the Rajha did not rise to receive us, nor pay us any attention, further than a *saláam* with one hand and an intimation that we should seat ourselves in the chairs provided for us.

Annoyed at the slight thus put upon us, I ventured, before I took my seat, to address a few words to the self-important gentleman, signifying that I was apprehensive that sickness deterred him from quitting his *charpáhi.* This was certainly not borne out by his appearance, and he replied to the insinuation by saying that it was not the custom of his family to do so. We had no inducement to prolong our visit to this man beyond a few minutes, and without waiting for the dismissal, which is customary with the natives, we withdrew, disgusted alike with his arrogance and his ill-concealed vulgarity. All we had to admire in him were, his finely-proportioned frame, as far as it was visible to us, and his very handsome countenance: with little ceremony, therefore, we mounted our horses and departed: and I was certainly glad to find myself outside his gates; for Sackville was sadly out of temper at the unceremonious manner in which we had been treated, and I feared that some rash conduct on his part might have embroiled us in a quarrel.

In the evening, we were sitting outside our tent, enjoying the cool air, which blew down from the mountains, smoking our cigars, and sipping the thin mixture commonly called *brandy-pani*, when one of my domestics, with a smile upon his countenance, came to inform me of some news which he had learnt among the Rajha's dependants in the bazaar. It appeared from the man's story, that the gentleman, who had so affronted our dignity in the morning, was after all no chief, but the *moohktcya*, head-menial, of the Rajha; who, being ambitious of receiving homage from his superiors, or being otherwise inclined to play a trick upon the *sahib lōg*, had ventured to personate his superior. This was the first specimen of 'high life below stairs,' with which I had met in India; I have since heard of other instances.

Sackville was out of humour at the trick which had been put upon him, vowing vengeance against the *moohkteya* for his insolence, and all my best efforts failed to restore him to his usual serenity, or to make him consider the thing as a joke; the more I laboured to allay his wrath, the more he frowned, and at last, treating him as a froward child, I took no notice of him; so there we sat in silence, looking at the sky and the landscape before us, but never once towards each other. How incomprehensible is the human mind! by what trifles is it influenced! That which I had found it quite impossible to effect, was brought about through the agency of a hoary old he-goat, in the simplest manner possible.

Whilst Sackville was eyeing the floating clouds, the old goat was eyeing his tumbler, which stood upon the ground beside him. Step by step, with stealthy and suspicious pace, did the old fellow advance towards it, and having observed Sackville not unfrequently apply it to his lips, concluded, I suppose, that what was good for the master, would be good for the goat also. The beverage was nearly finished, when old Buckra,* fearing possibly that he might lose his opportunity, made a bold push and thrust his head into the glass.

Sackville, impatient of this second infringement upon the respect which he thought due to him, started from his seat to punish the intruder, and away went the goat, with the tumbler sticking to his nose. Sackville instantly gave chase at his best speed, and after a dodging run, over at least a mile of country, he brought Buckra up by the tail. "Buh—hur—hur—r—r," cried the old goat,

* *Buckra*, male goat: Hindostani.

twisting his head first on one side, then on the other, as if determined to keep possession of the stolen glass, while Sackville did his best to recover it; this he ultimately effected, but not without much difficulty, and at the expense of some hard blows from the horns of the unruly thief. With the glass, however, he regained his good humour, and to prevent similar depredations in future, he ordered a bell to be hung upon the goat's neck: this the animal received as an especial mark of favour, and from that time he exalted himself to the honour of leader in the herd.

From Lundhoura, having altered the plan of our route, we struck across the country, in the direction of the Ganges, for the purpose of shooting through the Kadir, on our way back to Merat. We entered the junguls at Jogiwalla, a village upon the western bank of the river, celebrated for the number of its tigers: but we found the swamps and morasses still too wet for us to do much execution among them. We slew two at this place, and taking our way through Jáedpore, Selimpore, and Maerzapore, we destroyed three more, one of which we found to have been severely wounded with balls apparently some weeks previously to his death.

By most people who frequent the Kadir with the object of shooting, the deer and wild hogs are injudiciously destroyed in vast numbers; I remember to have gloried in the number I had killed during my first expedition: but the evil of this indiscriminate slaughter is quickly apparent to the sportsman who strikes at higher game. If the prey of the tigers be rendered scarce, they will seek it elsewhere, and, therefore, if the deer and the hogs are annihilated, we shall have no tiger-shooting in the Kadir. I do not think that sportsmen generally are sufficiently alive to this: I have known old hands, excellent shots, and men whose opinion in all sporting matters was considered law, bring home to camp no less than five-and-twenty hog-deer, and half-a-dozen of the swine tribe. Surely this cannot be defended; if the system is pursued, the tigers will remain in the fastnesses of their own forests, and there will be an end to the exciting, fascinating sport, which so greatly benefits the poor *raiuts* of the junguls, in diminishing their personal risk and saving the flocks and herds from spoliation.

While upon the subject of tiger shooting, I may as well mention in a few words the issue of an excursion of this sort which I undertook in the following month of June. I introduce it here, as the current of my narrative might otherwise be checked by it.

Notwithstanding the hot winds and vertical sun of a month so near to midsummer, I could not resist the temptation of once more taking the field against the tigers, Mirchi having brought news of eight or ten in different parts of the Kadir, over whose haunts he had placed scouts. He also told us that a second wild elephant, as formidable as that which had been slain there the previous year, had made his appearance at Selimpore, and was committing dreadful havoc and devastation in the villages.

A fine young man, of the name of Hodgson, in the civil service, was my companion on this expedition; and we set forth with the understanding that we should be joined at a day's notice by one of my brother officers, if we were fortunate enough to come up with the elephant. The fact was, that we were rather suspicious of Mirchi's information upon this point, and we, therefore, thought it unnecessary to increase our force until the truth could be ascertained.

Think not, gracious reader, that I am again about to lead you through all the junguls and morasses of the Kadir, as I did in my last tiger campaign; or that I shall recount the order of the chase and charge as heretofore. Suffice it to say, that with excellent and varied sport, we marched through the junguls during three days, and upon the morning of the fourth day, came upon the track of the wild elephant, of which our guide, Mirchi, had forewarned us. We followed this track in the direction of Selimpore; but as we advanced, we found at each village that the elephant continued his journey northward, keeping, as if purposely, two or three days' march a-head of us. This continued to be the case until we arrived at Jáedpore, where, to our surprise, we found the monster had taken up permanent quarters in a dense jungul, in which it would have been dangerous indeed to have encountered him unaided. We therefore despatched a messenger to summon our friend, who had promised to join us. He came without loss of time to our assistance; but ere he reached our position, the elephant had decamped, and was in all probability half-way towards the forests of the Dhoon; for, suspicious of our close proximity, he appeared to consider his present quarters anything but safe.

Until the elephant had taken his departure, we

had remained perdue, not even venturing to discharge a gun, lest we should alarm him; but he possibly caught sight of our tents, or the mustering of our followers. No sooner was he gone, however, than we sallied forth in search of a couple of tigers, about seven miles distant; these shewed us excellent sport, and we had exciting work with them before they were brought to bite the dust.

Between the scene of this action and our camp, lay a flat sandy plain, four or five miles in breadth, without a blade of jungul, or vegetation of any kind; and, knowing that the time occupied in crossing this would be otherwise spent in idleness, I took with me in the *háoda* a book, which I continued to read upwards of an hour, while the sun was still high in the heavens. The heat had been intense during the day, so much so that it was painful to place the hand upon the iron bar of the *háoda*: the burning glare upon the white page was exceedingly painful to the eye, and was possibly instrumental in bringing on a fever, by which I was attacked upon my arrival in camp. I had just dismounted from my elephant, and was receiving my guns from the *mahawut*, when suddenly my brain grew giddy, my sight failed me, and, unable to support myself, I fell senseless to the ground.

I was immediately taken up by the servants, and carried into the tent, where Hodgson quickly recovered me by a most unmedical mixture of claret and water. "Why, my good fellow," said he, jokingly, "surely you don't intend to desert me now? must I send into cantonments for a prayer-book? I have not got one here, and should hardly be up to repeating the service *vivâ voce.*"

Poor fellow! as he stood by my bed-side in the full enjoyment of health and spirits, he little thought that, within a week from that time, the solemn rite of which he spoke with so much levity would be performed over his clay-cold body.

A burning fever succeeded to the symptoms already described, and determining not to await the issue, without making an effort to reach medical assistance, I instantly gave orders for my horses to be taken forward upon the road, in order that I might be able to ride into Merat the next morning. Jáedpore is forty-five miles distant from Merat, but I was compelled to venture upon the journey. A few hours sleep during the night very much refreshed me; and at two o'clock, finding that I had still some strength left, I arose and dressed myself, taking a cup of hot tea, while my elephant was being put in readiness. The morning was beautifully moonlight, and without much inconvenience I got over the first ten miles by five o'clock; dismounting from the elephant, I found myself so very weak, and my limbs so unmanageable, that I almost despaired of accomplishing my object, when I thought of the long thirty-five miles before me. It was, however, too late to consider, and taking in my pocket a rope wherewith to bind myself to the horse's neck, in case I should find myself fainting; I mounted my horse, and spurred him along the road. The exercise and excitement, I believe, kept off the effects of the fever for a time, and this was indeed fortunate, for although I had two other horses upon the road, I was misdirected by the villagers in my route, and missing both, I did not reach cantonments until nearly ten o'clock.

Immediately upon my arrival at my own house, I sent off a servant for the doctor; but before he could arrive, I had become delirious. Copious bleeding, and, I believe, nearly all the contents of the pharmacopœia, were resorted to, and not without success: my life was in all probability saved by the promptitude of my medical attendant, and the vigorous measures which he adopted.

Three days afterwards, my two sporting companions were brought into cantonments smitten with fevers of a most deadly kind, and a day or two afterwards, Hodgson was laid, a corpse, in the grave. As soon as I was myself sufficiently recovered, I went to visit the other sick man; he was delirious, and did not know me; indeed, I scarcely knew him, so greatly was he altered in a few short days. He lay upon the ground, his head shaved, his flesh wasted, his eyes fixed and vacant, and exhibiting every symptom of approaching death. The surgeon who attended him quite despaired of his recovery, but the strength of his constitution carried him through the disease, although his restoration was looked upon almost as a return from the grave.

CHAPTER VII.

ANCIENT DEHLI AND SHAHJEHANABAD.

I MADE it a rule, during my sojourn in India, to remain as short a time as possible stationary in any one place, more especially after Merat became, as Sackville expressed it, so "sadly shrunken." From the time of my arrival at Merat, the city of Dehli, which is only thirty-six miles distant, continued to be a perpetual haunt of mine; but until the present time I have refrained from leading the reader thither, preferring to wait for some especially propitious opportunity. Whether or not the inducements held out for the trip, at the particular season now selected, be of due importance, it would be difficult for me to decide, as it is probable that no two of my readers will be precisely of the same opinion.

In the month of October 1834, I was tempted by a most vulgar curiosity to visit Dehli, in expectation of witnessing the execution of Shumsh-ud-Deen, the Nawab of Ferosepoor, upon whom we daily expected sentence of death would be passed; he having been convicted of instigating, aiding, and abetting the murder of Mr. Fraser, the Resident and Representative of the British Government; an event which from the importance of the victim, the noble rank of the perpetrator, and the peculiar nature of the circumstances, created great interest and excitement throughout India. But I am running over my ground a little too rapidly. First, it will be necessary to get to Dehli, and when there, I may by chance be tempted to hang the Nawab first, and tell the tale of his crime afterwards; a summary method, decidedly preferable to the dilatory, apathetic measures pursued by the local government in this case.

In visiting a native city, whether Moslem or Hindu, nothing is to be lost, and very much will be gained, by the display of a little consequence and dignity: a man with a full train of attendants, numerous horses, handsome equipages, and the like, will meet with every possible attention from natives of all ranks, and their deference for importance will gain him many privileges and attentions, which otherwise he could not hope to enjoy. Upon this consideration, I determined to make myself comfortable, if possible.

I have before mentioned that, at Dehli, the Begum Sumroo had a very handsome mansion, which for several years she had not frequented: this I coveted as a residence during my stay at Dehli, and a note to my good-natured friend, Dyce Sombre, at once secured it to me. With his usual kindness and good-nature, moreover, Dyce sent extra servants over to Dehli, with orders to the *moohkteya* to get every thing in readiness for my arrival. I should say, our arrival; for I was to be accompanied in my visit to Dehli by a young friend, and by his wife also—the young and handsome Septimus Sackville, sobered down into a patient steady husband, some six months past the honeymoon. Almost immediately after our return from Hurdwar, he had proposed to and been accepted by his old friend, Mrs. Leicester, whose husband had died about ten months previously to her second wedding. Within six weeks of their engagement, the nuptials were consummated, and thus Sackville, the gay and admired Sackville, became a Benedict and the father of two noisy riotous boys, with nothing but a subaltern's poor pittance for their support. He bore his altered fortunes with wonderful equanimity, and with excellent philosophy, borrowed from the black menials about him, he exclaimed, "*Hum kia kurrenge? kismut hi.*" "What can I do? It is my fate." His wife was quite the person he had formerly described to me, in beauty and in fascination of manners; but, alas! she was —— let her speak for herself.

It was agreed that, unless we previously grew weary of each other, we should spend the whole month together at Dehli; and all the preliminaries having been arranged, the last consideration was the method of our journeying thither. In my mind, this was the least difficult part of the affair; I had been accustomed to ride to and from Dehli within three hours, having five horses on the road; but the lady could by no means entertain a thought of riding six-and-thirty miles direct before breakfast; and as to a palki, she had a religious antipathy to the very idea of such a thing. Sackville had sold his tandem, the springs of the buggy were hardly safe, and the motion of an elephant was quite intolerable. Her only alternative therefore was, to go on horseback and march by easy stages. By good fortune, I slipped the collar, being particularly engaged at Merat until the last day of their march, which would bring them within a few miles of Dehli, allowing three halts. After muster-parade on the first morning of the month, I saw my friends fairly upon the road; and when I beheld the mismanagement and discomforts of their mode of marching, I was not a little rejoiced at my escape. No method of travelling can be more agreeable than that of marching in India, provided every thing is well ordered and under good regulation; but without this, it is the most harassing and the most intolerable of all others.

I was under an engagement to overtake my friends upon their last march, for the purpose of conducting them to their destination; for they, being unacquainted with the city, and likewise ignorant of the language, would probably have found great difficulty in managing for themselves, upon their arrival at the place.

On the morning of the 3rd., at two o'clock, having sent three horses forward on the road, I rolled myself into my palki and was carried to Begumabad, the first stage towards Dehli, about thirteen miles distant from Merat. Here I arrived at five o'clock, and found my horse awaiting me. Making a hasty toilet in one of the little niches of the *serai*, appropriated to the accommodation of all travellers, I mounted my horse and was about to set forth, when I was accosted by the *durroga*, who had charge of the *serai*. He first inquired my name, which, as it was asked with becoming humility and respect, I condescended to give him; he then begged to know if I had lost anything upon the road a few weeks previously, and I at once answered in the affirmative, mentioning and describing a pistol which had been dropt by one of my servants. Upon this, the man produced the weapon and tendered it to me.

Here was one of the very few instances of honesty, in a native, with which I met during my sojourn in India; and in another respect the man displayed a trait of character decidedly opposite to that of most of his fellows; his cautious reservation of the property until I had, in a measure, proved my claim to it, betokened suspicion of my integrity, which is very rarely found to exist among natives towards the English: generally speaking, they have implicit reliance upon our honour, however dishonest they may themselves be. This must be felt by all who have had any dealings with them; but how, or why it should be so, it is very difficult to determine, when we recollect the numberless deceits which have been practised upon them from time to time.

I accepted the pistol from the man, and for his honesty's sake, offered him a suitable recompense; but even this he refused as long as he understood it to be in return for his services: when I assured him it was a *buckshis*, a gratuitous present, he immediately took it; for the refusal of the gift under such circumstances would have been deemed an insult to me, according to the etiquette of his nation. He regretted that he had then no offering worthy of my acceptance, but he promised to send me the first produce of his vines and fruit-trees; and in this he kept his word, which I have very seldom known performed by others of his class. I found that the *durroga* had discovered me to be the owner of the pistol through the agency of my *súes*, who had been making inquiries for it.

After quitting Begumabad, I galloped my horse seven miles over the level turf by the road side, and then mounting a second, I galloped him also seven miles, but over a less pleasant road; and this brought me to the small town of Furrucknuggur, overlooking the river Hindon, from the little eminence upon which it stands. Here I found my friends, who, instead of being close upon Dehli, as I expected, had only just arrived here, having been detained upon the road by all sorts of imaginary difficulties, and by the supposed illness of one of the children. They were just making preparation for breakfast when I joined them, but their tents were unfortunately pitched in a most disagreeable spot, scarcely tenable by reason of the bad odours: I therefore proposed that we should have them removed to the garden of a native gentleman of my acquaintance, Meer Saiud Alli, who had his country-residence here, and in the interim that we should claim the shelter of his roof.

This was presently managed, and we were most hospitably received by my friend, who made it his business to shew particular attention to the lady, and who supplied our table with many delicacies, which we should not otherwise have been able to procure. With all his kind assistance, however, we were lamentably deficient in the usual appertenances of an English breakfast; neither could his anxious services supply us with comforts of another kind, or furnish the beautiful Mrs. Sackville with patience sufficient for the endurance of those little inconveniences, which are the infallible lot of a subaltern's wife in India.

The scene was amusing, though uncomfortable. The chief requisites for the breakfast were either half a stage in the rear, or altogether forgotten; the children kept up an incessant screaming and squalling; the good lady vented her displeasure upon her patient husband, who, in his turn, employed himself in abusing the servants in the few words of Hindostani with which he was acquainted.

"Now, Septimus," cried the lady, "will you bring me some milk for the child, if you are not too busily engaged in picking that hat to pieces?"

"My love, the *bukries* (goats) have not yet come up, and the *khidmutgar* says there is nothing but smoked milk to be had in the village."*

"Well then, my dear sir, will you have the kindness to ask your black friend, Mr. Alli, or whatever his name is, to get us some? do please, or the poor child will starve."

"Certainly, Mrs. Sackville; you shall have some milk in five minutes."

"Now, Septimus; do look at the child; I never saw such a plague as you are, putting the boy down in the dirt: do take him up and amuse him—now, leave him alone—give him to me—

* The natives of India invariably smoke the milk as soon as it is taken from the cow, not only because they prefer it thus flavoured, but because they believe that the process preserves it longer good.

you're of no use in the world, and are quite unfit to take care of yourself." Then turning to me: "Will you oblige me by scolding that *kahnsuma?*—you know Sackville can't speak a word of the language, and if I attempt it, he only laughs at me; really it's quite vexatious."

"Oh! I'll scold him for you;—but what is it for?"

"What for? why for everything: the stupid fellow has left the tea-kettle behind, in the first place, and then——"

"Here, *soonno* you *haremzeada, toom kis-wasti kettli* not bring?"—which very grammatical sentence might be thus construed: "Listen, you rascal, why did you not bring the kettle?"

"Oh never mind, Mrs. Sackville, we will boil some water in an earthen pot."

"No, no, it won't be nice."

"Indeed it will; the vessel is quite new and clean. Where have you put the tea?"

"Oh! dear me! the nurse took it with her upon the elephant, and won't be up these two hours to come."

"Well, never mind; I think I have got a little in my *pittarra*, which I ordered to be sent forward, in case your's should happen to be behind."

"Really, you are so kind and thoughtful; but then I fear we have no teapot, or cups, or sugar, or spoons, or anything. Dear me, Sackville, I declare you are the stupidest man in the world; Leicester never used to treat me in this manner."

At last all things, or their substitutes, were provided, and breakfast was placed upon the table, in a style which did great credit to the kindness of our host and to the skill of our menials, considering the shifts to which they were put.

Towards evening, Mrs. Sackville fancied that her little boy was becoming worse and worse, and she therefore begged that we would forthwith proceed with her to Dehli; she felt quite strong enough to ride; the distance was only nine miles; and she was very anxious to have medical advice immediately. This sudden resolution came a little too late, and although the sun was still above the horizon, I warned them that they could not possibly reach their destination before dark, having the river Hindon and two channels of the Jumna to cross upon the road. This advice was at once thrown aside, as absurd; the distance was only nine miles, and although they must remain with the children's palki it might easily be accomplished in three hours. With all possible despatch, therefore, preparations were made for moving: the European nurse and the two children were put into the palki, and the Sackvilles set forward on horseback. I remained behind to see the camp struck, and to get the necessary equipage sent forward immediately; anticipating that the probable delay upon the road would leave us without beds or any of the necessaries for dinner.

I overtook the party upon the bank of the river Hindon, scarcely a couple of miles beyond Furrucknuggur, and although the stream was at this season fordable, they were completely at a loss as to the method of getting over. The palki-bearers, knowing the ford, had proceeded on with their charge, but were checked in the centre of the river by the cries of the mother, insisting upon their returning, when she saw them exalting the palki upon their heads, to preserve it from being wetted. As for herself, it was out of the question her riding through such deep water, and she gave orders for an immediate return to Merat. This was combated by her husband, and at last, seeing that crossing in the palki presented less terrors than riding through the water, she turned the nurse out of it, saying, that she would trust her children to no other person's keeping, in such imminent peril. Thus, with her husband riding beside the palki, she was conducted safely to the opposite bank; and being then convinced that she was too much fatigued to remount her horse, she kept possession of the palki, and abandoned the poor nurse to her fate.

The woman was a soldier's wife, and not at all inclined to be annoyed or alarmed by trifles; so taking off her shoes and stockings, she made an attempt to ford the water; but she set off at an unfortunate spot, and ere she had advanced three paces stuck fast in the mud, and the difficulties of her situation got the better of her courage.

"Oh! deary me! deary me! sir; for pity sake, don't let me be left here. Oh! deary me! deary me! missus is gone on in the palki, and master's ridin' on afore her. Oh, sir, tell me what I'm to do; I can't let them nasty black brutes carry me, and I'm sure the water's very deep. Well I'm blest if missus and I don't have a rumpus about this; leavin' me to be drown'd like a dog. Oh! now, pray don't go away, sir; I shall die of fright if I'm left alone with they savage Moors."

"Well, come then, nurse, you must let the men carry you across. and then——"

"Lauk, sir, no, that I won't never let them foul black fellows handle me, sir: I can't, indeed."

"Very well, then, are you afraid to jump up behind me, upon my horse?"

"Oh! no, sir, I'm not afeard; only he'll kick, maybe."

"Pooh! stuff and nonsense, kick! he's as quiet as a lamb; that's only play. Here you *sáes lōg, mem oothao*—but will you sit before or behind?"

"Lauk o'mercy! sir, I'm 'most afeard I'll tumble down; see, sir, he's movin' his tail so. Oh! I'll go before if you please, sir, and then you can hold me on, if I be like to fall."

"Very well, then, give me your hand, and give your foot to that *sáes: pawun se oothaki churhao, pagul:* never mind the shoes; there you are, now."

In order the better to support herself, the dapper little woman put her arm firmly round my waist, and as we floundered through the water, I was more than once within an ace of being dismounted by her. The joke ended here, though it had like to have gone a step further; for the horse, putting his foot into a small hole, stumbled, and at once immersed us, till our heads and shoulders alone were visible above the flood, and we had well-nigh been sent sprawling in the water, much to the consternation of my charge, who almost squeezed me breathless as she clung to me for support.

The river Jumna we crossed in boats, and here again we had troubles little short of those already suffered; for the night being unfortunately very dark, we had great difficulty in getting the horses into the boats, and were continually sticking upon the sand-banks, the light of our torches being of no use to the boatmen in enabling them to see the shallows. We should certainly have been a picturesque group, to any person looking at us from the banks of the river, as we stood huddled together in the boat, horses and all, with the strong light of the torches catching upon the outlines of our figures, in contrast to the naked persons of the boatmen, as they plied at the heavy implements intended for paddles; the other end of the clumsy old barge being piled up with the baggage and grotesque carriages of some merchants, also bound to the capital of the district.

Travellers to Dehli are not subject to the annoyance of crossing the river in boats at all seasons of the year, pontoons being annually constructed by the sappers and miners, who have their head-quarters in the city. The stream, however, has too much the character of a mountain torrent during the monsoon to allow the bridges to remain; the very first fall of rain, after the breaking up of the hot winds, carries them away; and until the termination of the wet season, it is quite impossible to reconstruct them, on account of the violence of the flood.

I had been present at Dehli this season, in the month of July, when the monsoon set in, and had witnessed the sudden rise which took place in the waters of the river: the rains opened at nine o'clock in the morning, and before noon, the Jumna, which had hitherto been almost fordable, had overflowed its banks, and was in many places four and five miles in breadth. Away go all boats, bridges, huts, houses and gardens, in some cases leaving the inmates scarcely time to save their persons: it is not, however, very frequently thus, the greater part of the habitations within reach of the flood being constructed of planks and mats, which may be removed at a moment's notice. The havock in the melon-gardens is always a picture worth beholding; every elephant in this city, so overstocked with them, turns out to take advantage of the general spoliation, and all along the banks are seen these monstrous brutes, wading or swimming about, in search of the fruit, which they at once appropriate. The streams of the Jumna had now retired to their proper beds, but the pontons had not yet been constructed; they seldom are earlier than the middle of October, as, until that time, the weather is never fully settled.

We arrived at the Rajh Ghát just as the evening gun fired, that is, at nine o'clock, and having disembarked, I escorted my friends to the Begum's palace. This we found in excellent order for our occupation; but, with the exception of a few pieces of old massive furniture, for which we could find no use, the spacious apartments presented little beyond bare walls and nicely swept floors, a few odd chairs of antique fashion here and there, together with mirrors and paintings of the same heterogeneous patterns, both ancient and modern. Beds there were none, with the exception of the dirty *charpáhis* belonging to the native soldiery, who were stationed in the palace as a guard; and as for dinner, we had neither servants nor materials, nor could we expect them until early the next morning: all this I had foretold, and therefore the grievance was less patiently borne by the beautiful Mrs. Sackville.

The fact was, that Mrs. Sackville was hungry

and cross, and Sackville was silent and sulky, and the children were fretful and terribly noisy. I used my best efforts to soothe and restore good humour, but my endeavours were repulsed, and I therefore thought that the better plan would be to leave them to themselves, to regain their composure, while I went in search of those good things of which we were really in great need.

One corps only is quartered within the walls of Dehli; the remainder of the garrison, consisting of a company of Foot Artillery and three regiments of Native Infantry, being cantoned about two miles distant from the walls: to the former then, the Sappers and Miners, I had recourse.

Remounting my horse, I galloped off to their mess-house, and being intimate with every officer at table, I was cordially received, and had no hesitation in confessing myself a beggar. My wants were no sooner made known than active measures were taken to supply them. In a very few minutes, a weighty *banghi*-load of provisions of every kind was despatched to the palace, and servants were sent forward to prepare the feast. In the interim, an oyster pâté, a chicken salad, and a glass or two of iced claret, were by no means unwelcome restoratives; but in the discussion of these I was induced to over-stay my time a little, and I thought it not unlikely that, before I could get back to the palace, the dinner, which I had been at such pains to procure, would disappear without my assistance.

This consideration prompted me to make a short cut in returning to the palace; but in the obscurity of the night, I had no difficulty in losing my way among the back streets. I rode and turned, and turned and rode, in all directions, without being able to extricate myself, nor could I see any minarets by which to guide my way. Again and again, I enquired the road, and was directed and redirected, but still without avail, and at last I began to think that all the world were in league against me. "Whereabouts is the Begum Sumroo's palace?" I angrily enquired, for the fiftieth time.

"In the Chandni Chouk," said one man.

"Opposite Akbur Shah's palace," said another.

"Close beside Alli Mirdun Kahn's canal," exclaimed a third.

"Just above the bridge," replied a fourth.

"Very near Roshun-ud-dowla's Musjid," said a fifth.

"Behind the Lall Ra," answered a sixth.

I galloped up one street, cantered down another, trotted through the next, walked over one more, and then came to a stand-still, to make new enquiries. A native horseman crossed the road at a little distance before me; I dashed forward and seized him by the arm. "Where is the Begum Sumroo's palace?"

"A little beyond the —— but do not drag me from my saddle, and I will tell you; it's a little beyond ——"

"Peace, dotard! put spurs to your horse, and conduct me thither instantly, or assuredly I will cast you headlong into the drain below."

"Sir, I am an aged man, and your cruel grip suspends the blood in my veins; unhand me, and I will do your bidding; but let it be at a sober pace, for my horse is as infirm as his unfortunate rider."

"My son," said I, "I have ridden far this day, and am very hungry; moreover, my moments are precious; put your old nag to his best speed and I will quit my hold."

The man did so, calling me his 'father and mother,' and by many other equally flattering and endearing titles: two minutes' ride brought us to the foot of the Jumma Musjid, looking doubly grand and solemn in the mysterious obscurity of the partial light cast from the shops around it. My road was now familiar to me, and having bestowed a small *bukshis* and many thanks upon my guide for his services, I was about to gallop off, when he stopped me. "One word, sir, if I may be forgiven; by the foam upon your bit, and the soiled condition of your equipage, you appear to have travelled far and hastily: bring you any tidings of the unhappy Shumsh-ud-deen, the Nawab of Ferozepore?"

An angel either of light or of darkness prompted my reply; or else I know not why or wherefore I uttered it: "The Nawab," said I, "will be hanged to death on Thursday morning next;" and away I galloped, but not without certain uncomfortable twinges of conscience for the falsehood I had so inconsiderately, I might almost say unwittingly, spoken. "How came I to make the old man such an answer?—not a word has been heard as to the Nawab's fate—strange indeed that I should have been guilty of such an invention."

When I arrived at the palace, I found Sackville and Mrs. S. sitting in the viranda with candles on the table, the board spread with abundance of good things, plenty of servants in attendance, and every thing that hungry people might wish for, except good humour. The pair sat opposite to each other, in silence, broken only by the rattling of their knives and forks, and the clashing of glasses and crockery, as they continued to satisfy their appetites, with a display of interminable voracity, which promised a scanty share to those who came in at the tail of the hunt.

"Well," said I, seating myself, heated and fatigued, at the table, "I hope you have got all you want. Mrs. Sackville, may I trouble you for the leg of that chicken?"

"Help yourself, sir," said the lady.

"Sackville, Sackville, you're very entertaining; come, a glass of claret with me."

"Thank you, I've had sufficient."

"I am glad to tell you, Mrs. Sackville, that I have a *charpáhi* coming for you: I fear you are very much fatigued."

"You are very polite, sir; I prefer sleeping in the palki."

There is nothing so charming as a woman in smiles; but, is there anything so perverse, so perplexing, as a cross woman? In the absence of the *hookka*, a cigar is an excellent stand-by on such occasions, and to this I had recourse; then stretching myself upon one of the rugs, I gave myself up to speculations on the folly of marriage; till Somnus took me by surprise and made me 'the happiest of men,' by sending me to the altar, the delighted bridegroom of a beauty and a fortune, of the latest importation.

The sun's first rays, aided by the bellowing of camels, the trumpeting of elephants, and the clamour of the servants who had just arrived with the baggage, aroused me from my rest. I jumped up and shook myself: why, but a moment since it was evening—where were the Sackvilles? where the dinner of which I had just partaken? Mrs. Sackville, all smiles and good humour, made her appearance to answer these questions; she had enjoyed an excellent night's rest upon the *charpáhi,* and had risen to inhale the morning breezes.

Modern Dehli, called by the natives Shahjehanabad, in honour of its founder, the Emperor Shah Jehan, is one of the largest Moslem cities throughout India. The population is computed at 160,000, but this is by no means a fair criterion of the importance of the place; for the commercial advantages which it enjoys, render it the chief mart to all the western provinces, and hence the resort of merchants and petty traders is found to swell the number of inhabitants to an amount nearly double that of the fixed population.

The Emperor Shah Jehan was the grandson of Akbur the great; he ascended the *musnud* in 1628, and his first act was to undertake the building of a new city upon the ruins of ancient Dehli. He selected the eastern extremity of the old works as the most advantageous spot, on account of the river Jumna, which now washes the walls. The plan of the city is irregular: its circumference within the walls is seven miles, and there are seven handsome gates by which its fortifications are passed. The plan of the original defences is still retained, but they have been completely renovated by our government, and faced with a high escarp of granite taken from the fallen tombs and other ruins. At intervals along the walls, where the curtains (the distances from bastion to bastion) were found too great for our modern system of attack and defence, small martello towers have been constructed, for the purpose of bringing the foot of the high walls under the fire of musketry: the gates and bridges have been repaired or built anew, and the city has been otherwise restored and beautified by order of our liberal governors. The names of the gates are the

Dehli-gate, the Lahore-gate, the Ajhmere-gate, the Agra-gate, the Toorkomán-gate, the Mohur-gate, and the Cashmere-gate: this latter has casemated apartments for the accommodation of the city guard, which is stationed there. The inner gate has been almost completely rebuilt lately: the work was entrusted to Captain Smith of the Engineers, who has displayed his taste and skill to very great advantage, in the suspension of a very beautiful, but fanciful arch, over the entrance.

The principal street is the Chandni Chouk;—the name may signify either 'the place of moonlight,' or 'the place of silver-smiths';—it reaches in a direct line from the Dehli-gate to the Emperor's palace, a distance of nearly three-quarters of a mile; in breadth it is about fifty yards, but it is divided by a small raised aqueduct, which runs through the centre of the road, supplying a stream of pure water from the canal. This valuable duct had been suffered to fall into complete decay, until our government, having cleared and rebuilt the great canal of Alli Mirdun Kahn, it became again available, and the rejoicing inhabitants of the Chandni Chouk eagerly undertook the repair of it. The houses and shops in this street are much handsomer, and constructed of better materials, than in any other parts of the city, and here is the principal market for all descriptions of wares.

The second street, which is of dimensions equal to that already described, leads from the south-west entrance of the palace to the Lahore gate, and it has an aqueduct similar to that in the Chandni Chouk; but this has not been restored, owing, in some measure, to the comparative poverty of the inhabitants of this neighbourhood, and further, to the local difficulties of leading the water to it. This street is not so likely to attract the attention of the visitor, in consequence of its poor and dirty appearance, and the want of bustle and traffic, which give such an air of life and importance to the other.

The great canal, already mentioned as the canal of Alli Mirdun Kahn, after passing through the centre of the city, pours its waters into the stream from which they were taken at Kurnal, more than a hundred miles distant; having flowed through a foreign channel, one hundred and eighty miles in length. For very many years, this noble water-course remained choked, and in some parts completely buried; and it is probable that it would never have been put in repair at all, had not our government taken the matter in hand. Wells were exceedingly scarce, in consequence of the great depth at which water is found below the surface, and the waters of the Jumna were unserviceable, both for the purposes of agriculture and for domestic uses, being strongly impregnated with nitre; thus the whole district of Dehli became sterile for want of irrigation, and the inhabitants were impoverished in proportion to the decline of agriculture. Representations of the extent of this evil, and of the infallible consequences, were reported to Government, and at last, in 1817, an order was issued by Lord Hastings, for the restoration of the canal, and the task was entrusted to Captain Blane, of the Engineers, an officer well suited for the undertaking by his skill and activity. The expense incurred by the Government in the work scarcely amounted to two lahks and a half, about £25,000, and this was repaid by the increased revenues in a very few years.

No sooner was it known that the water was turned into the channel, than nearly all the inhabitants of Dehli and the neighbouring towns went forth to meet it, with music, and processions, and every possible demonstration of joy. Captain Blane informs us, that the sluices were opened, and the water admitted in the new bed on the 22d of January, but the stream did not reach Dehli until the 12th of February, the water being copiously absorbed by the loose arid soil through which it ran, and also being drawn from the canal in very large quantities by the land-owners and villagers as it flowed past. So great a blessing was this esteemed by the natives, not only of Dehli, but of the whole district as far as Kurnal, that everywhere in the vicinity public rejoicings were held, and songs of praise were sung in honour of the English.

This canal is sometimes called by the natives Feroze Shah's canal; this is erroneous, however, it being only a branch led off from the canal properly so called, which is still choked and unserviceable: it used to run from Kurnal through Hansi, in the direction of Bikanir; and as this tract of country is capable of high cultivation, it is to be hoped that the government will ere long see fit to have this cleared also.

The Sackvilles having never before been in Dehli, I gladly undertook to *lionise* them through the city. The first place to which I took them was the palace of the Emperor Akbur Shah, not because I deemed it the best worth seeing, nor on

AKBUR SHAHS PALACE AND OLD FORT, DELHI.

account of its possessor's rank and dignity, but because it would be little admired after having seen the Jumma Musjid and other buildings. It is necessary for all Europeans to apply to the Resident for an order, before they can be admitted here.

The palace was built by Shah Jehan, at the time that he undertook the foundation of the city, and he certainly made a regal residence for himself. Its courts and enclosures occupy the space of one mile in circumference, surrounded by a moat, and a wall of fine red granite, forty feet in height, flanked with turrets and cupolas, very beautifully built, and kept in thorough repair. It is connected with the old fort of Selimghur, by a narrow bridge thrown over a branch of the Jumna; and within this are some of the most ancient remains of architecture to be found in Dehli, being apparently of Afghan structure, or perhaps that of the earliest Patan kings: the style is very weighty and massive, unrelieved by any ornament, beyond very rude carvings, here and there, about the mouldings and cornices.

The entrance to the palace is through a succession of noble and very lofty gateways, also built of red granite, and very beautifully sculptured in parts; the doors are of solid wood, studded with brass; and after passing through several of these which divide the courts, we came to a large pair of doors entirely of that metal, below a fine arched passage of elegant architecture, more ornamented than any of the former. Here our sticks and whips were demanded by a *chobdar* in waiting for that purpose, and being told by the man to make a humble *saláam* the moment the gate was opened, we complied, and found ourselves in presence of the *Dewani Khas*, the imperial hall of judgment. This is a very elegant building of pure white marble, sculptured into delicate screen-work, and inlaid with precious stones in the patterns of wreaths, flowers, birds, insects, &c.: the design is very chaste and simple; it consists of a light dome supported by double rows of marble pillars, highly ornamented, and beautifully proportioned. Upon this we were not suffered to set foot, until after having a second time made a humble obeisance to the vacant throne.

Within, the ceiling is wrought in enamel of every brilliant colour, inlaid with small pieces of looking-glass, and elaborately gilded in patterns and devices purely Eastern. In the centre of this apartment, or, more correctly, pillared terrace, is the Emperor's judgment-seat, hewn out of a solid block of natural crystal, about twenty inches in breadth, and the same in depth; it stands below an archway of larger dimensions than the others, and in front of it three jets of clear water are kept continually playing, whose waters are carried through the hall on either side by a duct formed of the same beautiful material as the rest of the building. This exquisite place is now rarely made use of by the Emperor; never, indeed, unless for the reception of some personage of exalted rank. It is abandoned to the crows and kites, and is left in a filthy state of impurity, while the paltry expenditure of three rupees monthly would allow of its being kept in order, or at least cleanly.

In a small court, leading from the quadrangle in which the Dewani Khas stands, is the Emperor's private place of worship, the Moti Musjid, or mosque of pearl, and well does it deserve its name, so chaste and rich is it, both in design and execution. It was built by the Emperor Aurungzebe, the son of Shah Jehan, and is in better preservation than any other part of the imperial palace, probably on account of its sanctity. The domes only are seen above the walls which enclose the chapel, until the opening of two small brass gates, and then the whole gem is exposed to view. It is in the style of most places of Moslem worship, having three domes, the centre one of which is the largest, supported by as many double rows of columns rising into open arches in the front, and being closed by niches of the same order in rear; thus giving it the appearance of three distinct apartments when viewed in front: at the corners, and between each of the domes, are very small minarets, in this instance scarcely higher than the domes themselves. I had hitherto been under the impression that the Mussulmans would never, under any circumstances, permit their places of worship to be invaded by the feet of infidels, more especially by such as might be shod; this, however, I found to be erroneous, for the guide, who professed to be a devout man, made no objection to our entering every part of the place. This they will not on any account suffer in tombs of peculiar sanctity, and I have more than once been denied, in places of the same kind as the one in question.

The gardens around the palace are very extensive, and are adorned with pavilions, baths, aqueducts, fountains, grottos, reservoirs, and the most ingenious contrivances of the like sort; many of the numerous streams about the place being led into courses, representing snakes revolving and in pursuit, of one another, here disappearing below the surface of the ground, and again issuing in a new form. The trees are of splendid growth, and are fortunately likely to flourish after all the rest has gone to complete decay, for they thrive in the irrigation employed in rearing the produce of the garden ; the orange groves and other beds of fruit trees being let to fruiterers at a handsome rent. With the exception of these, which are cultivated simply for the sake of their price in the market, the whole place is abandoned to ruin and neglect ; the buildings are overgrown with weeds and rank mosses, the tanks are stagnant and corrupt, the channels are broken up and choked, the fountains are silent, the beautiful marble baths are filled with dried leaves and rubbish, and the grottos are for the most part half buried ; even the palace courts are turned into bazaars, half choked with dirty huts and temporary stabling, and the whole place is overrun with noisy children and old women. Nothing but desolation and decay is to be found among these once proud emblems of regal magnificence, and this is to be attributed to the miserable poverty of the present Emperor, who receives from our Government a wretched pittance, barely sufficient to feed his family and to support his paltry train.

As we were returning through these courts, we met old Akbur Shah, the Emperor, returning from a visit to the tomb of Zufdir Junge, where he had been residing a short time for change of air. We happened fortunately to fall in with the procession where there was room to go aside, or otherwise we should have had cause to repent the honour we enjoyed in the sublimity of his presence; for as it was, even with a lady in company, which would on most occasions have proved a protection, we were thrust about and turned away, by the horsemen and *chobdars*, with very little ceremony.

In front came three or four elephants, covered with tawdry housings and bearing gilded *háodas* of state, very much the worse for wear, the *mahawuts* clad in dowdy suits of brown, and they, as well as the elephants, exhibiting an unequivocal appearance of poverty and low diet. Then came two horses saddled and appointed, one for the Emperor, the other for his son; they simply performed a part in the pageant, being never used. Immediately after these came the *Badshah* himself, borne in a *ton-jaun* of state, a sort of tray, having a scarlet canopy trimmed with faded gold lace; this was profusely gilded, but had little of the magnificence and intrinsic costliness, which formerly distinguished the noble race of monarchs from whom he is a lineal descendant.

The old man is upwards of eighty years of age, and although greatly bowed, he bears evidence of having been a very handsome man in his youth. His features are aquiline and finely proportioned; his complexion is fair and fresh, and this, together with a light brown eye, and hair and beard perfectly white, renders his appearance more that of a Persian than a native of Hindostan. He did not notice us as he passed, nor did he even deign to return the smiling *saláam* of the beautiful Mrs. Sackville. I know not why it was so, but, contrary to the usual custom of princes in the East, he arrived at his palace in silence, without the usual acclamations of the populace, or the shouting of his titles and attributes by his own attendants; the only public manifestation of his great rank was in the firing of a salute at the entrance to the palace, and a guard-of-honour, consisting of British *sipáhis*, drawn up at the gate to receive him. Beside the royal *ton-jaun* rode the English officer commanding the palace guard, who has the honour of acting the part of bear-leader to his majesty on all occasions, being an honorary sort of jailer.

Behind the Emperor came his favourite son Mirza Sulleem,* who, though the third son, is looked upon as heir to the dominion of his father, the two elder being represented as incompetent to rule, where no rule is. He is a fine man in appearance, very unlike his royal father, having black hair and beard, with very dark eyes and a swarthy complexion. Though the least debauched of the Emperor's sons, he has the appearance of dissipation in his air and countenance, and is reported to be inordinately addicted to intoxicating drugs.

This prince was followed by the state treasurer and other officers of the household; then came a troop of *sawars*, native matchlock-men mounted upon camels; and after them the cavalry, about fifty troopers, ill-mounted, ill-clad, and ill-armed, positively in rags and tatters, and bearing indiscriminately every sort of weapon, in rear, came a train of elephants and a number of led horses, all in keeping with the rest of the display. A crowd of the inhabitants were collected round to see, and to pay their obedience to this remnant of the mighty Mogul dynasty, which once held sway over the greater part of Hindostan.

* The death of this prince, whose favour with his father was the source of so much jealousy and heart-burning among the other members of the royal household, is just announced.

After quitting the palace, we took with us the *chobdars,* who had been appointed by the resident to attend us, and whose further services we required in gaining admission to the Jumma Musjid, the chief mosque; no person except the Moslems themselves being admitted here without an order from the Resident, and an empty permission from the Emperor, who has still many forms of respect and submission paid to him, and who loves to fancy that his acquiescence is necessary, in such cases, within the city: this prerogative is merely nominal, however, and any objection on his part, unless upon good grounds, would be at once set aside by the British Resident.

The Jumma Musjid stands upon a rocky eminence at the back of the Chandni Chouk; the position is not felicitous, being in a low dirty part of the city, amid narrow streets and meanly built houses. The little hill upon which it stands was originally a high conical point of rock; but no undertaking being too great for the architects of the days in which it was built, the upper part of the rock was cut away, and made serviceable in filling in below; and thus a large table surface was obtained, upon which the foundation of the present building was laid. This was executed in the year 1632, by order of Shah Jehan, then reigning, and the mosque itself, so deservedly admired by all, for its exquisite symmetry, is said to have been the emperor's own design. The body of the temple, and the walls around the area, as also the three beautiful gateways, with their gigantic flights of steps, are all constructed of red granite, very skilfully jointed and put together; but the domes, and the cupolas of the minarets, are of white marble, and there are some cornices and mouldings of the same, about the facing of the building.

Richly as the carvings and ornaments are wrought about the gates and lower walls, the upper parts, the minarets and domes, are altogether free from decoration, except in the very simplest form; and this most happy circumstance adds greatly to the imposing grandeur and magnitude of the work; for it thus gains an air of distance and mystery about the highest points, which brings ocular delusion to the assistance of the already sublime reality. The minarets are exquisitely proportioned, and, in contrast with the circular domes, have a double value, and the fabric must be looked upon with feelings of veneration as well as admiration; even those least susceptible of pleasure in such sights never fail to be struck with the beauty and solemn grandeur of the edifice. In the centre of the quadrangle is a reservoir of water, in which three fountains play, and which is found necessary in the performance of the ceremonies of worship. The groups of figures performing ablution about this tank, the knots of sage venerable *padris* standing in earnest confabulation in different parts of the court, and the *pundits* squatted below the arcades teaching their scholars, form a scene which, in connexion with the building, is highly interesting and picturesque.

There is also a large well belonging to the *musjid*, which was excavated by Shah Jehan, soon after the completion of the building; the shaft is sunk to a great depth through the solid rock, and the water is raised to the surface by means of a number of wheels and complicated machinery, the greater part of which appears to be superfluous, but is still kept up as at first erected. The interior of this well affords shelter to great numbers of pigeons, who build their nests in the interstices of the masonry: with the natives they are tame and familiar, and will suffer them to approach almost within arm's length; but the moment an European makes his appearance in the *chouk*, away they all fly in eddying circles to the summits of the pinnacles: they are respected by the natives, who are universally fond of all sorts of animals, and who never refuse them a share of their own food, however scanty.

I could not induce my fair friend to venture to the top of the minarets, but I was unable myself to resist the temptation; the bird's eye view of the city from hence is very entertaining, and parts of it are really rich in crowded mosques, palaces, and battlemented walls. I could not help comparing some groups of the buildings with those of Constantinople, so light and elegant, yet so grand and awe-inspiring.

In the Chandni Chouk is a small mosque, named Roshun-ud-dowla ki Musjid, from its founder, the Light-of-the-State. It is not remarkable for its size or architecture, but simply as being the spot from whence Nadir Shah looked down upon the massacre of one hundred and twenty thousand of the inhabitants of the city, which he had ordered to be prosecuted without mercy, until by a motion of his sword he should give the signal for the slaughter to be suspended. This horrible deed was perpetrated in the year 1739, during the reign of the Emperor Mohummed Shah the third, who was surprised in his capital by Nadir Shah, at the head of an immense army of Jhauts; a tyrant, who, having put to the sword more than two-thirds of the inhabitants, plundered the city coffers and private treasuries, of property, to the amount of £6,000,000; and then withdrawing his troops, retired again to his own fastnesses.

The historical tale connected with this musjid deterred Mrs. Sackville from visiting it, and the very sound of the priest's voice within, as we were passing, rendered an application to the vinaigrette necessary.

Besides these, the visitor should not omit to explore the dilapidated palaces, musjids, and tombs, which are to be found in every quarter of the city; they will amply repay him for his toil, even though he should attempt it under a summer sun. The principal are, the old residence of Sahadut Kahn, which is in the Cashmere quarter of the city; and then there are those of Kummur-ud-deen, and Alli Mirdun Kahn, with many more *quos enumerare longum est*. Such are the lions best worthy of notice within Shajehanabad; others well worthy of inspection, though scarcely within the limits of verbal description, will be touched upon as soon as we can find leisure to pay them a visit.

CHAPTER VIII.

ANCIENT DEHLI AND SHAHJEHANABAD.

IMMEDIATELY after our arrival in Dehli, a report gained general circulation and credit, not only in the city, but through the military cantonment also, that the Nawab Shumsh-ud-deen was condemned to suffer the extreme penalty of the law, for the crime of which he had been convicted. It was affirmed that the execution would take place on the following Thursday morning: the rumour was honoured with almost universal belief, because it was from a most authentic source; yet no one knew whence, or by what means the news had arrived. No author could be discovered; the local officers of the government, who should be the first to hear it, were still in the dark, and had received no official communications from head-quarters, although intimations of the possibility of such a thing had been forwarded by private letters. The natives whispered that a secret emissary had arrived from Calcutta, bearing the death-warrant, and that the ignorance of the English was merely affected for the sake of keeping the natives quiet, until the moment of execution, so as to prevent conspiracies or intrigue; and thus the rumour spread, and gained strength among all classes.

It may be believed that I was at no loss to account for the popular error, nor was I at any pains to undeceive the public mind, preferring to remain as much as possible in the back-ground: my friends, the Sackvilles, were the only persons to whom I had mentioned the circumstance of my being myself the author of the report, and the manner in which it had fallen out; we could not help feeling a vicious pleasure in the commotion it excited. What then was our surprise, when, by a singular coincidence, a warrant did in reality arrive for the death of the Nawab upon the very day, Thursday the eighth, which I had mentioned to the old horseman, and which had been so universally talked of!

All the grandees and men of authority were confounded. How did the natives get the news? They were always a day or two before the government despatches with their information; secret agency—intrigue at head-quarters—surreptitious means — insurrections — conspiracies — rescues — and the like, were the only topics of conversation and argument. Fifty different measures were proposed for the correction of the evil in future; and precautions were taken to prevent the issue of any mischief which might be brewing in the present instance. Rumours were afloat that a rescue was already plotted, and one version affirmed that fifty native gentlemen of rank had bound themselves in a solemn league to set the Nawab free, or die in the attempt; others told that the whole city was preparing to rise in confederacy against the British power.

These flying reports probably had birth in the city, whence they were carried to and disseminated in the cantonment by the merchants and *box-wallas;* and there, among the officers, they grew by circulation into detailed and circumstantial accounts "upon the very best authority." Whether or not they were fully credited by the chiefs and civil functionaries, I cannot say; but the most vigorous measures were taken for security, and for the peace of the city; every precaution which care and forethought could suggest was put in practice, and the whole business was executed with a promptitude and secrecy highly creditable to those who conducted it. A double guard was stationed over the person of the Nawab, who was then imprisoned in a small guard-room in the cantonment; more troops were called in from Merat; and a body of Skinner's Irregular Horse, together with a large force of the police, and mounted soldiers from various native chiefs, formed an array, sufficient to defy the best concerted schemes of the natives.

But before we proceed to the execution of this unhappy young nobleman, it would be as well to state the circumstances of the crime for which he suffered. On account of his high birth, and his many agreeable qualities, Shumsh-ud-deen had been admitted to a free and familiar intercourse with many of the European officers and gentlemen, in and around Dehli. He was not more than three-and-twenty years of age; in person, he was handsome, possessing an air of superiority and good breeding, as infallibly distinctive of high birth and education, among the natives of India, as it is with the more polished nations of the Occidental world. His *jaghir* at Ferozepore was rich, being valued at from ten to fifteen *lahks* per annum; he was particularly hospitable and generous, and appeared never so happy as in the exchange of good-offices with his English acquaintance. Mr. Fraser, the Commissioner, and Agent to the Government, who fell a victim to his treachery, had been his chief and foremost friend, and had rendered him many essential services; and it was proved, in the course of the Nawab's trial, that he was professing the warmest esteem and devotion for his kind patron, while, in his heart, he was concerting schemes for his destruction.

On the 22d of March, Mr. Fraser having to pay a visit of ceremony to a native of high rank, residing within the city walls, Kullian Singh, the ex-Rajha of Kishenghur, quitted his residence, as was his habit, with no attendants, beyond a single *sawar* (armed horseman) and his *sáes*. It was about sun-set when he set forth, and entering the city by the Lahore-gate, he proceeded to the house of the Rajha; here he remained in conference about an hour, and when he again mounted his horse, it was nearly dark. He returned by the same gate, and with only the same number of attendants: why he did so, it is difficult to conceive, as the way leading through the Cashmere-gate would have been both nearer and more pleasant, and was, moreover, his usual route. Just as he arrived at that part of the road, without the city, where it joins a similar one leading to the Cashmere-gate, a disguised horseman overtook him at a gallop, who, wheeling his horse suddenly upon him, presented and discharged a matchlock at him, the contents of which entered his side and killed him on the spot, before he comprehended the man's intention. The assassin then, putting spurs to his horse, which was evidently one of very superior speed and mettle, dashed past Mr. Fraser's attendants, and galloped back at full speed, entering the city, it was supposed, by the Lahore-gate. The *sawar* gave chase, but the murderer had got too much the start, and rode too fleet an animal to be overtaken, and as he was already lost in the increasing dusk, the man returned, in the hope of being able to afford assistance to his fallen master. He found him, however, without a sign of life, his head resting in the lap of the *sáes*, who continued to bewail his death with loud lamentation and curses upon the murderer, which soon brought in the assistance of passengers. A *charpáhi* was immediately procured, and the body was carried back to the house, which it had so lately left in the enjoyment of health and vigour. These are the material points of the case, as taken from the evidence of the servants who accompanied him. On examination of the wounds, it appeared that the injury had been inflicted by a charge of slugs, and not by a single ball; the heart and lungs were so lacerated as, in all probability, to have induced instant dissolution without agony.

The most active and searching means were immediately set on foot by the magistrate for the discovery of the assassin, and from Mr. Fraser's well-known popularity among the natives of the district, the presumption was strong that the deed had been committed by a hired ruffian, acting under orders of some man of rank or fortune, from private motives of revenge; or possibly, in retaliation of dissatisfaction given in the commissioner's awards, or in the discharge of other official duties. In this case, the best clue to those concerned would be found in the records of those measures of his policy, which might be considered to have given cause for vengeance, or to have excited resentment, in quarters possessing the means of resorting to mercenary assassination. Hence, and from various corroborating circumstances, which it is unnecessary fully to detail in this little sketch, suspicion attached to the young Nawab Shumsh-ud-deen.

A *bunnia*, or petty shopkeeper, upon his *jaghir*, had, not long since, been found murdered under circumstances, the mystery of which Mr. Fraser had taken great pains to remove, but which the Nawab had endeavoured to conceal; and being unable to bring the affair at once to light, Mr. Fraser thought it his duty to deny the Nawab his presence, until he should give up the offender, or aid him in his apprehension. This, together with other fancied causes of dissatisfaction, first directed the attention of Mr. Simon Fraser, the magistrate, to the Nawab; and when the news of this suspicion came to be bruited about, the interest already excited in the public mind was very greatly increased, by reason of the exalted rank of the suspected perpetrator. The native community were strongly moved by the imputation thus cast upon one of their nobles, but they consoled themselves with the belief that he was too high to be touched by the law, and that the government would not dare to bring to condign punishment a man of such princely birth and fortune.

So strong was the suspicion against this man, and so many circumstances were elicited in support of it, that Mr. Metcalfe, the successor in office to Mr. Fraser, thought it necessary to take him in custody, and this was done in a manner far from consistent with the dignity of our government, or with the high honour which should distinguish it. Of all who lamented the death of Mr. Fraser, none appeared to feel more sorrow and regret, than did Shumsh-ud-deen; and among many other natives of rank and wealth, who voluntarily came forward with princely rewards for the apprehension of the murderer, he himself appeared most generous. Of this Mr. Metcalfe took advantage, when it became advisable to secure the Nawab's person: he sent him an invitation, begging him to come over to Dehli and assist in the investigation; on the Nawab's arrival, he received him within the Cashmere gate, where he gently intimated that he must consider himself a prisoner.

Two followers of the Nawab were found skulking in disguise in different parts of the district; these were apprehended and brought to trial. Unnia, a Mehwatti, turned king's evidence against his accomplice, Kurreim Kahn; and through his deposition, the murder was brought home most clearly to the latter: he was, in fact, the horseman who had done the deed, and so irresistible was the evidence, that, without any difficulty, he was found guilty, condemned, and executed. He died with the most solemn declarations of his own and his master's innocence still on his lips, and by many of the native gentlemen and merchants about Dehli, he was considered innocent, and was looked upon as a sacrifice to the revenge of the English.

It appears from the evidence which was laid before the court by Unnia, that Shumsh-ud-deen, at whose instigation the murder was committed, had entrusted the immediate plotting and direction of the affair to his father-in-law, Mogul Beg, and to his *sawar*, Kurreim Kahn, than whom two more cool and crafty villains, or two more appropriate instruments, could not have been selected; the former particularly remarkable for his duplicity and subtle invention; the other for his cold-blooded hardihood, and tried secrecy and devotion to his lord.

Kurreim Kahn was sent over to Dehli by the Nawab about six weeks previous to the murder, with the ostensible commission of purchasing grey-hounds for coursing; but from papers and correspondence found upon his person after apprehension, there can no doubt remain as to the real object of his visit. The design of the murder was sufficiently brought home to him, even without the testimony of Unnia, who affirmed that Mr.

Fraser had frequently before his death escaped destruction by the most narrow chances; such as returning by some other route than was expected, or by the fact of some friend joining him on the road, Kurreim Kahn having been in wait for him more than a month, before he could find an opportunity to effect his object.

Unnia further acknowledged having been in the neighbourhood when the shot was fired, and he directed the magistrates to a well, in which they discovered the matchlock which the ruffian had used in the accomplishment of his bloody design; he also pointed out a place in which was secreted about three inches of the end of the barrel, which had been cut off by a blacksmith in the bazaar, by order of Kurreim Kahn; this the smith confirmed, and the barrel was found to correspond with the fragment: every point of the evidence was satisfactorily supported, and the murder was fully brought home to the assassin.

It was further elicited from this man, that if not actually the instigator, and supposing Mogul Beg to have been such, Shumsh-ud-deen must at least have been privy to the conspiracy; for, immediately after the consummation of the affair, he despatched a second *sawar* to look after the safety of Kurreim

Kahn, and to give him intelligence of the search which was instituted ; but the scout came upon the ground just in time to witness the apprehension of the villain to whom he was deputed, and with this news he returned to his master.

The Nawab finding his myrmidon in custody, and fearing that his guilt might be wrung from him, and that he himself might be involved in his confession, appointed a secret agent to communicate with the prisoner, and used all possible means to stifle the case, but without avail. This emissary was also seized, and afterwards assisted greatly in exposing the Nawab's plans. Independent of this witness, however, the whole chain of evidence was perfectly connected, and was so lucid as to leave no room for hesitation, as to the extent of the Nawab's guilt : he was plainly the prime mover of the conspiracy. After this complete exposure of "the head and front of his offending," however, the government appeared to pay little attention to the affair ; and it seemed as though they had satisfied themselves by the execution of the slave who had perpetrated the deed, without passing a similar sentence upon the instigator.

Week after week passed over, and yet no orders were issued for the public trial of the Nawab. It is true, he was detained in close custody, and those who had attended the trial of Kurreim Kahn, or had heard the evidence of Unnia, entertained a full conviction of his guilt: still, the authorities at head-quarters continued inactive, and the whole Anglo-Indian community became alarmed, lest through the weak policy and non-interference system of the governor-general, the criminal should be allowed to escape justice. The public prints and periodicals teemed with calls and appeals to the government to rouse itself and bring the offender to trial; on their part, the most lamentable apathy was displayed; and so much indecision and delay occurred, as could only be construed into a positive disinclination to undertake the punishment of a person of the Nawab's consequence, even in expiation of so atrocious a crime. The natives, at least the inhabitants of Dehli, did not hesitate to declare this opinion openly; and, in other parts, a more lamentable proof of the same sentiments manifested itself, for those chiefs who gave the government credit for this weakness, took a ready advantage of it, and did not neglect to wreak vengeance, wherever they thought fit, with a comfortable anticipation of impunity.

An instance, however, very soon occurred, which

succeeded in bringing the government to a conviction of the fearful tendency of its slothful indifference; and also of the necessity of adopting the most determined and unflinching intervention, in order to crush the spirit of insubordination and crime, which its own imbecile conduct had fostered; and which had been generated by Lord William Bentinck's systematic degradation of the European character in the estimation of the natives. The occurrence to which I refer, is the desperate attempt which was made at Jeypore to assassinate Major Alves, the political agent of Rajhpootana, and three other officers who were with him. One of the four only fell a sacrifice in the affray, but the circumstances are truly horrible. As connected with the foregoing remarks, the reader will perhaps suffer a short digression, that I may state the leading features of the transaction; a hasty outline will be sufficient.

Lord William Bentinck had been compelled, though, as he confessed, with great reluctance, to enter upon a partial interference in the affairs of Jeypore;* on the death of the late Rajha, who was supposed to have been murdered by his vizier, Joota Ram, a "crafty three-headed thief," as ever

* Jeypore is an independent state; the capital having the same name.

ruled a kingdom by the hands of his sovereign. The accusation of this murder was variously supported: the women of the harem declared positively that the Rajha had been poisoned, and that they, instead of being permitted to attend his dying bed, were thrust forth from the apartment by Joota Ram, as soon as they became suspicious of villainy; that the minister had refused to comply with their oft-repeated entreaties to be allowed to receive the Rajha's last commands; and that the royal physicians had been expelled from the palace by violent means, and the only apology for a medical man who was permitted to visit the Rajha was a quack, who sold drugs, and spells, and magic philters, in an obscure quarter of the city.

This minister, Joota Ram, whose crimes are said to have been countless and unparalleled, whose wholesale murders and villainous machinations had excited popular wrath and detestation to its extremity, was professedly taken under the British protection. Both the Ráni (widow of the Rajha) and the minister applied simultaneously to the political agent for his assistance, and after some little hesitation, Lord William accorded his sanction to a limited interference, a halting, uncertain, wavering, irresolute interposition, which could only debase our character in the opinion of the natives, and would infallibly do the very mischief, which it only required a strong and determined arm to check.

When Major Alves arrived at Jeypore for the investigation of the affair, tales of violence and bloodshed were revealed to him, equalling the terrors of the most romantic fictions. Every thing was in disorder; the populace riotous and discontented, the soldiery in declared mutiny, the sacred places defiled, and the treasury plundered; so that it became necessary to enter into a negociation for a loan of fifty thousand rupees, on British security, for the disbursement and supply of the royal household. Joota Ram at once resigned his office, and placed himself under the protection of the Political Agent.

While the affairs of Jeypore were in this state, Lord William Bentinck quitted India, and Sir Charles Metcalfe assumed the reins of government. A directly opposite plan was now pursued, with a policy most ruinous in such a juncture; but, at the same time, one, which, had it been put in practice at the commencement of the affair, would, in a measure, have saved the credit of our government, and have averted the mischief in question. Not that this was the high ground which our government might have been expected to occupy, in virtue of its supremacy, but that it would have been preferable to that which was acted on by Lord William. A decided interposition could alone have put an effectual check upon the spirit of crime and rebellion which was spreading, not only at Jeypore, but in other independent states, as well as in our own territories.

Instructions were forwarded to Major Alves to withdraw from the belligerent parties at Jeypore, all interference on the part of the British. After that interference had once been granted, and an acceptation on the part of government, of the office of arbiter, had taken place, it is difficult indeed to conceive what motive could have induced Sir Charles to adopt such a measure as this.

The Political Agent was under the necessity of paying a visit to the royal family, for the purpose of showing cause why he did not, in accordance with the Ráni's requisition, surrender into her hands the person of the ex-minister, being anxious at the same time to keep the instructions he had received from the knowledge of the Ráni, until a fitting opportunity should occur for the disclosure.

But, however secret he might have believed his orders to be, correct information of the same had been, by some means, conveyed to the Ráni; and she, enraged at the removal of our arbitration, determined upon revenge: indeed, both parties lost their confidence in the British protection, and from the moment that the news was received, insurrections, tumults, and conspiracies broke forth.

Major Alves, on his visit to the palace, was attended by his two assistants, Messrs. Blake and Macnaghten, and by Captain Ludlow. The Ráni received them in person, but she did not so far set aside the religious prejudices of her nation as to appear before the *purda*, or screen made use of on such occasions by all modest women of her rank. They found the lady in great wrath, and in a state of excitement which instigated her to treat Major Alves with unrestrained insolence: she even went so far as to threaten him with vengeance, if he persisted in refusing her the assistance which she demanded. The Major, nothing moved by her abuse, was about to retire from the *durbar*, when a man from the crowd which thronged about the audience-chamber, rushed forward and cut him down with a *tulwar* (a heavy kind of broad-sword). A terrible tumult succeeded, with cries of murder, and shouts demanding the lives of the English; and if the first blow was not struck by one of the Ráni's people, they now in a body joined the mob, and lent their assistance in the outrage, exclaiming that violence had been offered by the English to the inmates of the palace, and that the royal *zenána* had been defiled.

Major Alves was severely wounded, but he effected an escape by the assistance of some of those assembled, who were well disposed towards him. With great difficulty they succeeded in smuggling him into a palki, in which he was hurried out of the crowd. Captain Ludlow and Mr. Macnaghten evaded the fury of the mob by a like good fortune; but the city gates were closed on Mr. Blake ere he could make good his flight.

He was in the very centre of the riot, and its whole vengeance fell upon him; stones, clubs, bricks, spears, and all sorts of missiles were hurled at him, and sorely was he bruised and wounded. In company with his *chupprassi*, who behaved most gallantly in defence of his master, he, by great exertion, managed to force his way to the elephant upon which he had ridden to the palace; and having mounted it, he directed the *mahawut* to make for the Tripolea Durwása, a gate not far from the palace. But at this place they were met by a guard of the *Rajh*, armed with spears and swords, and these likewise joined the insurgents, as they followed the elephant, with shouts of "*Mar! Mar!*" (Kill him! Kill him!) The mob, finding that they could not effect their bloodthirsty purpose while the elephant continued to move on, now commenced hacking and chopping at his hind legs with their weapons: upon this the *chupprassi* desired the *chuŕrakutta* to beat them away; and this the brave fellow attempted to perform single-handed, making use of the little ladder which is slung by the elephant's side for the purpose of mounting and dismounting, but he was quickly cut down by the mob. A *sawar* belonging to Major Alves had remained by Mr. Blake from the commencement of the fray, and he now rode in front of the elephant, endeavouring to clear the way with his sword; him Mr. Blake deputed to the Agent's residence, to bring assistance.

With great perseverance and resolution, they forced a way to the Tripolea Durwása, but this they found closed; and not knowing where to turn for safety, Mr. Blake now gave directions to the *mahawut* to drive to the house of Poorahit Ramnaut, a native gentleman, on whose protection he thought he could depend; but the elephant was so cruelly mangled and disabled by the wounds inflicted upon him, that the *mahawut* declared his inability to proceed so far. And now the only hope of escape which presented itself was that of taking sanctuary in some sacred building, and Mr. Blake, therefore, gave orders to make for the temple of Poorahit, which was close at hand. Here also they found the doors closed; but, with the assistance of two persons within, they succeeded in climbing in at the window; and now they considered themselves safe from further violence, and awaited calmly the arrival of assistance from the agent.

Both Mr. Blake and his faithful *chupprasi* were severely wounded in different places; they were fatigued and worn out by their exertions; and the occupants of the temple taking pity upon their sufferings, conducted them to a room in the *chouk* below, and supplied them with water. The only door in this small apartment opened towards the street, where the populace were still gathered, demanding in a loud clamour, and with threats of vengeance to their own priests, a surrender of the fugitives. The door, however, was well secured, and they continued in perfect silence for some time, hoping that the mob would disperse, or that aid might be brought to them.

Presently, some person from the exterior, whether friend or foe has never transpired, came to the door and said, "Do not alarm yourselves; you are now safe." At this instant, the door was burst in, and large stones were poured in upon the unfortunate victims. They defended the entrance as well as they could, sheltering themselves behind the walls, as opportunities occurred, until at last, a violent effort was made by the assailants to carry the entrance. Desperate, yet firm, Mr. Blake seized a spear, which was aimed at him, from the hands of the owner, and, thus armed, he kept the whole mob at bay for more than half an hour, killing several of the foremost.

At length, the dastardly crew, fearing the vengeance of their intrepid antagonist, commenced breaking down the masonry at the back of the temple, for the purpose of opening a new attack upon their victims, whom they thus surrounded; and not even the religious prejudices of these holy Hindus could restrain them from consummating a sacrifice, by which they defiled their sacred altars with the polluting blood of a Christian. The faithful *chupprassi* was slain while still defending the person of his fallen master, but the life of the *mahawut* was saved by the interference of the *Rajh hurkarras*, and from him the foregoing account was learnt. After the *chupprassi* had been slain, Mr. Blake's corpse was dragged into the street, and literally chopped into fragments by the savage populace, after having been subjected to other more disgusting indignities.

Such was the affair which at last forced upon the attention of our Government the necessity of using more determined measures for the preservation of their public servants, and for the suppression of the open contempt and contumely cast upon themselves and their actions. The following paragraph, copied from the Merat Magazine for the month of July, will exhibit pretty clearly the sentiments of the community, both British and Indian.

"After the part taken by the rulers of India in the settlement of Jeypore, how can they demand satisfaction for the insult offered to the whole British nation? Protecting Joota Ram from the justice of his country, how can they demand vengeance upon the actors in the late scene, as an offering to the outraged laws? Casting off, as they have done, the high office that devolved on them by right of supremacy, how can they reconcile, either by policy or by international law, the capricious interference and non-interference successively pursued. Would that the lethargy which has so long entranced our Indian officials could be dispelled; that they would see and acknowledge the real jeopardy in which our power is placed; that they could be made conscious that a middle line of conduct is not practicable, while the native population bears a proportion of thousands to units of Europeans; fostered as the passions of these nations have been within the last eight years, and encouraged, as we have seen them, to regard Europeans as oppressors, as the scourge of the country, as tyrannical task-masters, and meditating, as very many do, the day of revenge!"

Even this second instance of rebellious outrage among the natives, failed to arouse our Government as it should have done. They saw that something must be done, but they were a long time coming to a decision as to what that something should be. Instead of calling upon the *Rajh* of Jeypore, and fearlessly demanding a thorough sifting of every circumstance connected with this bloody transaction, they, after much delay, during which all the political agents in the country might have been assassinated, commissioned Major Alves to investigate the case.

Major Alves commenced his work by the execution of the man who had struck him down, and the same punishment was awarded to one or two of the ringleaders of the riot. But all his conferences with the Ráni ended in smoke; and up to the time of my departure from India, nothing satisfactory was elicited as to the cause or plot of the conspiracy.

But enough of this: I must to the issue of the former case;—and I trust I shall not shock the nerves of the too sensitive reader, by proposing to conduct her or him to the scene of the Nawab's execution; premising, as an example of the sloth temperately commented upon above, that the murder of Mr. Fraser was committed in March; the trial did not commence till July; and the Nawab, having been found guilty, was not executed until October.

Willing to obtain a good view of the execution, I gladly accepted the invitation of the officer on guard to sleep the previous night at the Cashmere-gate, upon the plain immediately opposite to which the scaffold was erected. One or two other officers did the same, and after dinner we met at our rendezvous. We seated ourselves at the table to discuss our cigars and *brandy-pani*, before going to rest, and conversation naturally turned upon the scene to be enacted the next morning. While we were thus engaged, the officer on duty was suddenly summoned to the gate by the *subadar* of the guard, who informed him that a body of British *sipáhis* demanded admittance. An occurrence so unusual at that late hour, excited our surprise; but it was quickly explained. The brigadier, in order to prevent any attempt at rescue, or any commotion in conducting the Nawab from the cantonment to the scaffold the next morning, had issued a sudden order for his person to be removed from its former place of confinement, to the Cashmere-gate, under an escort of a hundred men, so as to have him upon the spot without the populace being aware of it. Thus, if a rescue was at any time meditated, the design was frustrated by this unexpected movement.

When the Nawab was first made aware of his sentence, he was so completely astounded by the intelligence, as to be quite unmanned, and to receive it as a calamity which he never anticipated. In the agony of his despair, he dashed his head against the wall, and unless he had been prevented by his guard, he would have destroyed himself. For many days he watched an opportunity to commit suicide, but again becoming calm and collected, he took refuge in his pride, and behaved with the most perfect indifference, as though his existence were worthless in his estimation: but lest his violence should be resumed, an increased guard was placed over his person, and three European non-commissioned officers from the Sappers and Miners were kept constantly in his presence, for the purpose of proving every thing which was brought to him, lest poison should have been secreted, or lest intrigue should be attempted by the *sipáhis*.

Soon after the officer on guard had answered the summons to the gate, the Nawab, having alighted from his palki, entered the room where our party were assembled. His deportment was natural and easy—I might say it was cheerful—but I was much struck with the change which had taken place in his person. Instead of the hale powerful man I once had known him, he appeared cadaverous and sickly, owing to the effects of confinement, upon one accustomed to incessant exercise and activity. Previously to his imprisonment, I had met him at the table of Colonel Skinner and elsewhere, and he had frequently invited me to pay him a visit at Ferozepore: this, however, I never had an opportunity of doing. He recognised me instantly upon his entrance, and first salaaming to our party generally, he advanced towards me and shook hands in the English fashion. We offered to retire, and leave him in undisturbed possession of the room, but to this he objected, saying that he had been so long without society, that our presence was a relief to him, and he would enjoy it by smoking a *chillaum*, and by joining in our conversation before he went to rest. He then ordered his *charpáhi* to be brought in, and upon this he seated himself cross-legged, with his *hookka*.

"It was not kind," said he, "to disturb my rest to-night; the last sleep which I can enjoy in this world, should, for decency's sake, have been unbroken by such an intrusion. I had eaten a dinner more than usually hearty, and after smoking my *chillaum*, had fallen into a most comfortable slumber, when I was awoke and taken from my rest, to be brought here, under a guard strong enough to have taken the city by storm. I think, at least, they might have left it till the morning."

Soon after this he said to me, "Do you think that Metcalfe Sahib will allow me to wear the costume of my rank to-morrow morning? I cannot bear the idea of being hanged like a dog by the neck, in a common white muslin dress, such as my own slaves wear: they do well enough for dishabille, but for a public execution such as you will witness to-morrow morning, I should certainly prefer something better suited to my rank."

To this I could only reply, that he had better speak to Mr. Metcalfe in the morning, as I could give no opinion. He said he had already made the request, but that it had hitherto been denied him: he would, however, renew his petition in the morning. When he had finished his *chillaum,* he bade us good night, and turning himself round upon his *charpáhi,* he was *mulled** to sleep by two of his servants. We also retired; but although the Nawab, with a certain prospect of death before him, slept soundly, I confess I found it quite impossible to

* To be *mulled,* from the Hindostani word *mullána,* "to rub, to thump;" colloquially applied to the operation termed shampooing. It is a luxury indulged in by nearly all Europeans in India; but hardly to be estimated, except during the langour induced by exertion, or unusual excitement, in a tropical climate. In such case, it is indeed a treat to lie down and be squeezed, and rubbed, and thumped, and pinched, and drummed upon, till every muscle relaxing, and becoming supple and easy, sleep gradually steals over the body.

rest while thinking of the dreadful fate which awaited him.

When gun-fire announced the dawn of day, we arose and found the Nawab also performing his toilet; this he did with more than usual care, and as soon as it was finished, he seated himself upon his *charpáhi,* with his *padri* opposite to him, and commenced the recital of his prayers, which appeared to exist more in form than in petition; for while still muttering the words after the priest, he saluted us cordially, and soon found an opportunity of inquiring if Mr. Metcalfe had arrived, and of putting other questions regarding the movements without. He was habited in a spotless suit of fine white muslin, and when Mr. Metcalfe made his appearance, he again sued to be permitted to wear the costume of his rank, but this it was deemed expedient to refuse; and the question was once again put to him if he confessed himself guilty of the crime for which he was condemned to die: in reply, he still adhered to his affirmation of innocence.

After expressing to Mr. Metcalfe his last wishes, with regard to his family and the disposal of his affairs, he returned to the occupation of his toilet, dressing and combing his beard with great care, and examining himself, again and again, in a small looking-glass, as if he were really sorry to part with that, which in a few short minutes would be corruption.

Twice or thrice, he inquired impatiently if the preparations were not concluded, and at last he begged that a message might be taken to the Brigadier, requesting him to form up the troops with as little delay as possible; but all this was done deliberately, and with perfect self-possession. Eight o'clock was the hour appointed for the execution, and as the city clocks struck, the Brigadier sent word that all was in readiness. The Nawab, without bidding farewell to any about him, but simply giving to his servants and his priest a few articles of dress from his own person, such as the scarf, *kummurbund*, &c., quietly got into his palki, and attended by Mr. Metcalfe and two other civilians, was carried to the scaffold.

From the ramparts I had an uninterrupted view of the scene. At the distance of about three hundred yards, in the open green, the fatal tree was erected; around it the troops were drawn up, forming three sides of a square, the rampart completing the enclosure. On the west, were a regiment of Native Light Cavalry, and one of Native Infantry; on the east were three regiments of Native Infantry, and the north side was occupied by a battery of Foot Artillery, and a squadron of Colonel Skinner's Irregular Horse, constituting altogether a very spacious square.

Very few spectators had assembled, not more than about two thousand in all; this was attributable to various causes. The Nawab had very many friends within the city, who would not be present at his death; others staid away from prudential motives, fearing to be involved in some popular commotion; but the chief cause existed in a misunderstanding among the inhabitants of the city. The magistrate had given orders for the closing of the Cashmere-gate, in order to avert the press and confusion which would ensue, if egress and ingress were permitted so close to the place of execution; and either the gate-keepers mistook their orders, and closed all the gates, or otherwise the inhabitants, finding their exit stopped at one gate, fancied that it must have been so at all the others, and therefore remained within the walls, while they might have been witnesses of the scene.

Among those present were several chiefs, men of high rank and consequence, who had attended the trial throughout, and who considered it due to the British Government, that they should thus exhibit their concurrence in the justice of the finding and sentence. These were bedecked in all the glitter of their most costly equipages and costumes, as though they came to a gala; the most remarkable among them were, the Gwalior chief Maha-rajha Hindu Ráo, the Puttiala, Nabur, Khittul, and Ulwar Rajhas, together with many others of almost equal rank and splendour, unknown to me by name. Altogether, the scene was one which, under other circumstances than the present, would have been highly animating. I should not omit to mention, that a large concourse of people had assembled, and were waiting at the place of imprisonment first occupied by the Nawab, and were still in expectation of his being brought out, long after the poor man had ceased to exist.

When the Nawab arrived at the foot of the gallows, he stepped out of his *palki*, and with an air of dignified indifference, asked Mr. Metcalfe if he should ascend; Mr. Metcalfe bowed, and with a firm step he mounted the ladder, at the top of which he was received by two men, his executioners. With perfect calmness, he at first submitted his neck to have the rope adjusted ; but suddenly, from the low *parria* looks of one of the men, he felt that his person was defiled, and for a moment he became apparently agitated. " What !" said he, " are you a *mehter ?*" with an intonation which it was not difficult to construe into its true meaning.—Am I to be polluted by the touch of this foul wretch at the very moment of death ? a filthy degraded monster, who could not have stood in my presence formerly !—The pang was a short one ; the noose was quickly tied, and the cap, a red one by-the-bye, was drawn over his face ; the next moment the drop fell, and Shumsh-ud-deen was no more. He died without a struggle ; his slippers even did not fall from his feet.

For several moments after the fall of the drop, a perfect silence prevailed ; it was broken by an officer standing next to me. " By Jove !" said he, " the villain takes it as coolly as if he had been accustomed to be hanged every morning of his life." Thus terminated the short existence of this young nobleman, who, until his conviction of the crime, was " the last man in the world, who could have been supposed capable of doing such a thing."

The body being left suspended for the usual time, I mounted my elephant, and entered the crowd. I was accosted by Hindu Ráo, with whom I was acquainted. "Ah! Sahib! I see you everywhere; that is, whenever there is any *tamásha* (fun) going on—he behaved very well; did he not? Will you come to my *nauch* this evening? Punna, whose singing you so much admire, will be there. Besides, I can offer you another inducement; you shall have something more substantial than our usual style of refreshment. I have just got a new cook from Calcutta, and will give you a first rate oyster pâté with your wine. Ha! ha! I know how to tickle the over-refined taste of you English."

Although glad at any time of an opportunity of hearing Punna sing her sweet Persian songs, I readily excused myself from partaking of the hospitality of this uncouth chief, who could hardly be accused of the over-refinement which he imputed to the English, unless extreme looseness and debauchery may be esteemed such. I told him I was engaged to dine with Colonel Skinner. "The very thing," said he; "the Colonel has promised to bring his whole party; so, of course, you will come."

CHAPTER IX.

ANCIENT DEHLI AND SHAHJEHANABAD.

Colonel Skinner (familiarly called Secundur Sahib, by a Hindustani corruption of the name, signifying the Happy, or Fortunate) has long been known by persons connected with India, as one of the bravest and most distinguished soldiers in the East-India Company's army. The Colonel's father was an Englishman in the service of a native prince, and his mother was a *Mussulmani;* his complexion is, however, darker than that of most Mussulmans, although in his youth he is said to have possessed a skin more indicative of his mixed origin. He has for many years commanded a regiment of Irregular Cavalry, known as Skinner's Horse, which is generally considered the best disciplined and finest corps of the kind in the service.

In Lord Lake's time, and at many subsequent opportunities, both the commander and his men have done valuable and distinguished service for their honourable masters; more especially on the banks of the Sutlege and at Bhurtpore; and right handsomely have the Company rewarded him, not only with his commission as Brevet-Colonel and the command of his corps, together with the dignity of C. B., but also in the presentation of a handsome *jaghir* at Belaspore, which yields him a splendid income, and has enabled him to amass a princely treasure. He is fortunately as generous as he is rich, and besides living in magnificent style, indulging in unmeasured hospitality, his purse-strings are ever most cheerfully loosened in favour of public institutions, and for charity. Altogether, the old gentleman is looked upon as one of the oldest, and ablest, and bravest, and most fortunate, and most distinguished, and happiest, and best rewarded officers holding a commission in the name of the Honourable Company. He is a most pleasant companion, full of anecdote and good-humour, with no mean smattering of natural wit; and for his many excellent qualities, he is met by his brother-officers of the regular army, with perfect good-will, notwithstanding his Eastern origin: not that this behaviour on their part is deserving of any particular praise;

but that an opposite course of conduct would be highly disgraceful to them: he is esteemed and admired by all who know him, either personally or by character. At Belaspore, he has erected some small fortifications, on which are mounted about eighteen or twenty pieces of heavy ordnance; and although this is merely a toy of the old man's, it might be turned to very efficient account if need be. Under cover of this épaulement is a handsome house, his country residence, and the factory, with offices, &c.; these, no less than his house at Dehli, display his wealth.

The Colonel has three sons, the elder of whom, James, is adjutant of his corps, and displays a skill and activity in horsemanship and feats of arms, scarcely inferior to that for which his father was in his youth so celebrated, and to which he has still some just pretensions, though growing very stout, as well as old. His second and third sons are occupied in the management of the *jaghir*, and they are also known as sporting characters about Dehli; they were educated at the Dehli college, and are not wanting in general information, and a show of cultivation. The younger, I must not omit to mention, was the cause of the beautiful new church being erected at Dehli. The circumstance was in this wise.

For many years, the want of a church in Dehli had been complained of, and very much had been talked, from time to time, of the expediency of building one; but, unfortunately, churches cannot be built without money; the Christian community were too poor, and the Government would not advance more than a very inadequate sum for the purpose. Thus stood the ecclesiastical affairs of the station, the service being read weekly by the chaplain, in an old deserted bungalow, when Joe Skinner was taken very dangerously ill; and having been given over, without hope, by the medical men, his father, in the anxiety of his parental affection, made a solemn vow to the Almighty, that if his son should by divine interposition be raised up again to life, he would build a handsome church in commemoration of so signal a mercy. Strange it is to our every-day ideas, but it is no less true than strange, that the son was restored from his sick-bed, and although the vow had been made in secret, the father was not unmindful of it, but immediately set about the erection of a very beautiful Protestant church, at an estimate of a *lahk* of rupees: it is still unfinished.

The head-quarters of Skinner's regiment is at

Hansi, a town and fort about ninety-five miles west from Dehli, where are daily practised all those athletic exercises, for which the Irregular Cavalry are so celebrated. The most striking of these are, bearing from the ground a tent-peg, fairly driven, upon the point of the lance; cutting a brass utensil in two, with the sword; striking a bull's-eye with a matchlock ball; picking up from the ground a card or small coin; all of them performed while the charger is at full speed. The whole regiment execute these exploits with wonderful dexterity, but some few are so nicely skilled, as to excite the astonishment of all the beholders; among the first of these is James Skinner, the Colonel's son.

The uniform of the troopers is truly picturesque; they are clad in blue and scarlet, having the Mussulman cut of surcoat, trimmed with silver lace; a steel casque armed with a pike, which is shadowed by a drooping plume of black hackles, or horse-hair; they have also greaves and armlets, and some few are appointed with surcoats of chain mail. Their weapons are, the matchlock, which they handle with wonderful facility, considering its great length and weight, the lance and the broad-sword, in the use of which they are more than a match for any of our European soldiery; and, if the combat depended on skill alone, would generally come off victorious. But there is one little trait in the character of our British troops which will ever uphold their superiority; I mean their proud, invincible, dogged intrepidity, which quails before nothing human, whatever the odds may be.

On the evening after Shumsh-ud-deen's execution, I dined at the Colonel's ample board; we sat down a numerous party, and being fortunate enough to be seated next our host, I had an opportunity of leading him from one anecdote to another, touching his various campaigns in different parts of India. It is with a true spirit of chivalry that he recounts his valiant deeds, and those of his regiment, together with similar stories of his contemporaries, long since passed away: his performances were rendered doubly interesting from the tone of unaffected modesty with which they were told, and the humorous scenes occasionally introduced.

At ten o'clock, we all adjourned to the tents of the Maha-rajha Hindu Ráo, where the *nauch* was to be held; and as Dehli is considered, throughout India, as the place of all others where native dancing is to be seen in perfection, the reader will, perhaps, excuse my giving a little outline of what is there to be seen and heard in these displays of music and finery.

But first, a word or two about our royal host. Maha-rajha Hindu Ráo is the brother of the Ráni Baiza Bháe, and by inheritance the rightful sovereign of the principality of Gwalior; but he was deposed by his ambitious and intriguing sister, under an allegation of imbecility or of incapacity through debauchery, and for malepractices. He now resides at Dehli, and makes the most of his comparatively narrow income. The state allows him one *lakh* annually, or about £1,000 per month; this, and more, as far as his credit will go, is all swallowed up in wantonness and debauchery; a very small portion of it being devoted to the maintenance of his establishment. Of display there is sufficient, but it is tawdry and imperfect, and there is a *débordé* air about all his retainers and the rest of his household, which marks the man's character. In person, he is short and very broad made, quite of the bull-dog cut, as Joe Skinner said, and showing indications of great personal strength: his features too are coarse, and expressive of sensuality and cunning.

The tents, where the *nauch* was given, were very spacious, and laid out purposely for this amusement; though without the grand ornaments and gay paintings generally adopted by the natives in their camp-equipages, the formation and plan of the canvas mansion distinguished it as thoroughly oriental. We found the Maha-rajha seated in state, under a scarlet canopy, with the usual attendants about him; and he certainly formed a picture of eastern luxury, as he lounged with his *hookka* by his side, listening, in a half state of stupor, to the tale of a bard, who was seated on the ground at a little distance before him. On our entrance, he rose and cordially welcomed each of us, first by the English shaking of hands, and then by a hug something after the fashion of that which is in vogue upon the continent, but with a bear-like squeeze which would have crushed a Frenchman's ribs; then, having seated himself in a gilded chair in the centre, he motioned us to take our seats on either side of him.

The tent was most glaringly lighted; *mussaulchis*, or torch-bearers, stood here and there, ready to attend any person who might require them, and other flambeaux, upon a sort of trident, were fixed in the earth around the canvas walls. Before us was spread a snow-white cloth for a carpet, upon which the *nauchnis* were to perform. We had scarcely seated ourselves ere two of them made their appearance, floating into our presence, all tinsel, coloured muslin, and ornaments: they were followed by three musicians, and attended by a couple of *mussaulchis*, who held their torches first to the face and then lower down, as if showing off the charms of the dancers to the best advantage.

Advancing to the front, the girls made a humble obeisance to the Maha-rajah; and then giving a signal to their minstrels, they raised their hands and arms, and at the first scrape of the instruments, broke into the favourite song "*Taza buttaza náo bunnáo*," in a style which was highly applauded by the admiring company. The music approaches nearer to that produced by the hurdi-gurdy than anything else to which I can liken it; the interminable sawing upon one cadence, accompanied by the everlasting *tom-tom*, so expressively named, is wearisome beyond measure to those who have failed in acquiring a taste for it; and then the shrill ear-piercing notes of the women's voices, jarring occasionally in different keys, do most cruelly offend the tutored ear of an European; while the natives are becoming enraptured and excited, far beyond anything that may be witnessed in civilized concert-rooms.

The players more especially, as their interest rises into the highest excitement, vie with each other in producing the loudest notes; and the vehement grimaces, of which they seem perfectly unconscious, while every thought is absorbed in admiration of the *nauchni's* skill, or of their own excellence, is ludicrous beyond description. So vehement, so wild, and energetic are their movements, as to have the appearance of intoxication, and when the dance is concluded, these men are quite as much fatigued as the dancers themselves, who have been borne up, till quite exhausted, by the smiles and cheers of their audience, and, ever and anon, a peep into the little mirror worn as a thumb-ring.

The movements of the dance are extremely graceful; we have nothing in England to which I can compare them. At first, the action is quiet and expressive of soft delight; then, as the dance proceeds, the music rises in tone, and the countenance and gesture grow more animated, suggesting love, then adoration, then alternately, or in accordance with the humour of the song, fear, homage, affection, hatred, and other ardent feelings, until both music and song, ascending in force and sentiment, inspire the dancers with most passionate gesticulation, speaking the language of fervent love and sometimes even of despair, and this I have more than once seen depicted with a truth we could hardly expect from them. So warmly do the dancers enter into the spirit of their own performance, that their excitement produces complete suspension of the faculties, and they are led away by the old matrons in attendance, to be plied with more and more stimulants, so as to prepare them for a second appearance. The wear and tear of this constant labour and excitement, together with all sorts of excess and dissipation, breaks up the constitution and despoils the person of its charms, in a very few months. No *nauchni* is expected to wear longer than three or four years, after which she is cast aside, or exercises her art among the lowest of the low.

Among those who acted for our entertainment on the evening in question, was an exception to this rule, and a second, who also seemed to promise the same. The former was Alfina, the Catalani of the East; in volume and compass of voice superior to all her competitors, and who, by virtue of her charms and accomplishments, had been taken into great favour by Lord Combermere. She is now more than a little *passée,* but still her voice is without a rival; and this, together with her very graceful action, excites universal admiration, notwithstanding her faded charms. She was, on this occasion, very splendidly dressed and adorned with jewels of great price, in place of the tawdry imitations usually worn by the women of her class; the dress and ornaments in which she danced, were said to be worth 40,000 rupees, about £4,000, her own property; her nose-ring was particularly costly, being set with diamonds and emeralds of the most valuable kind; it was also much larger than they are usually worn. My fair countrywomen would, I fear, be sorry to be compelled to add such an appendage to their charms, and yet it is certain that those who are accustomed to the ornament, consider that it enhances the beauty of the wearer, rather than the contrary.

Another strange custom, to which these women have recourse in their toilet, is that of rubbing the interior edges of the eye-lids with a black powder, called *soorma,* a preparation of antimony; this gives a languishing softness and apparently additional length to the eye, it being carried a little beyond the corner of the lids; they likewise stain their nails and the soles of their feet rose-colour, with the juice of the plant called *mihndi*.

The other singer, who particularly attracted my attention on this evening, and frequently at similar entertainments, was Punna, whose Persian songs are very sweet, and in a very different strain from those of the Hindostani, being softer, and possessing a more cultivated melody. The style in which she sings them too is truly bewitching, as all have confessed after listening to her "*Guf-ta-gu;*" upon this occasion, it was encored again and again, and only dispensed with when the poor girl was unable from fatigue to continue it any longer. In person, Punna is attractive, but by no means so handsome as many of her class; her figure is very diminutive, but beautifully formed; her hand and arm, and foot and ankle, are such as a sculptor would love to study; so small, so delicate, so exquisitely rounded, and so perfectly easy are they, in whatever attitudes they may be displayed. Her countenance is very pleasing, but different from the usual Jewish style of most *nauchnis*, and not so regularly handsome; her eyes are the chief attraction in her face, very lustrous, yet soft; and then the smile of the whole countenance, so happy was it, that those who gazed generally confessed that, for a moment, they were beguiled from listening to the sweet tones of her voice.

Punna was an universal favourite with the whole company, and the more so from her modest and unobtrusive deportment, so unlike that of the others. She was very splendidly dressed, and, in the constellation of gems about her person, were tokens of the admiration of her hearers. The most prominent was the nose-ring; it even outshone Alfina's. Ah! laugh as ye list, ye who have only seen swine with rings in their noses! had ye beheld Punna, ye would never again have thought of a pig when a nose-ring was mentioned.

The song is not unfrequently a duet, in which a boy takes a part, but of this the audience are seldom aware, as none but the best experienced are able to detect the cheat under the female attire, unless it be in the greater modesty of his deportment; for while the woman is making rather a liberal exhibition of her charms, by unwinding and winding again the *chuddur* of coloured muslin, which covers the upper part of her person, the boy wisely refrains from any such display. The voices of these lads are invariably sweeter than those of the women, and they seem to have more the tact of modulation, or else a better taste in music, for they seldom offend the ear of the European with the false screaming notes which the women seem to be at some pains to produce.

When Punna withdrew, we had a short interval of comparative quiet, while a handsome supper was served; it was something more in the European style than is generally prepared by natives; but there was no lack of luxuries peculiar to the East, for those who preferred them to hermetically sealed fish, and carrots, or parsnips, brought from England in the same way, and placed upon the table as choice fruit. Hindu Ráo paid little attention to the substantials, nor did he in any way appear inclined to indulge in the champaign, burgundy, claret, and other costly wines, liberally supplied for his visitors; his whole affection seemed absorbed in the cherry-brandy, a beverage highly esteemed by those natives whose religious prejudices have little rule over their appetites, and before our refection was concluded, three or four pints of this had disappeared under his sole care.

When the *nauch* was resumed, finding that the Maha-rajha, having taken his *hookka*, was dosing into a most celestial stupor, I threw myself upon one of the couches and composed myself to sleep, amid the screaming, scraping, and drumming, which appeared so deeply interesting to the rest of the audience. I slept long and soundly, and should probably have continued to do so much longer, had I not been awoke by my servant, who came to inform me that the company were dispersing.

A most uncomfortable scene was presented to my waking senses. The rays of the morning sun were striking through the openings in the awning, forming a most sickly mixture with the declining glare of the few torches still burning. The last set of *nauchnis* were just making their *saláam*, and their jaded looks and soiled apparel formed a miserable contrast to the brilliant illusions of the previous night. Groups of yawning ghost-like officers were standing, stretching themselves, and discussing the means of conveyance back to cantonments, or the possibility of another similar entertainment elsewhere. The spotless white carpet of the previous night was strewed with the remnants of the feast, soiled with crushed fruit, and stained with wine; empty bottles, broken glasses, and destroyed ornaments were scattered about in all directions, and upon a *charpáhi*, brought in for his accommodation, lay the Maha-rajha himself, stretched in a heavy sleep, which the united clamour of all his retainers, to say nothing of sundry blows and thumps bestowed upon his royal person, failed to dispel. On the ground beside him was his *hookka* of state, capsized, and an expiring lamp disclosed a whole regiment of empty cherry-brandy bottles lying near; and, to close the picture, in one corner, with his face upon the bare soil, his arm thrown over his head, lay the Meer Sahib, the Maha-rajha's spiritual adviser, the priest of his household, who, lest his lord should take more than a becoming share, had been assisting him in the consumption of the intoxicating beverage, "albeit his lips were scarce wiped, since he had drank last."

Having seen most of the lions within the new city, I persuaded the Sackvilles to accompany me upon a little excursion, to visit those which are to be found among the ruins of ancient Indraput (Dehli), which was formerly the seat of empire under the Patan, Afghan, and Mogul dynasties; and an authentic history of which is preserved from the time of its subjection by Kootab-ud-deen, the first of the Patan monarchs who exalted his *musnud* here, in 1193 A.D.

This superb city, when in the height of its glory,

extended over twenty square miles of country, the ruins of which present a scene of decayed grandeur and magnificence which it is not possible to describe properly. As far as the eye can reach, it wanders over a sea of ruined palaces, gardens, pavilions, gateways, mosques, towers, courts, and sepulchres, in all stages of decay, the crumbling vestiges of human power and wealth, long since obliterated, which brought forcibly to my mind that line of Byron's, in Childe Harold, I believe,—

"Stop! for thy tread is on an empire's dust."

The heart of the gazer swells and sinks alternately with pride and dread, as these fallen images of the fullest extent of human might declare the emptiness of man's proudest works. But little more than two hundred years since, this gigantic city was in the height of its noblest beauty and majesty, and now it is a heap of ruins. It was destroyed by the Maharhattas, after the death of the Emperor Akbur, and at the accession of his son Jehanghir, which occurred in the year 1605.

I proposed that we should first visit the tomb of Zufdir Junge, which is about four miles from Shahjehanabad; but before I bound myself to keep in company with my friends, I extorted a promise that the *baba-lōg*, with all their annoyances and encumbrances, should be left at the palace. This point was very unwillingly yielded, because the sweet little things might never have another opportunity of examining the ruins and curiosities, and really some of them were very pretty, only so black and overgrown with weeds, that perhaps they would be frightened at them.

This point gained, it was with something approaching to a hope of comfort, that we set forth upon our trip; but, alas! a new source of dispute and disagreement arose, for Mrs. Sackville came forth in the new character of a virtuoso; carrying with her, in all our peregrinations, a large trunk full of sketch-books, note-books, rough sketch-books, rough note-books, fair sketch-books, fair note-books, and divers varieties of the same, together with a library, by no means portable, of chronology, history, biography, mythology, mineralogy, entomology, botany, &c. &c. &c., upon all of which both she and her good husband were most profoundly ignorant, and therefore most unbending in dispute.

The tomb of Zufdir Junge is a very chaste and symmetrical edifice, though perfectly simple in its style of architecture, and unadorned with the profuse carving and deeply wrought mouldings common in this part of India. The building is formed of solid blocks of red granite, squared and mortised with great nicety; its plan, like that of most cemeteries of those days, is octagonal, inclosing a high vaulted apartment in the centre, and smaller ones of the same figure at each of the angles. The interior is finished with a coating of the finest pearl *chuna*, a preparation of calcined shells, resembling marble so closely, as to be scarcely distinguishable to a superficial observer. In the centre of the principal apartment, is a small oblong block of fine white marble, cut in the most perfect style of art, and inlaid with gems of great value, with a beauty and exquisite delicacy truly surprising to those who have been unaccustomed to such sights. The building is faced with mouldings of white marble around the principal arches, and the domes are also of the same material. Altogether the structure is decidedly handsome, but there is a defect upon the side on which the architects of the East seldom err: the minarets at the angles of the principal figure are of insufficient height for their diameter, having the appearance of a work discontinued, or rather finished off by the addition of the cupolas, when they were only half-built; this destroys much of that elegance for which the Moslem buildings are remarkable.

In the gardens surrounding this tomb are beautiful reservoirs of water, supplied from wells of very great depth, and within these are fountains, which give an exquisite freshness to the air; they are seldom set playing, however, on account of the labour in drawing water, and it was not without very considerable difficulty, and the application of sundry rewards to the *durroga*, and others, about the place, togetherwith double hire for the bullocks employed in the draught, that I at last succeeded in obtaining this luxury. We took up our quarters in one of the pavilions in the garden, and so commodious, so pleasant a residence did we find it, that Mrs. Sackville at once gave orders for her head-quarters to be established here, and withdrew all her train from the palace at Dehli, declaring that the swarms of flies and my native friends rendered it quite intolerable.

The day following our arrival at Zufdir Junge's tomb, we devoted to the inspection of the Kootab Minar, the celebrated relic of Patan architecture which attracts all visitors, whether learned or simply curious. Mrs. Sackville undertook the former of these characters, but I hope the reader will pardon my ranking myself among the latter, as I am hardly prepared to support the former, by any very profound knowledge of the subject under discussion, neither have I Mrs. Sackville's tables at hand.

About eight miles from Modern Dehli stands the Kootab Minar, (I speak with all submission to the more learned,) the most ancient and perfect specimen of a Patan structure in India. It is a gigantic pillar, built of red granite, upon the plan of a polygon of twenty-seven sides; the extreme diameter at the base is fifty-four feet, and the column rises to the height of two hundred and twenty-six feet, exaggerated by travellers to as much as two hundred and eighty feet. It was built by Kootab-ud-deen, at the beginning of the thirteenth century, and tradition affirms it to have been one of the minarets attached to a gigantic mosque, the body of which has been destroyed; and the natives in the vicinity point out the foundation of a second tower, not far distant, in support of this hypothesis.

With the assistance of my learned friend, Mrs. Sackville, I carefully examined this ruin: but from the relative position of the two, the figures of their plans being of unequal numbers of sides, and the faces of these being irregularly disposed, in fronts having a different aspect, we settled the matter, in a note appended to the lady's sketch, that there were no grounds for the above surmise; that the pillar was originally isolated as it is to this day, unconnected with the other ruins about it; and this decision was based upon the remark, that the inscriptions which surround the pillar are perfect on all sides, and apparently of the same date and workmanship, so that no wall or other masonry can have been detached from it. These characters are of gigantic size, and are not to be deciphered or classed by any of the *pundits* and learned men of the day: even Mrs. Sackville confessed herself at a loss. The column consists of five stories, each having a balcony jutting from the floor, entered by a small arch. A winding staircase, of three hundred and eighty-four steps, leads to the top, but this being quite dark, except at the doorways and small loop-holes, I was unable to persuade either of my friends to ascend.

"You know I don't mind going into a bear's den, or shaking hands with a leopard," said the gentleman, in his natural strain of modesty, "but I never go aloft; I should feel an inclination to throw myself off at once, and had therefore rather remain where I am: besides, if you will observe, the pillar is anything but perpendicular."

Sackville was right; the Kootab Sahib (as it is usually denominated by the natives) shows signs of decay, notwithstanding its great solidity and the strength of its materials. It is very much out of the perpendicular, having two or more bends in its height, and near the base many of the stones have become loose and crumbling; even the hardest granite gives way before such extremes of heat and cold as are here experienced at different seasons, and the strongest of human works must be made to totter by rolling earthquakes, and hurricanes from the very muzzle of Eolus' bellows.

Not long since, it was repaired by Captain Smith, of the Engineers, by order of our Government; and the work which he executed appears to have been a bold undertaking, indeed; for a very large portion of the masonry at the base of the pillar must have been removed, before the new could be substituted. All these scientific works, however, are undertaken upon such nice and certain calculations, that I suppose the architect himself had little apprehension of bringing it down, although the native masons, generally a most hardy and adventurous set, were with the greatest possible difficulty brought to put their hands to the labour. The repairs are finished in a style which, like all his other works, do the engineer the greatest credit.

The spiral staircase, leading to the top of this pillar, is certainly far from being pleasing to ascend, being almost pitch-dark; and the stairs, which are of unequal breadth, are rendered the more difficult, by heaps of dirt and filth, from the many myriads of bats and vampyres which have their homes in this eternal darkness, and who resent the intrusion of a stranger, by cuffing him about the head and face with their offensive wings; the squeaking, and flitting, and flapping of these innumerable beasts is anything but agreeable; and the higher the adventurer ascends, the more intolerable does the nuisance become, the air being very foul and tainted, in consequence of the accumulated filth. All these annoyances are amply compensated by the magnificent view which greets the traveller when he arrives at the top. The Kootab is pretty near the centre of the old city, and all around, as far as the eye can go, is ruin, destruction, and desolation, with here and there a relic, less decayed than its fallen rivals, standing out in melancholy solitude.

I stood upon the top, resting against one of the pillars of the cupola, cogitating upon all these striking wonders, and wishing that Mrs. Sackville was not quite so nervous, when I was surprised to find a man at my elbow. He was a native, a Mussulman, and hoping that the old man was some *cicerone,* who would be able to explain the names and histories of all before me, I entered into conversation with him. The old man—he was very aged—could not help me to what I wanted; but considering himself the greatest curiosity, and among the best of the antiques, he voluntarily supplied me with a little of his own history. He told me he was a tailor by trade, and being a stranger to this metropolis of the Western Provinces, he had come up the pillar to look around him, and see all the fine sights at once, in order that, when he should return to his home—if it pleased God that he should live long enough—he might be able to tell his sons and daughters, and his many grand-children, of the great things which he had beheld.

The old man was very asthmatical, and it cost him long to tell his simple tale; so that, ere he had come to the termination of it, I was again entranced in contemplation of the scene. Still the old stranger's countenance haunted me; I was certain that I had seen it somewhere; it was in a degree familiar, but associated with ideas of difficulty, confusion, and mystery; and while my mind was only half-employed, I could not at all recall the circumstances under which I had before met him. The village he named as his home was unknown to me; he had only lately arrived in Dehli, and therefore it was hardly possible that we could have met; still, without thinking much about the matter, I could not help being sensible of rather uncomfortable impressions recalled to my mind. I turned with the intention of ascertaining the circumstance by further scrutiny, or by direct inquiry; but, ah!——a piercing scream at that instant attracted my eye to the spot where he had stood; he was gone: a little cloud of smoke from his *kullian* still lingering on the air, was all that remained of him. A fearful crash below told his cruel fate; he had probably been seized with the *ghoomti,* as the natives call giddiness, and the fence which guards the edge being no higher than the knee, he fell over. Poor old fellow! what were his family to him now?

I ran hastily down the dark staircase, and had like to have broken my own neck in my descent. I found the body literally dashed to atoms, scarcely a bone was left entire, and pieces of the skull had, by the force of the concussion, been thrown to a considerable distance from the body; one fragment which I picked up was perfectly clean, and with only a few small specks of blood upon it.

The sight of the mangled body brought forcibly to my recollection the sad fate of Major Blundel, whose corpse I had looked upon under somewhat similar circumstances, just twelve months before, at Mussoori; and, notwithstanding the latter had been personally known to me, and was in the same walk of life, yet I could not help feeling, even more acutely, the untimely fate of this poor man than I had done that of the Major: possibly from the circumstance of the feeling he displayed, when talking to me of his family, a few seconds before, and the probability that thoughts of home occupied his mind at the very moment of his fall. Nothing of his face remained by which to identify him; but I had now no difficulty in recognising him: it suddenly became evident to me, that this was the same old man who had acted as my guide to the Begum Sumroo's palace, on the night of our arrival in Dehli.

Having remained a couple of days at the Kootab, turning over the ruins, and exploring all sorts of dirty places, we directed our camp, about eleven

RUINS [illegible]

miles further to the south, to Toglukabad, the name of which has been strangely perverted by the English into Thuglikabad. It takes its name from its founder, the Emperor Togluk Shah, one of the Afghan princes, of whose short reign history makes very little mention. He ascended the *musnud* in 1321, and died by assassination in 1324, during which time he erected many strange and incomprehensible buildings, in a style of architecture distinct from the fashion of those times; being even still more weighty and cumbrous in his designs than were his contemporaries. The ancient town of Toglukabad is now a heap of ruins, which by their vast solidity, and the enormous blocks of which they are composed, excite our surprise that they could ever have been overthrown. Time could not have done the mischief; an earthquake seems to be the only power which could have effected it; and the circumstance of all the remains, with their gravings and cuttings, being still in good preservation, seems to sanction this opinion.

The whole town is composed of enormous masses of red granite, (which is the chief material of the ruins all around Dehli); the relics of palaces, baths, &c., many of which are still sufficiently entire to excite our wonder, induce us involuntarily to put the question; "Were there giants in those days?" Some of the subterranean apartments are of great extent, and are exceedingly curious in their structure, the roofs being formed of immense slabs of granite, so put together as to support each other by their inward pressure, in a manner rather uninviting to a nervous person: from their plan, it appears impossible that these chambers should have been excavated; they appear rather to have been built, and subsequently buried; otherwise, we cannot by any means conceive how some of the masonry could have been disposed in its present position.

These ruins have been too little explored by scientific travellers; throughout all the remains of this once mighty empire, I met with nothing which so deeply excited my interest; not even the ruins of Futtehpore Sikri, which I subsequently visited: nothing else which I have seen is half so gigantic, with the exception of Kanarak, and that is one single building, whereas Togluka-bad presents a small city of such wonders.

The principal of these is the mausoleum which the founder built for his own imperial person; this is detached from the town, and appears to have been defended by a fortification of its own: the remains of an old covered way, by which it was approached from the palace, are still to be traced. But I regret I cannot offer the reader my sketch of this tomb; Mrs. Sackville, being dissatisfied with her own, maliciously destroyed mine, when it was too late to repair the evil: a bit of the old *serai* is all I have preserved of this place, and I am sorry to say, it gives no adequate conception of the magnitude of the buildings.

We next visited the tomb of Hummaione, an Emperor who came to the *musnud* in 1540; he was the eldest son of Babur, and the father of Akbur the Great, and, after the example of his forefathers, made it his especial care to prepare a handsome resting-place for his body after death. He is said to have laid the foundation stone with his own hands, in the year 1550; the work, however, remained for his son Akbur to complete, for the Emperor died in the year 1556, when the tomb was scarcely half-finished; the old man having stopped the work, for the purpose of erecting a similar building on a smaller scale for his barber: this remains perfect to the present day, and is pointed out, with great conceit, by all the tonsors of Dehli, as a proof of the high estimation in which they were once held by princes.

That which records the mortality of Hummaione is much upon the same plan as that of Zufdir Junge, but by no means so elegant, or in such good repair. Parts of it are ornamented with brilliant mosaic work of all colours, made of an enamel which bids defiance to time and the seasons, being still perfect both in colour and polish. In the centre of the cemetery is the usual block of white marble, sculptured with the name and attributes of the great man; and in different smaller crypts are similar stones, in commemoration of the Emperor's favourite wives and daughters, and other members of the royal household. The basement plan, which forms an arcaded terrace to the upper part of the structure, is built in a succession of small vaults, in each of which is the tomb of one or more persons.

About a quarter of a mile from this building is a small tomb of very exquisite workmanship, in memory of Nizam-ud-deen Olea, one of the Afghan princes who flourished at the beginning of the fifteenth century. This beautiful specimen of the arts of those days is built entirely of white marble, of the most spotless quality, carved into screen-work of the most delicate design, and in every way most highly finished. The lattice-work around the sainted shrine is so very slight, and so finely wrought, as to make the admirer tremble lest the next puff of wind should shiver it to atoms; yet it has remained here since the year 1415, and is now without a single chip or scar of any kind.

The verandah around the principal shrine is, perhaps, the most beautiful part of the work, if it be possible to make any selection where all is so very perfect; the pillars are most highly carved, not only in flutings, and the ordinary decorations of the bases and capitals, but also with flowers, and the most delicate representations of butterflies, birds, &c. The covering to this verandah is formed of large slabs of the same spotless material, and the interior is enamelled and gilded in the same manner as I have described the *Dewani Khas*, in Akbur Shah's palace; the dome is also similar.

There are several other tombs around this, of design and workmanship scarcely inferior to it. The doors of one of these particularly attracted my notice; they are formed of two immense slabs of white marble, swung under an arch of the same, and the whole so very richly sculptured, that the flowers, insects, and other devices, appear to have been separately cut and to have been afterwards fastened upon their ground.

The whole of what I have here described is on a miniature scale, very seldom employed by the natives in the commemoration of great men or of great deeds: in all other instances which I can call to mind, they appear to have measured the size of their buildings by the grandeur and importance of those in whose names the structures were raised. The relics in question are the more valuable on this account, and also for their perfect preservation. There is, moreover, something so chaste, so simple, and yet so elaborate, about the place, that the very contradiction enhances the admiration when seen; such a sacred care seems to have been bestowed upon it, that it is difficult to fancy that it has been entrusted to any other keeping than to the light hands of fairies or angels: time has placed no mark upon it; it is as fresh and perfect as if it had only just been finished by the artist. Mrs. Sackville declared it to be a little darling, worth fifty of the Kootab.

At the entrance to these tombs is an old *serai*, within a small court of which is a *bowli*, or tank of water, upwards of fifty feet deep; the water is enclosed on all sides by high buildings, in which a set of men reside, who, for a trifling reward, will leap from the highest walls into the gulf below them. The leap is truly terrific; the greatest height from which they spring is fifty-five feet. The spectator is stationed in a gallery, about twenty feet above the water, exactly opposite to the buildings from which the leap is taken; and on looking up, he beholds a naked human being, (I am about to state a fact which I have beheld, otherwise, according to Garlic's system of credit, I should have confessed myself a little sceptical,) crawling up the rounded surface of a circular dome on all fours, with as much apparent ease as a fly would do the same. Having reached the summit, which is crowned with a coronet, he draws himself up upon it, and then stands for a few seconds balancing himself on one foot, with his arms aloft; then taking a run down the face of the dome, he springs with a frightful bound into mid-air; down he comes, nearer and nearer, throwing his limbs about in the most energetic manner; down he comes, close to the lookers-on; then down he goes, lower, lower, using the same terrific gestures, as if in agony, until within a few feet of the water, when the limbs are suddenly straightened, and, feet foremost, he disappears beneath the surface, like an arrow.

So very frightful is this leap, that my breath

was suspended at sight of the man's awful situation; and Mrs. Sackville's eye being by chance directed another way at the moment that the leap was made, so nervously did I endeavour to draw her attention to the sight, that the impression of my fingers remained upon her delicate arm for many days afterwards.

When the man had been a few seconds below the surface, he again came above, and swam ashore as coolly as if the heavens and the depths were his own proper elements. There are very many of these jumpers and divers, all of whom are said to make a handsome living out of the bounty of visitors; and this is not unlikely, for, if we pay willingly for anything, surely it is for a sight of the frightful and the marvellous, rather than for the beautiful. It appeared to be a thriving trade, if we may judge by the hale, muscular fellows engaged in it, and by the numbers of young candidates in training, for there were thirty or forty young boys, and youths of all ages, practising the art, and hanging about the wakes of the men, in the hope of picking up some of the largesses showered down upon them; sometimes as many as a dozen of these little imps might be seen flying through the air all at once, from a height of, perhaps, twenty or more feet, according to their age and proficiency. They display astonishing quickness in scrambling for the money; if a pice be thrown into the air, it will, in all probability, be secured before it reaches the water; or if it should by chance escape their hands, they pounce into the water after it, like so many water-fowls, and one or other of them is sure to catch it before it reaches the bottom.

Poor Mrs. Sackville afterwards declared, that she never spent her money to less advantage, for her rest was broken by the images of these jumpers and divers, taking all the most frightful forms of demons and goblins: "No sooner do I fall asleep, after tumbling and tossing till near daylight, than down comes one of those little black imps upon me, and puts me all in a tremble."

"Tremble!" said Sackville; "you may call it a tremble, but I call it kicking. Why I'm black and blue from the hip downward, and never have I had an hour's quiet sleep since we visited that detestable *bowli*. Look! here's a nose! while she was dreaming the other night, she struck me with the back of her hand; and because I returned the blow in my sleep, she calls me a cruel, unmanly monster!"

The ruins we have just visited are only four or five miles from the modern city, and as Mrs. Sackville was already tired of the head-quarters which she had fixed at Zufdir Junge's mausoleum, we again turned our steps towards the Begum's palace.

About a mile distant from Hummaione's tomb is a dilapidated old ruin, the observatory of Jey Singh, the celebrated astronomer of the East, who flourished in the reign of Mohummed Shah; this man was a great favourite at the imperial court, and the Emperor just named, delighted with his skill, erected the enormous observatory, which is now visited by all travellers to Dehli, as one of the greatest wonders of the place. A few of the more massive instruments remain to this day, being constructed on a scale resembling Stonehenge, to which they are also something similar in appearance: they are evidently intended as triangles for taking altitudes and distances, and have been made use of for that purpose by some of our modern moon-starers. The place is said to have been formerly supplied with magnificent instruments of pure gold; but these, if they ever existed, were plundered by the Maharhattas, in their many incursions upon their more civilized neighbours.

On our road back to Dehli, we visited the *poorana killa*, or old fort, which was built by Feroze Shah, also one of the Afghan dynasty. The foundation of this fort was laid in 1290, and some of the remains are scarcely less gigantic than those of Toglukabad; the gateways, though nearly all destroyed, have here and there an arch or two left, which are of size and elegance likely to attract the attention of all visitors. There is also an old amphitheatre on the south side of it, unlike anything else which bears the same date: a portion of it only remains, and it is difficult to say for what purpose it was intended, there being only an open sort of verandah, surmounting a broad arcade, which is perfectly dark within; the whole is built of red granite, the surface of which shews plainly that even this solid material is subject to decay.

In the court opposite to this building is an extraordinary pillar, apparently metallic, but which the learned ones have declared to be "a kind of red sandstone, nearly approaching to freestone (and not granite), bearing a silvery bed in it."* It is called Feroze Shah's *laht* (walking-stick), is about thirty feet in height, above the surface of

* Vide *Journal of Asiatic Society of Bengal*, No. 27, March 1834, p. 105.

the ground, and buried very many feet in the earth. There is one exactly similar to this at the Kootab Minar, and another at Allahabad: they are all supposed to be of the same origin, but their history remains obscure; for, although the characters with which they are inscribed, have, after many years' labour and research, been deciphered, still no mention is made in the original writing of any date, nor have we any clue to the era in which those whose names are recorded may have flourished; these are Samudragupta and Yasovarman, of whom we know nothing, and whose very names had never been heard of by us, until the deciphering of these mysterious writings. The inscriptions are in various characters, and of as many different ages, bearing the marks of innovation and re-inscription at the hands of successive generations.*

* For the information of the curious, I subjoin an extract from the Journal of the Asiatic Society of Bengal, concerning the inscription upon the *laht* at Allahabad, which was published antecedent to the discovery of the character, noted as No. I; and again another short quotation from the same work, subsequent to the perusal of the inscription, by the Rev. W. H. Mill, D.D.:—

"However ancient the inscription No. 2, may be, it is very certain that the character No. I boasts a still higher antiquity. This may, I think, be proved. First, by the position it occupies on the Allahabad column, as well as on that of Dehli, called Feroze's Laht; in both, it is the principal, and, as it were, the original inscription, the others being subsequently added, perhaps, on some occasions of triumph, or visit to the spot. Secondly, the simplicity of this character, and the limited number of radicals, denote its

When the Jhauts invaded this part of the western provinces, they took possession of Dehli; and, after dismantling and spoiling all the sacred edifices on which they could lay their rapacious fingers, they made strenuous efforts to overthrow these pillars; but all their exertions proved abortive; they could neither destroy them, nor deface the characters; Artillery was directed against them, and the scars

priority to the more complicated and refined system subsequently adopted; while, thirdly, the very great rarity of its occurrence on ancient monuments, and the perfect ignorance which prevails regarding its origin in the earliest Persian historians, who mention the *laht* of Feroze Shah, confirm its belonging to an epoch beyond the reach of native research. The only other inscriptions identical in character, which have been met with in India are, I believe, the *laht* of Bim Sen in Sarun, and that of the Khandghiri Rocks in Orissa, of which a fac-simile is given by Mr. Stirling, in the Researches, vol. xv. p. 314. The Ellora and other cave inscriptions appear to be considerably modified from it, and in fact more to resemble No. 2 of the Allahabad column; and the latter inscription has so many points of resemblance, that it may be fairly traced to a derivation from the former. It is not yet ascertained whether the character No. 1 denotes, is Sanscrit."—*Jour. As. Soc.* No. 27, March 1834 p. 116.

"Until further lists be obtained, therefore, the apparent absence of all dates, on this part of the column, must preclude anything like exact determination of the time that elapsed between its hero, Samudragupta and Yasovarman. As far as it is possible to form an opinion on internal evidence, concerning the age of so short an inscription as this, from the enumeration of deities, or the traces of manners that may be discovered in it, I should be inclined to think that it was written after the hero-worship (which the sacred epics first introduced) had begun to take place of the simple elementary adoration, visible in the ancient hymns of the *Vedas;* yet before it had altogether its present shape, and apparently before the worship of the *linga*, and that of the *sactis*, the most impure parts of an impure system, had attained the footing which they had in India, at the time of the first Mohummedan invasions."—*Jour As. Soc.* No. 30, June 1834, p. 268.

of two or three balls are still visible upon that at the Kootab. This was of no avail, and they then commenced excavating; but the depth of the pillar prevented them from executing their purpose, and, in their haste, they fortunately abandoned the attempt. After all, method alone was wanting; had the powder expended in their guns been applied in the form of a mine, they would have gained their barbarous object, and these curiosities would probably have been buried in oblivion, until brought again to light by the chance-stroke of the spade or plough.

We entered Dehli by the Ajhmere-gate, and on our road inspected the old *madrissa*, or college, and the *serais* in the neighbourhood, some of which are very picturesque. All are much in the same style, and the little sketch annexed, though the subject was not selected from the most important, will give a pretty correct idea of the form and disposition of these old buildings.

On our arrival at the palace, we found our hospitable friend, Meer Saiud Alli; he had heard from our servants of our intended return, and had hastened to make his *saláam*, and offer his services. He brought us a singular anecdote, which we afterwards found to be no exaggeration. The

SERAI, near the AJHMERE GATE, DEHLI.

story is very absurd, though truly pitiable, and it is not easy to relate it without appearing almost unfeeling, so difficult is it to separate the comic from the tragic: it is impossible to refrain from smiling at the very moment that the heart is filled with commiseration for the victim involved.

The murder of Mr. Fraser, and the execution of his assassins, had created so great a sensation around Dehli, that for the usual life-time of such rumours, nothing else was talked of by high or low. A pretty correct report of the circumstances reached a small village, a few miles distant from Dehli; and there, among the rest, the tragic tale excited the deep interest of a school of young boys, all under twelve years of age, and these little urchins determined to act a *tableau vivant*, representing the whole affair from beginning to end. Parts were drawn and assigned, with as much importance as debutants usually attach to the character allotted for their first appearance. Having gone through the form of shooting Mr. Fraser, with bow and arrow, they proceeded to the trial of the youths personating the conspirators, Unnia and Kurreim Kahn, and having found them guilty, they were dealt with after the award of the court. Fortunately, while they were conveying Kurreim Kahn to the scaffold, his mamma or his papa wanted him, and he was reprieved. He who represented the Nawab, however, was not so fortunate; he was tried, found guilty, and condemned, and as no mamma or papa wanted him, he was not reprieved; but was led forth to execution upon a buffalo. The little fellow, as he rode to the scene of his last dying speech, mimicked the cold indifferent bearing of his illustrious prototype; and having arrived beneath a large *bannian* tree, his executioner tied his hands behind him, and drew a cap over his face; they then adjusted a rope around his neck, and tied the other end of it to the branch of the tree, and then the buffalo was driven away, leaving the poor child suspended by the neck. The drop had not been sufficient to dislocate the boy's neck; but he was fast strangling, and in the agony of terror and pain, he screamed and struggled most pitiably, amid his cries and convulsive gasps, entreating a release from death. But, alas! he was misunderstood.

"*Wa! Wa!*" screamed his little executioners; "*wah khoob tamásha kurta hi. Phir khello Mungloo; bahoot uchhi-turri nuhkul kurte ho tūm.* (Excellent! excellent! He makes capital sport. Do it again, Mungloo; you perform your part admirably.) Alas! poor little fellow, he could do it no more; his limbs refused to struggle any longer; his cry died into the death-rattle; one last convulsive heave shook his whole frame, and the spirit fled, much to the horror and consternation of his companions, who now ran to the village for assistance. Two or three of these children were brought before the magistrate for examination, and the above account is taken from their united depositions.

Towards the end of the month, Mrs. Sackville grew weary of Dehli, and declared that no civilized being could exist longer among the flies, dirt, sweetmeats, and odours, for all of which Dehli is notorious, and has been, probably, since the days of Kootab-ud-deen. In obedience to her commands, we put our marching equipage in order for our return, for she was anxious to visit other scenes; indeed, I fear the reader, too, may have thought me too long in one place, and have been looking out for a move; and much do I regret, in this case, being obliged to disappoint him; for I have only to escort my friends back to Merat, and then I revisit Dehli again, in my route to the Presidency, being homeward-bound for Old England. One word more before I march out of the city.

It was here that, in 1804, Holkar, having besieged the city with his whole army, General Sir David Ochterlony held out the walls for many days, until the arrival of succour; and this he did with a very weak and insufficient garrison, having only a small detachment of Infantry, and a few Sappers and Miners, to man the extensive defences of this large city. This brilliant achievement secured to the British a stronghold from which we should have found it difficult to dislodge so powerful a body, and which has so fine a command of all the Western Provinces; and when we consider all the circumstances of the case, this defence appears to be one of the most splendid military exploits on record in modern history; and yet how little do we hear of it!

CHAPTER X.

VOYAGE DOWN THE JUMNA.

About a month after my return from Dehli, with the Sackvilles, I took leave of all my friends at Merat, which place (one good word at parting), in spite of all that Sackville can say, or write against it, and although a mere shadow of what it once was, is still the most delightful station upon the Bengal side of India; and although with dear England in my eye, it was not without many regrets that I turned my back upon a place which had been so long a home to me, and wherein I had experienced so much of good and evil.

Having travelled up the Ganges, in my route to Merat, I chose the Jumna upon my return to the Presidency; not simply for the sake of novelty, but for the reputed beauty of its banks, and in order that I might visit the celebrated cities, with which its course is dotted, from Dehli down to its confluence with the Ganges. This arrangement would, I was well aware, at that season of the year, curtail my comforts on the way; for, there being scarcely sufficient water in the river for the purposes of navigation, I was compelled to stow myself, and baggage, and servants into the smallest possible space, in order that we might be kept afloat; as it was, in a mere nut-shell, I was not unfrequently two and three days upon a sand-bank. But I am anticipating, and the reader has yet to return with me to Dehli, where my boats are in preparation.

Here I will make no long tarry; but I cannot pass without remark, a display of native splendour, which I witnessed during this my last visit to the place, far more magnificent than anything which I had previously beheld, and which I conceived to exist in the history of former days only, after what I had seen of the train and tawdry pomp of the Mogul Emperor himself.

Expecting to be only a few days in Dehli, I took up my quarters with a friend at the Residency, and thus it was that I had an opportunity of seeing, to the greatest advantage, what Indian magnificence really is, when the means are equal to the love of display.

Three native princes, the most wealthy in the

land, met in the neighbourhood of Dehli, for the purpose of fulfilling a contract of marriage between certain members of their families: these were the Puttiála Rajha, the Nabur Rajha, and the Kishenghur Rajha; and, great as were their riches and their pride, like dutiful dependants, they came to pay their tribute of honour and submission to their protectors, after the celebration of the nuptials.

Mr. Metcalfe, the representative of the British power at Dehli, being absent, his assistant received the princes at the Residency. Never before had I witnessed anything at all to be compared to the costliness and brilliancy of their equipages, and the appointments of their *jullouse* (retinue). The procession entered by the Cashmere-gate; in front came about fifty armed *sawars*, on noble prancing chargers, the choicest of the stud, most splendidly caparisoned; the riders were clad in entire suits of the richest crimson velvet, thickly embroidered with gold; the trappings of the horses were of the same materials, set off with scales of polished steel, and gilded chains. These, with the equerries on foot, the slaves of these noble steeds, cleared the way for the Rajhas; who, preceded by their own chargers with empty saddles, advanced on elephants, each so gloriously arrayed, that it was impossible to say which most attracted wonder and admiration.

The dresses of the Rajhas themselves were of the choicest Cashmere shawls, and their turbans were also very costly, but there was not that prodigality of decoration, which the rest of the train would have betokened; they wore few jewels about their persons, but those few were said to be worth a prince's ransom. The *háodas* in which they were seated were covered with the purest embossed gold, profusely set with gems of every kind. The *jhules* of the elephants, hanging down to the ground on either side, were of the richest velvet, embroidered with gold, in beautiful border-patterns and medallions, in which the colours of flowers were depicted by precious stones of various hues; round this beautiful cloth ran a heavy fringe of gold bullion, and tassels of the same, dragging in the dust. Upon their heads the proud elephants wore an ornament wrought in the same manner, but in this the gems were more lavishly set; the tusks of the animals were bound with rings and amulets of pure gold. The *mahawut* was as extravagantly arrayed, carrying in his hand a *hankus*, or goad, also of gold; and in the *káhause* was another man supporting a very splendid *chatta*, which, as the emblem of royalty, was made to exceed in glory all that has yet been described. In rear of the Rajhas came about a hundred and fifty more mounted soldiers, some clad in the colours already mentioned, others in sky-blue velvet, trimmed with silver, all alike in gorgeous finery and flashing steel.

I was present at the *durbar*, which was held in the audience-room of the Residency, and was greatly entertained by the conversation which we enjoyed with our princely visitors. Carefully steering clear of all political subjects, they scarcely trusted themselves to speak of the execution of the Nawab Shumsh-ud-deen, except in the most casual manner, nor did they venture upon any remarks about the Jeypore affairs. The topics of conversation were selected with great caution, and in the instance of his mightiness with whom I had the honour of conversing, I found it quite impossible to get beyond Runjeet Singh, the Begum Sumroo, the Baiza Bháe, tiger-shooting, agriculture, and the two grand resources of colloquy in the East, money, and the gratification of the appetites.

It is the etiquette of Indian society for the person receiving a visitor, to intimate when the conference has been of sufficient length; and, until that has been done, a native could not withdraw without giving offence. A short half-hour seemed to satisfy my friend, and he informed the great princes, who sat before him, that they were at liberty to take their leave. Upon this they rose, and we walked with them to the portico, where they were to mount their elephants; here a ceremony was gone through, which I could have wished should have been something more than a mere form. In turn, the Rajhas offered each of us an *inám*, or gift of friendship: three very superb horses, each bedecked with appointments worth a moderate fortune, were led forward; and, with the strain of Eastern compliments usual on such occasions, one was first offered to the official big-wig, not as an offering to the Government, but simply as a private token of goodwill. A very humble *saláam* was returned by my friend, who avowed himself to be crushed to the earth by their godlike munificence, but that he was prevented by the strict commands of his noble masters from availing himself of the honour intended for him. The same ceremony was repeated towards myself and another officer present, and in a similar manner declined, though, perhaps, with hardly so good a grace as that shown by our courtly friend, who had learned, by daily practice, to keep the tenth commandment without chagrin. With much ceremony, the Rajhas now took their leave; and half an hour afterwards, a messenger was despatched to their camp, with gold-bespangled letters, intimating to them that as they were about to quit Dehli on the morrow, the representative of the British Government would do them the honour of a visit at sunset.

When the hour arrived, the *sawarri* (*cortége*) of the mighty power to be represented, was marshalled to the door; it was impossible not to smile at the contrast exhibited between this and that of the black men who had been with us in the morning. The gentleman upon whom, in virtue of his office, this honour devolved, habited in a genteel suit of black, mounted his elephant of state, a noble animal, muffled in a threadbare *jhule* of scarlet cloth, with an old tarnished gilt *háoda*, and a *chatta* which would have been a fit emblem of the poverty-stricken royalty of the Mogul court. The train consisted of four ragamuffin *sawars* habited in rusty brown suits, mounted on pitiful hacks, little better than my pony at Munglour. I mounted my horse and stole away from the state retinue, until it reached the Rajhas' camp.

It was evident from what we saw of the encampment even at a distance, that the pageantry of the morning was not more magnificent than the rest of the establishment of these princes. The extent of canvas was tremendous, and apparently sufficient for the accommodation of the whole city before which it was spread. It occupied at least two miles of the glacis, stretching round the walls, from the Cashmere-gate to the Lahore-gate; and yet, amid all the confusion of the elephants, camels, horses, and camp-followers, we had no difficulty in distinguishing the tents of "the Presence." *Hirkarras* (running messengers) came forth to meet us, and clear the way as we advanced; others were continually running to and fro, with the tidings of our advance, shouting all the usual titles of which they conceived our dignity deserving.

We were conducted first to the tents of the Puttiála Rajha; these were of very large dimensions, constructed entirely of alternate stripes of crimson and white velvet, and most extravagantly embroidered with gold, having ropes and tassels of the same: the ground, not only within the tent, but over a large space in front, was spread with crimson velvet, fringed with gold bullion, at least six inches deep, and the spear-heads of the poles were similarly decorated. We were welcomed with great ceremony, and the same desultory conversation ensued as in the morning. When the Rajha had seen enough of us, he rose, and the ceremony of *rohksut* (leave-taking) was performed, first by a shaking of paws, as is the English fashion, and then after the Eastern manner, of presenting *pawn* and sweetmeats, being at the same time sprinkled and besmeared with rose-water and the *attar* of roses.

We next made our *saláam* to the Nabur Rajha, whose tents, though equally splendid, exhibited more taste and elegance than the other: this was of sky-blue and white velvet, in alternate stripes, embroidered with a running pattern of silver upon the blue, and having its hangings and trimmings also of silver. At one end of the tent, in a dark corner, hung a portrait of the King of Oude, a little shrivelled mean-looking figure, dressed in the robes of royalty, copied exactly from those of a portrait of George the Third. Who the artist might have been, the Rajha could not inform me, and the man, whether native or European, had the good sense not to affix it to the canvas: the painting put me in mind of a caricature I once saw of a beggar in the Lord Mayor's carriage. Here the same ceremonies were performed as at the Puttiála Rajha's tent, and we then paid our visit to the Kishenghur Rajha, whom we found much in the same style as the others: his tent was not perhaps so costly, or in such good taste; it was of purple and yellow, with very little of gold or silver about it. I had heard much of native magnificence and courtly splendour in India, but all that I had hitherto seen had been paltry indeed compared to this.

On the 20th of this month (December 1835), we experienced, at Dehli, a very severe shock of earthquake. I was sitting at breakfast with my host, and during a pause in the conversation, we were made to stare at one another by a sudden trembling and rattling of all the doors and windows in the house; this continued for several seconds, increasing in violence, until, at last, the floor beneath us began to heave in long successive undulations, like the swell of the sea, accompanied with a loud rumbling noise, as of innumerable carriages driving to and fro over a hollow bridge of metal (I can liken it to nothing else); the whole building rocked to its foundation, and the joists of the walls opened as if it were coming down upon us. We rushed into the open air, and there beheld a dreadful scene of confusion; the natives, who are generally indifferent to an ordinary shock, were rushing in all directions, screaming and crying "*bhoomchal! bhoomchal!*" (earthquake! earthquake!). Many of the old offices in the Residency compound were falling, and we expected every moment to see the house itself go, for it is an old rickety building, which was erected by Sir David Ochterlony. The shock did not last more than a minute, but it was very severe; more so than any earthquake which had been felt at Delhi for many years: several of the old buildings in the city were overthrown, and some few lives were lost. It came in a direction from north to south, and its influence appears to have extended over an immense extent of country, having been slightly felt in Calcutta on the same day, though several hours afterwards. When we returned to the house, we found broad fissures in the corners of all the rooms, and it really appeared a marvel that it remained standing; strange to say, that in the course of a day or two afterwards, the chasms had closed, in a great measure, so that a little plastering was all that was required in repairing them.

I found great difficulty in providing myself with a suitable boat at Dehli; there was certainly no fear of my being puzzled in the selection by a multiplicity of advantages: of the few to be had, all were either too large for the draught of water, or too small for my convenience. At last, I settled matters by hiring one, the smallest specimen of an *oolahk* I ever saw, scarcely deserving of the name; the mat hut built over it was hardly the height of my shoulder, and but just broad enough for my little *charpáhi*. This was to serve as my dining-room and bed-room, and as I could not make up my mind to use it as a drawing-room also, I purchased a small four-oared wherry; in which, as long as the weather continued moderate, I intended to spend the hours of daylight, in fishing, shooting, sketching, and the like, according to my humour.

On the 22d of December, I set sail from Dehli, having found it necessary to reduce my train and followers, from two or three-and-twenty, to three; and now for the first time, since my arrival in India, I learned to dress myself, and behave like a rational being; instead of paying slaves to see and think, in fact to do all but eat and drink, for me. But then it was cold weather, bitterly cold, and the bracing air blowing over the water, together with the occupation and excitement of navigating my own little wherry, and the prospect of Old England in the distance, made me forget that I had ever been called a *koi hi*.

Those alone who have travelled in a small native boat, can sympathise in all my privations and discomforts, so keenly felt when contrasted with the luxurious mode of life in which I had been indulging, during the few previous years. I was stowed in a little floating hut, scarcely twenty feet in length, with three black servants, a *manji*, six *dandis*, two goats, a Persian cat, an otter, and a puppy for a friend; and happy should I have thought myself, had these been my only companions; but, unfortunately, I found the boat pre-occupied by a vast population of musk-rats, mice, cock-roaches, fleas, centipedes, and countless other loathsome vermin; moreover, it was much overloaded, and very leaky. All these additional miseries remained undiscovered, until I was many miles from Dehli; for, during the whole of the day, I had remained in my little wherry, bowling away before a spanking breeze. It was not till I sought my dinner, that I knew the full extent of my bliss. A curry and rice were the only viands spread upon my humble table (bullock-trunk I should say, for I had no room for a table), to the great chagrin of my solitary attendant, whose chief inducement to so arduous a task, as sole manager of my *cuisine*, had been in all probability, the prospect of the *dustoor* in purchase, rather than the extra wages he received.

Upon the lid of an old trunk a white napkin was spread, shewing here and there need of the tailor's craft; upon this, the curry, in a common blue-patterned vegetable-dish, was laid, so as to hide the most conspicuous of the rents; the wine and glasses were placed upon the deck, as were also the numerous other appurtenances of the table. An inverted washing-basin, with a music-book placed over it, served me as a chair; but my *vis-à-vis*, an old black goat, preferred lounging after the fashion of the ancient Romans, resting his chin upon the edge of the trunk, the better to watch each mouthful of my meal.

"Here you *khidmutgar*; are there no better napkins than this? Why have you placed such a thing before me? Where are the rest?"

"Your slave cannot tell, sir; they were always in the keeping of your tailor, and therefore I know nothing about them; to-morrow I will see."

"What wine is that?"

"Sir, I cannot tell; *the aubdar* used to understand the seals, but your slave is ignorant."

"Well, never mind: bring me a wine-glass."

"The *kahnsuma* packed the glass, sir, and I do not know in which chest to look for it."

"Well, then, turn all the cases up to-morrow; try each, until you get the right one."

"Protector-of-the-poor, your slave is a weak man, and unable to lift those large boxes; and the *dhobi* (washerman) refuses to assist me, because it is not his *kám* (work)."

"Then, make the *tchokedar* help you. Why, that goat is starved; it is trying to eat the bones."

"Yes, sir, they will both die; for, since you discharged your *bukri-walla*, they have had nothing to eat, except their *gram* (a kind of pulse): the *tchokedar* will not fetch food for them."

"Then, why don't you do it yourself?"

"Sir, it is not your slave's *kám* to attend upon the goats."

Here the conversation was interrupted by a large rat dropping into the rice-dish from the roof, and a general scramble ensued in pursuit of it; a bit of his tail was all that we could secure, and that was bought at the expense of the bottle of wine, and the only tumbler.

After a night of incessant tumbling and tossing, I was glad to escape from my innumerable plagues and annoyances, as soon as the day dawned; taking my gun as a companion, I sought refuge in my little pleasure-boat, returning to my habitation for my meals only, and at night. It is astonishing how quickly the body adapts itself to all circumstances; I had hardly been a week on board, before I forgot one half of my troubles, and even the fleas and musquitoes were in a measure disregarded. My chief pursuits were those of shooting, and wandering with my sketch-book from place to place, along the banks of this beautiful river. Game I found even more abundant than on the Ganges, and there is scarcely a spot of ground, from Dehli downward, but would form a subject worthy of the powers of a Fielding or a Turner.

The twenty-fifth of the month being Christmas-day, I determined to celebrate it with a feast, and for this purpose gave orders to my *khidmutgar* to prepare a *burra kahna:* beef being out of the question, I desired a hind-quarter of kid to be roasted, and also sanctioned the man's petition for the concoction of a currant-dumpling, the goats having eaten the raisins; and the weather being very cold, my madeira gave place to port, which was ordered to be put before the fire. But, alas! I was destined to fare more frugally than usual that evening; for a tremendous *toofán*, coming on very suddenly, extinguished the fire, and filled the pudding with sand, giving an opportunity to a big *parria* dog for carrying off my hind-quarter of kid; so that, of all my promised feast, nothing remained to me but the *chuppatties*, a substitute for bread, and a hastily-grilled chop.

But I found more important matters to attend to, for the hurricane, instead of passing rapidly over, as may generally be anticipated when it rises so suddenly, continued to blow with great fury all night. My frail boat, in which my "little all" was launched, although secured to the bank with double warps and double rows of stakes, was dashed about with such violence, that I expected her every moment to go to pieces. Towards morning, the wind, which was from the south-west, abated a little; and, having weathered the worst of the storm, I began to calculate upon an escape from the wreck, which would certainly have befallen me, had the *toofán* continued an hour longer: this change for the better came just in time to save me the labour of unloading the boat, for which I had just given orders.

The day was breaking when I sought my couch, and, giving orders for the boats to be put in motion before sunrise, I lay down to rest. It was high noon when I awoke, and to my dismay, I found the boat in the same position which she had occupied over-night. I went out to ascertain the cause, and found the boat's crew comfortably seated round a blazing fire, cooking their dinner. My ire was greatly kindled: "You rascals, did I not give you my commands to get the boats under weigh at sunrise? How have you dared to disobey my orders? You *manji*, come here; what sort of a Mussulman are you? *nimuk-aram!*"*

"Does the rain fall because the earth cries out for moisture?" replied the *manji*; "do you not see that the boat is jammed upon the sand-bank?

**Nimuk-aram*; a term of reproach, parallel with our English saying, "not worth his salt;" it is compounded of the two Hindostani words *nimuk*, "salt," and *aram*, "ease," signifying, that although the ingrate has eaten his master's salt, he takes his ease, and will not exert himself to do his duty. The same figure is sometimes drawn more closely to our expression; "*Tūm-ne nimuk kahlea, lekkin khidmut nehin kurte ho.*" "You have eaten my salt, and yet you do me no service."

and here we must remain, until it is God's pleasure that we should depart."

"Fool, do you expect the God you quote to stretch forth his hand, and remove the obstruction? Collect every man immediately, and with ropes and levers we shall be able to get the boat afloat."

"Sir, we have tried our utmost, and cannot move it; now if God do not come to our assistance, we must continue on this sand-bank."

Finding the crew insufficient for the purpose, I sent to a village hard by, for as many *koolies* as would come, offering two *pice* (about three farthings) to each, and in less than half-an-hour I had more than a hundred hands at work upon the ropes; and thus the boat was run away with into deep water. "*Uchha!*" said the old *manji*, staring at the deed; "*yih kaisa hikmut?*" (what manner of invention is this?)

The first town particularly worthy of notice, at which I arrived, was Bindrabund, a large and populous Hindu city of peculiar sanctity. It was represented to me by an old Brahmin, as the most sacred of all spots throughout Bengal, not excepting Hurdwar, Allahabad, Benares, or even Juggurnaut, and it doubtless was so in his estimation, for he was a native of the place. He pointed out to me many points of the banks and trees, which were almost too holy to be mentioned to a Christian: these were formerly, according to tradition, the haunts of Kishen, or Krishna, or Vishnu, while he walked on earth. Here is a very ancient tree, the root of which forms a convenient seat, upon which the god used to sit and play his flute, while the women danced to his music; and so charming were the strains of his celestial *bánsulí*,* that all the wild beasts and reptiles of the forest assembled round him to listen. Here, too, is the *ghát*, whereon the said Krishna, while still a child, encountered and triumphed over the terrible serpent, Kalli Nágur, who, by lying across the Jumna, stopped its course and poisoned its waters, so that multitudes perished; after the performance of which exploit, Krishna restored to animation all who had died through fright or poison, by one godlike smile. Here, likewise, were pointed out to me many a spot upon which the god, with the assistance of his brother Ram, cured all manner of diseases, and healed every sort of affliction, under various forms. According to

* Krishna is the Apollo and the Hercules of Hindu mythology; his instrument was the *bánsuli*, whether a flute or pipe resembling the clarionet is uncertain, as the images of this deity are variously represented.

the best authorities, Krishna existed, in his various incarnations, about 1300 years before Christ.

The town of Bindrabund is beautifully situated on the western bank of the river, and contains some of the oldest and best preserved relics of Hindu architecture, in India, among its accumulated temples and *ghâts;* these are intersected with tufts and thick groves of bannian and mango-trees, which add greatly to the picturesque beauty of the place. The principal temple is built upon the plan of a cross, and presents very fine specimens of elaborate carving on a large scale; it is of red granite, and of this material there are lofty towers, in the same style of architecture as that of Juggurnaut. A distant sketch of one of these, and the southern extremity of the town, is all I have an opportunity of presenting to the reader, as an illustration.

The whole place swarms with monkies and religious mendicants, more numerous, I think, than I ever met with them before; and, however highly delighted the traveller may be, in gazing upon, or sketching, the very choice grouping of the old brahminical buildings and venerable trees, or in listening to the historical tales of the *pundits,* he will gladly make his escape from the corrupt atmosphere and filthy vicinity of Bindrabund. The monkies at this place are fed in a manner similar to that described at Saharunpore; but it is here performed by Brahmins, who do not love to be intruded upon by the inspection of the curious. The fish are also fed, and several acres of land are cultivated and sown with grain, for the exclusive possession of the peacocks. These three tribes are religiously venerated and protected by the Hindus throughout India; but, in the present instance, the especial care and favour bestowed upon them is in consequence of a handsome fund appointed for this purpose; the mass of which was bestowed by Mahajji Scindia, who has also built a splendid *ghát*. So greatly are these animals reverenced, that the traveller should be careful not to annoy or injure any of them, lest he be made to rue his cruelty. In 1808, two young officers from Muttra shot at, and wounded one of the monkies, upon which the infuriated Brahmins, attacking the elephant upon which they were mounted, drove it into the river, and both were drowned. The natives attribute this revenge to the monkies themselves, who, with sticks and stones, are said to have driven the elephant before them.

Only a few hours' sail below Bindrabund, stands

the fort and ancient city of Muttra, more properly Mathura, scarcely inferior to the former place in the beauty and extent of its Hindu buildings. Some of the marble pavilions and carved balconies along the smaller streets are well worth the noxious job of seeking them out. All Hindu cities are filthy: Bindrabund and Muttra are the filthiest of the filthy. The population of this place is large; and among the dirty shop-keepers are said to be men of wealth sufficient for the purchase of both towns, and of all the lands which are watered by the Jumna. Here it is that the waters of this river first begin to fructify the soil, being less impregnated with nitre than in the regions nearer to its source; this is ascribed by the Hindus to the purifying of the waters by Krishna, after he had destroyed the serpent at Bindrabund. The exploits and miracles performed by this god are said to have been wrought as frequently at Muttra as at Bindrabund, for here he used frequently to wander with his brother Ram, "finding more honour than in his own city." *

On the south side of the town is the military cantonment, where a large force was quartered a

* These words were made use of to me by the old Brahmin who acted as my guide.

few years since; but from which, by Lord William Bentinck's orders, all the troops have been withdrawn, with the exception of a regiment of native Light Cavalry, and a troop of Horse Artillery. I paid a visit to the station, and was most hospitably entertained by the officers of the 10th Light Cavalry, those of my own corps being encamped at some distance from Muttra, during the practice season ; so, for the first night since my quitting Dehli, I dined like a gentleman, and, what was better, I slept like a gentleman. In the morning, I allowed my boats to go forward, down the stream, in order that I might remain to see the city, without losing time. Having satisfied my curiosity in this respect, I rode out, in the evening, to the rendezvous appointed for my boats; a distance of about twenty miles, carrying a whole pantheon of little brazen deities in my pockets, which had been procured for me by my Brahmin guide, at a contract of eight annas each, for antiques.

Among the many delights of my stylish method of travelling, was that of being constantly taken for a pedlar, or, as the tribe are called in India, *soudágur*. I had not been half an hour in my boat, after riding from Muttra, when I received a note;

"Captain P—— will be obliged by Mr. Baker sending him three *seers** of bacon, if he has any which he can particularly recommend." Then came a note addressed to Mr. Bagom, for a pound of Windsor soap; then another from a third party, requiring a supply of kid gloves and lavender water, and to know if Mr. Beakem had any lap-dogs for sale; then came a fourth and a fifth note, from Abraham De Costa, Joachim De Sousa, or Reichardt De Crutz, inviting Mr. Biggin "as a bruther murchint—no opposition—and one of the same kidney, to come and take pot-luk, without ezzitation, and a bottle of prime whack." Before I reached Agra, I was so pestered with these applications, that I determined to push forward with all speed, and on my arrival at that city, to exchange my pedlar's boat for one more befitting my station, and such as would allow me a greater degree of comfort.

* *Seer*, two pounds weight.

CHAPTER XI.

AGRA, FUTTEHPORE-SIKRI, AND SECUNDRA.

On the morning of the 28th, I arrived at the ancient city, where this desired object was to be effected; and here I determined to remain several days, for the purpose of visiting the celebrated Tajh Mahal, and many other relics of antiquity, which had been represented to me as superior, in magnificence and in preservation, to those of Dehli.

At the time of the Mohummedan conquest, Agra was a mere village, without name or note; but the site was selected by Akbur, as the seat of a new metropolis, on account of its central position, and the advantage it enjoyed over Dehli, from the circumstance of the river being at no time fordable, and capable of navigation to boats of heavy tonnage throughout the year. In 1566, Akbur laid the foundation of the city, since which time it has been called by the natives Akburabad.

Under the patronage of this great Emperor, it sprung up and became a mighty city, in the course of a very few years; having an extensive, and to native attack, an impregnable fortress, together with exterior walls and defences, thrown up round the city and suburbs. At the present day, this fort is in perfect repair: it stands upon a rocky eminence, about eighty feet above the level of the river, and presents a striking object on approach to the place. This, like most of the buildings, is composed of red granite, similar to that of Dehli, Toglukabad, and other places already mentioned.

Within this fort, the founder erected many very handsome buildings; among the chief, we may notice his own palace, the marble halls and tessalated courts of which are still in wonderful preservation, though bearing many scars and mutilations dealt by the shot from the British batteries, at the time of its investment by Lord Lake, in 1803.* The white marble pavilion, overlooking

* The gigantic piece of ordnance, captured by Lord Lake at this siege, weighed 96,000 lbs.; and his lordship, wishing to preserve it as a trophy, had a raft constructed, upon which it was launched, with the intention of having it carried down to Calcutta; but it broke through the planks, and sunk in the sands of the river, where it remained unnoticed and forgotten, until the practice-season of 1833, when it was most cruelly experimentalized upon by the Artillery officers, who reduced it to fragments by blasting.

An equally grievous offence was committed, in the destruction of the Joud Bháe, a fine old ruin, about two miles from the city. Without regard the river, is a most chaste building, and put me in mind of the carved marbles I had so much admired at Dehli: the domes of this beautiful little chamber were formerly over-laid with pure gold, but this has been removed, and gilded copper is now substituted. The splendid audience-hall belonging to this palace has been converted into a storehouse for ammunition and small arms, and many other beautiful buildings are similarly misused.

The most perfect of them all, has, however, been regarded with a better show of consideration, being kept in repair by the British government; I speak of the Moti Musjid (pearl-mosque), the imperial place of worship attached to the palace. It is built of white marble, without a particle of any other substance; not only the mosque itself, but the court also, which surrounds it. No sooner is the beholder within the gates of this court, than he finds himself shut in on all sides by the same pure spotless material, the sky above him, and the pool of sacred water in the centre of the area, being the only exceptions. This *musjid* is reckoned

to the prejudices of the natives, or the reverend antiquity of the building, it was, for the gratification of childish curiosity, mined and blown into the air; one-half of it withstood the shock of twenty-five barrels of powder, and remains a monument of shame to its spoliators: the rest is a heap of rubbish.

one of the most perfect specimens of Eastern architecture extant; its proportions are certainly very just and elegant, and it is difficult for imagination to conceive anything more symmetrical.

Before I proceed to any mention of the other buildings about Agra, a short sketch of the character of the great Akbur will be necessary to the making myself intelligible. Sufficient for my purpose may be said in a very few pages.

Akbur is upheld by all ranks and castes as the greatest potentate, the wisest statesmen, and the most illustrious prince, who ever held sway in India. He was quite a lad, not more than fourteen years of age, when he succeeded to the *musnud*, his father, Hummaione, being then an exile from his own dominions among the Rajhpoot princes; having been placed in captivity by the tyrant Shere Shah, the Afghan. Even at this early period of his life, the young emperor appears to have been endowed with wonderful strength of mind and wisdom: his history is stored with examples of extraordinary genius, and of a noble and benevolent heart.

At the commencement of his reign, Akbur was under the guidance and restriction of his father's Vizier, Bhiram Kahn, a man distinguished by his shrewd penetration, and the keenness of his judgment, together with his quick resource in difficulty, and his prompt decision in action. Such faculties, had they existed in purity, would have rendered him the most eligible and invaluable agent for such an important state post; but with these he combined an overweening and insatiate ambition, and an inordinate love of intrigue, which nothing but a vigilant eye could detect, nor anything but a resolute arm have over-ruled. It appears, however, from history, that his first measures in endeavouring to draw the reins of government into his own grasp, were penetrated by the young prince, who, although disgusted at his treachery, preferred thwarting all his efforts by his secret interposition, rather than expose to public obloquy and destruction the favourite minister of his father's court. Every successive scheme of the traitor was forestalled and rendered abortive by the discrimination and consummate tact of the boy-emperor, until he had cause to be apprehensive of violence or treasonable designs against his own royal person, which was beyond his single strength to avert; and he then declared himself to his court, bringing evidence of the Vizier's malignant plots. This conduct on the part of the young prince gained him the fullest affection and confidence of his whole court, and the undivided support of all the most influential of his subjects; so that Bhiram Kahn, finding all his ambitious hopes crushed, determined to play the hypocrite, until a fitting opportunity should offer for open rebellion: he sued humbly for pardon at the feet of his gracious monarch, who nobly forgave him, and reinstated him in his office.

Very shortly after this, however, Bhiram Kahn, being about to take the field with a considerable force against some neighbouring chief, turned suddenly upon his sovereign, and made a desperate effort to seize the sceptre by force. The youthful Akbur was prepared for him, and meeting the disaffected force with a body of precisely equal strength, he speedily routed them, and took his faithless minister prisoner; and now, strong in his own foresight, and the devotion of his chiefs, ever more inclined to mercy than to vengeance, the imperial master once more granted a free and full pardon to his repentant slave; who, humbled to the dust by such undeserved mercy, being overwhelmed with confusion and remorse, solicited permission to make a pilgrimage to Mecca in expiation of his crime. To this petition Akbur not only gave a ready sanction, but, to exhibit the boldness of his confidence, he provided the Vizier with ample funds, and a train suited to the splendour of the state of which he was the chief servant; and, moreover, he placed at his command, as an escort, the very troops who by bribery had been won over to rebellion, in order that they too might benefit by the holy act. But, in the words of history, "God was not pleased that they should obtain absolution from their crime, for long ere they had reached the shrine of the divine prophet, they were slain, every individual, by a strong army of Pindarris, who having savagely hewn their victims in ten thousand pieces, plundered the camp."

Bhiram Kahn was succeeded in the office of Vizier by a more worthy and equally able man, Abul Fazil, a native of Agra, who had been educated at the court of Hummaione, and whose combined genius, as an historian, a poet, and a statesman, has rendered his name famous throughout all nations.

Akbur, with the devoted assistance of his skilful minister, turned his thoughts to the political and internal improvement of his over-grown dominions; preferring to maintain in subjection and good governance the vast tract of country of which he was the head, rather than expend the resources of the state, for the sake of making fresh acquisitions. Under his mild and wise control, his subjects made rapid advancement in the arts and sciences, as also in their taste for literature, while the agricultural interests were established upon a footing of security previously unheard of in the land. The revenue of the state was increased to 700,000,000 rupees annually, or about seventy millions of pounds. The splendour of the court, and the power of the monarch, became unrivalled throughout all Hindostan, and other princes thought it no indignity to do homage to so mighty and so merciful a prince. Innumerable public works, both of ornament and national benefit, were executed; canals were dug, roads were cut, forts were built, and schools were established in all parts of the empire; more especially at the seat of government, and at the second capital, Dehli.

Of the most stupendous undertakings of Akbur, at this time, we have still vestiges remaining; one of these we see in the ruins of a superb road of masonry, which extended from Agra to Dehli, a distance of a hundred and forty miles. This road was raised above the level of the surrounding country, and on either side of it were planted groves of magnificent trees, reported to have been brought in their full growth from the forest, by the assistance of elephants; within these groves, aqueducts of stone were erected, for the purposes of irrigation to the trees and the neighbouring land, and for the watering of the road, to lay the dust and cool the atmosphere, whenever the Emperor should travel that way. At every *kōs*,* a small tower was erected, called a *kōs-minar*, at the foot of which was the hut of a *tchokedar*, established as a patrol, to prevent the depredations of the robbers, who, from time immemorial, have been so numerous in these districts. Many of these towers still remain, and fragments of the aqueducts and of the road are also to be traced; there are also by the way-side, near Futtehpore-Sikri, the rapidly decaying remains of some gigantic trees, which, from their regularity of distance, and their position by the old masonry, are to be recognised as the same which, two hundred and eighty years since, were planted there, having outlived the

* *Kōs*, a measurement varying in its proportions, in different parts of India, from two-and-a-quarter English miles, to one mile. At Agra, the *kōs* is computed in late surveys to be about a mile and a half.

ravages of time, tempests, deluges, war, and the destroyer man.

Futtehpore-Sikri was the favourite country residence of Akbur. In 1570, he built upon the eminences around the old town a magnificent palace, and mansions for his court and retinue; which, as the dwellings of a royal household, may be traced by their ruins to have been vast beyond comparison in their extent, being, in fact, little short of a city. The distance of these ruins from Agra is about twenty-four miles, and among my brother officers I had no difficulty in mustering a pic-nic party to visit and explore them.

The Artillery were then encamped for practice in an open plain, about three miles distant from the city, and among their hospitable tents I took up my quarters. The dayselected for the excursion was the most cheerful and bracing I ever remember to have experienced in the plains of India; it was intensely cold, and small icicles were hanging from the canvas eaves of our tents, the frost upon the roof having thawed, and run down in moisture, in consequence of the fires which we found it necessary to keep up all night, until arrested, and consolidated in the act of dropping. The sun rose pale, and all the distances were bathed in floating mists, while the jungly ravines and weedy banks in the foreground were beginning to drop under the influence of returning warmth. Our cavalcade was strong, mustering about eight or nine; and having sent forward two relays of horses, we thought it no shame to keep our pace at the gallop, until we reached our destination: this we accomplished in something less than an hour and a-half.

The site of this ancient imperial abode is particularly picturesque, being raised above the surrounding country upon a low ridge of rocky hills, the approach to which is in places beautifully wooded and fertile, and again interspersed with crowded ruins, and mouldering temples. The first object which engrosses the attention of the traveller is a stupendous building, crowning the principal height, and overlooking the low country, the face of its walls terminating in a gigantic gateway, surmounted with domes and minarets. From a distant position, the effect of this enormous structure is to cause the hill on which it stands to dwindle into a mere hillock; but when the traveller arrives at its base, and can estimate the magnitude of the building by that of the eminence on which it is exalted, his admiration is raised to wonder and awe, at the startling height to which it rises.

The gateway was stated by our guide, a reverend old Mussulman, styling himself by the illustrious title of Ibrahim Kahn, to be the highest in the whole world, and he affirms that Lord Hastings is his authority for this assertion: it is seventy-two feet high, within the arch, and a hundred and twenty to its summit. The approach to this gate is by an immense flight of steps, leading up the face of the hill; these are now broken, and running fast to decay, for want of trifling repairs, which, as there is abundance of material at hand, is really a lamentable neglect; for, in the rainy season, the torrent of water which pours down over the steep, insinuating itself between the crevices of the masonry, bears it away stone by stone, and in a very few years, unless repaired, the proud gateway, which now stands almost without a blemish, must be undermined, and will be mingled with the general decay around it.

Within this gateway is an extensive quadrangular court, built, as is the gateway itself, of red granite; the whole interior is surrounded with a deep arcade, within which is a series of apartments, formerly appropriated to those who, from piety made a pilgrimage to the place; the court being rendered sacred by the shrine of Akbur's chief priest and ghostly minister, Sheik Selim Tchisti, to whose memory this beautiful sanctuary was erected by Akbur, in gratitude for the efficacy of the holy man's prayers, by means of which his Begum, after many years of sterility, became fruitful, and bore a son. The shrine is entirely of the purest white marble, and is sculptured as elegantly as anything of the kind to be seen in India. Its proportions are charming; and though small, there is an air of holy importance about it, truly striking, and which is admitted even by those least susceptible of such feelings. In a smaller quadrangle, leading by three small arch-ways from the one in question, are accumulated many tombs of various members and officers of Akbur's court: but these are neglected, over-run with weeds, and many of them buried in dirt.

The building just described is the only one of all the splendid edifices, which once stood here, now in preservation; all the rest have been overturned, or have fallen, and now present a continued scene of ruin on all sides within the walls of defence, which may be traced by their foundations to have extended from hill to hill, over a space six miles in circumference. Red granite is still the substance of these remains, with here and there mouldings and decorations of white marble.

Not far from the shrine of Sheik Selim, are to be discovered the walls and chambers of a similar court-yard, in which were deposited the remains of Abul Fazil, who, by a coincidence worthy of remark, met an untimely fate, like that of Bhiram Kahn, his predecessor, being slain by a horde of Pindarris, when travelling with a diminished retinue.

The old *dewan aum* (hall of justice) stands further to the eastward, on a separate hill from the foregoing. That which is still left of this stately apartment is very perfect in its minutiæ; but the cruel hand of the Jhauts and Maharhattas have sadly dilapidated the roof and galleries. All around, it is most gracefully adorned with deep cornices, and running patterns of wonderful device; and though by any but an eye-witness, granite may be thought a coarse material for such work, yet from the loftiness of the apartment, and the noble style of its architecture, this is not the case. In the centre of the hall is a massive pillar, of the same stone, in height about fifteen feet, with an elaborately-carved capital, the whole cut from one solid block; from this capital, transverse slabs are thrown across the four angles of the apartment, forming galleries of communication with passages running round the walls of the apartment, which are entered by arched doors, approached from the ground by spiral staircases: all this is so neatly put together, that it has the appearance of having been carved out of one enormous block. On this fanciful seat, Akbur used to sit, exalted above the heads of his nobles and those of his subjects who sought him; and here he in person gave audiences and dispensed justice to all who needed his aid, with equal impartiality and indifference, whether to the wealthy and noble, or to the meanest in degree. It is alleged that he had continually by him a bag of money, from which he distributed to the poor a sum equivalent to the value of their time spent in his presence, or whatever had been consumed in seeking the decision of his judgment. These *durbars* were granted during a certain number of hours daily, when all who had grievances to be redressed, or distresses to be relieved, were freely admitted to the imperial presence.

After wandering over an immense accumulation of ruins, all deeply interesting from the variety of their designs, and their dissimilarity of structure, we found ourselves at the foot of a most massive gateway, called the *Hatti durwáza* (the gate of elephants), commemorated in the writings of all historians, our guide told us, since the days of the great Akbur, who built it. The gateway is certainly elephantine in the enormity of its design; but it is not this which gives it the name in which Ibrahim Kahn so greatly gloried; it is so called from the figures of two elephants, of the natural size, which are finely sculptured over the arch. The attitudes and figure of these monsters are wonderfully true and perfect. When standing below them, I was inclined to criticise and condemn them as faulty; but when I exalted myself upon a neighbouring tower, so as to bring myself upon a level with them, I felt convinced that the nicest eye could not find a point for cavil. In other respects, there is nothing about this gateway to excite admiration.

A further ramble brought us to a small tower, about fifty feet high, built, our guide assured us, entirely of elephants' tusks, the animals to which they belonged having been captured or slain, at different times, in the ranks of his enemies, by Akbur himself. This tale is parallel with that of

Queen Anne's garden at Greenwich ; but it is only by close inspection that the fraud is detected, and even then it is hardly perceptible, except in places where the enamel has been broken off. The illusion is curious, particularly when we remember that the imitation has been exposed to a climate of intense extremes, during two hundred and sixty summers.

Having wandered throughout the day over all that was pointed out to us as best worthy of notice, we returned to the principal gateway, which we ascended, for the purpose of taking a bird's-eye view of the whole. The scene is indeed a lovely one, extending over an immense tract of country, the horizon of which is on all sides thirty miles distant from the beholder, on a clear day, such as that which we enjoyed. The low line of hills upon which the place is built, is seen creeping through the whole face of the level country, from east to west, crowned every here and there with ruined buildings or a hill fortress. Among these, Bhurtpore is just visible. On the opposite side is the Jumna, winding through the distance, and leading the eye to the glittering, though far off, towers and domes of Agra. The middle-distance is richly wooded and thickly spotted with ruins of every age and in every style of design, some exhibiting an undiminished front, and others crumbling rapidly to oblivion.

When the sun declined, my companions mounted and set forth upon their return to Agra; but having myself three excellent horses on the road, and being somewhat of an impatient horseman, I suffered them to depart without me. The sun set and the moon rose, while I was still fixed in contemplation of the landscape; and the servants having thrown away all remnants of our noon-day meal, hunger, together with the perishing cold, urged me to return; but there was a witching charm about the scene which chained me to the spot, particularly as I doubted the possibility of my ever beholding it again. At last, springing upon my eager nag, I put him to his best speed, and the same with the other two, crossing the four-and-twenty miles in an hour and twenty-eight minutes. I arrived at the mess-tent just as my friends had lighted their cigars, after the removal of the cloth; however, I recalled a few of the dishes, and fared excellently, while listening to tales and anecdotes of the renowned Akbur and his contemporaries.

After a glorious and happy reign of fifty-one

years, during which time he enjoyed the most perfect confidence and affection of his subjects, and experienced but little interruption of peace, Akbur the Great was gathered to his fathers. This event occurred in the year 1605, and this monarch's tomb closed over the brightest era of Mohummedan India. This great sovereign was succeeded by his son Jehanghir, the same prince who was sent on earth in answer to the petitions of Sheik Selim Tchisti, and who had hitherto been known at court simply by the modest cognomen of Selim; but now, putting on the glory of the state, he assumed also the imposing title of Jehan-ghir, 'king of the world.' The attention of the new monarch was first absorbed by committing to the earth, with befitting reverence and splendour, the remains of his illustrious father.

Akbur was buried at Secundra, and his devoted son erected to his memory one of the most magnificent mausoleums of which India can boast. Its plan is upon a square; it rises four stories in height, each diminishing in its area within the dimensions of that on which it rests; or it may be more explicit to say, that each story is but a smaller model of the one supporting it, so that the plans of all might be drawn one within the other.

The three lower stories are built of red granite, and the upper one of white marble, beautifully carved. It is altogether a noble pile, but the great attraction to travellers seems to be in the upper, marble story, and in the block of the same which stands in the centre of the quadrangle: this is certainly chaste and elegant, but I could not discover in it anything to justify the extravagant encomiums passed upon it by most who have visited it. How can it ever be compared to the shrine of Nizam-ud-deen at Dehli, or to that of Sheik Selim at Futtehpore-Sikri, or twenty others which I could enumerate! unless, indeed, we suffer our admiration to be more active, for the sake of the mighty prince whose name the marble bears. My interest was certainly enhanced by this consideration, but I could not enter into the spirit of the unreasonable eulogiums so frequently indulged in, on this account merely. The tombstone is an oblong block of the finest and most spotless marble, beautifully carved in devices of wreaths, flowers, butterflies, and the like, having the word Akbur interlaced with these ornaments.

The author of 'Sketches of India,' makes the following remark about this block of marble: "Natural in form, and naturally strewn, are the pale flowers which lie thickly scattered on it. For whom the sculptor scattered them, five small and beautifully formed letters declare :—AKBAR, you read (in Arabic characters), and read no more." A poetical idea certainly, if the sculptor had been fortunate enough to hit upon it ; but I fear it would hardly have been in the estimation of the applause-loving, title-loving race, for whose admiration it was designed. Had the historian been unhappy enough to have caught sight of the upper face of the marble, his beautiful idea would have been crushed by a long list engraven in the Persian character, also interwoven with flowers, &c., recording all the excellencies and noble attributes of the monarch, in the usual florid style of Eastern blandishment : 'Light of heaven! Protector of the world! Preserver of the State! Upholder of the Universe! Right hand of the Almighty!' &c. &c.

The gardens about the place are now a complete jungle, and both the walls and gateways are falling fast to decay. This is, indeed, lamentable. The government have more than once repaired this delightful place, and an old pensioner had charge of the grounds ; and now the disgraceful state of decay into which it has lapsed, is, in all probability, owing to the neglect of a proper representation of the matter by the government servants, to whom it is entrusted, in common with the rest of the district in which it stands.

The Emperor Jehanghir, though by no means to be compared to his father in genius or powers of mind, at all times maintained an unimpeachable character, both public and domestic. He died in 1628, and was succeeded by his son Shah Jehan, he who rebuilt Dehli, an amiable and a wise prince, universally beloved by his subjects, and a very pattern of excellence in private life. He had four sons, who, with one exception, the crafty Aurungzebe, followed in their father's steps and imitated his virtues. Aurungzebe, however, turned out a man of very different disposition, subtle, wily, and selfish, and upon him the father found it necessary to keep a strict curb and an ever-watchful eye. But even this vigilance was insufficient to frustrate his deep-laid schemes of treachery. After several abortive attempts to seize the reins of the empire from his father's hands, he threw off the character of a prince, and, under the pretext of expiating his crimes, he habited himself as a *fakhir*, and in that guise travelled all the way into the Deccan; there, by the incessant exertion of bribery, promises, and persuasions, he levied a large army and marched against the imperial city of his father, seizing the opportunity, while the attention of the state was engaged in another quarter. By an extraordinary concurrence of good fortune and skill, and by an inexplicable agency, wherein artifice and duplicity were his chief aids, he at last gained footing within the imperial city, and secured the persons of his father and one of his elder brothers: the other two, being absent from Agra upon an expedition, remained at large, and being at the time furnished with troops, made head against the usurper, but without avail. The Emperor, Shah Jehan, was incarcerated during the remainder of his days within the walls of his own fortress of Agra; in this manner he continued to exist, though broken-hearted, for seven years, and during these last unhappy days of his life, he employed himself in erecting the Moti Musjid already mentioned. He died in 1665.

In their style of structure, and in their execrable narrowness and filth, the streets of Agra resemble those of Benares and Hurdwar; in many of the principal thoroughfares, there is scarcely room for two persons to walk abreast. The artist, however, has a delightful treat in the bold projecting gables, the massive jambs and buttresses of granite, deeply carved in all the fanciful conceits of the ancient Indians, too elaborate for the pencil of an incipient artist, and to which nothing short of a Prout could do justice.

I have hitherto refrained from making mention of the Tajh Mahal, the choicest of all the relics at Agra, from the feeling that the reader once made acquainted with it, even by the faint delineation of my pen, would have little admiration left for any of those places which I have already attempted to describe. On my reaching Agra, I was anxious first of all to visit this far-famed mausoleum, having heard its beauties and its wonders lauded to the skies, from the time of my first arrival in India; but, for the reason which has induced me to give it the last place in my sketch of Agra, let the traveller reserve it until he has visited all the other curiosities. So much had I heard, on all sides, of this extraordinary edifice, that I had fully prepared myself for a disappointment; but when I stood in presence of the noble pile, I could not help feeling that, had fifty times as much been said in its praise, and had it been but one-half as exquisite, I should have allowed that all these rhapsodies had fallen short of its real magnificence. It appears absurd to attempt a description of such a structure. I am fully sensible of my own utter inability to the task, but I fear this would be deemed an insufficient apology for passing over it.

This celebrated specimen of oriental architecture stands on the western bank of the Jumna, about half-a-mile below the fort, exalted above the water upon a high terrace of red sand-stone and granite. But I would recommend that a person visiting it for the first time should not approach it by the water-side; let him rather take the old road leading from the fort, and, delaying only a few minutes at the beautiful gateway leading to the Tajh gardens (for day-light is too short for the enjoyment before him), let him advance onwards, without looking at the Tajh Mahal, until he arrives at the cruciform fountain-basin in the centre of the cypress grove, and there let him stand and gaze. I have had the curiosity to watch other visitors adopting this plan, and the invariable fact was, that the whole mind became absorbed in the object before them, and the silence of abstraction betokened their exceeding delight; while those who have wandered gazing in their approach upon all the other beautiful works with which the place abounds, may be heard uttering the usual exclamations of admiration, "How beautiful! How very exquisite! How grand! How solemn! How chaste!" Tush! they may talk till the millennium, they will never find words to indicate a tithe of the mingled emotions impressed upon the mind by the sight: this is not to be attributed to the circumstance of the building losing aught of its effect by a protracted inspection; on the contrary, every moment enhances the wonder and delight of the spectator, and whole days are inadequate to a full estimation of the work.

It is not to be supposed that those who have not witnessed it can, with any degree of truth, picture to their minds an immense structure of pure white marble, richly carved and elaborately inlaid all over with gems and precious stones, in the most graceful devices, and most finely executed. The proportions of the building are perfectly enchanting, and it is the symmetry which charms, as much as it is the grandeur which astonishes, the spectator.

The edifice is built upon the plan of an octagon, having four of its opposite faces larger than the other four; in these, are arches of immense height, reaching nearly to the cordon of the building, and circularly faced, so as to form a niche, within which is a second arch opening to the interior. It is surmounted with a beautiful dome of vast proportions, in the centre, and four smaller ones overlooking the inferior faces. Around the body of the structure is a quadrangular arcaded terrace, forming the basement; this is also of white marble, and at each corner of it is a minaret of the same beautiful substance: these minarets are justly the admiration of all who have beheld them, so light, so chaste are they, and yet in such perfect accordance with the rest of the building, that they do not interfere with, but rather assist its effect. These delicate towers are built in three stories, the uppermost of which is the highest; yet this singularity does not in any degree detract from their beauty, much as it is at variance with our established notions of proportion. The summits are crowned with open cupolas, particularly elegant, and here, as in all the rest of the building, the eye cannot rest on anything akin to a fault, or on that which gives merely cold content: the mind becomes altogether enwrapt in admiration and delight, intense as it is mysterious.

Below that already described, is a second terrace

of red granite, as though the architect would have intimated that this exquisite piece of workmanship is too pure, too delicate, to stand upon the common earth. The summit of the centre dome is said to be two hundred and sixty feet in height, from the foundation of the lower terrace; and yet, from the perfect proportion of the fabric, it does not appear to be more than one-half that height. The whole is so finely finished, and in such complete repair, that it seems to have come but recently from the hands of the artist. Some French traveller (not Jacquemont, certainly) has remarked, that the Tajh Mahal is so very delicate, that it ought to have been preserved in a glass case. It was long since I had read this, but the idea recurred most forcibly to my mind on seeing the building. When we consider that the foundation was laid two hundred years since, it is indeed difficult to fancy how it can have been so perfectly preserved; it is to all appearance quite unfit for exposure, and yet it has scarcely a scratch or blemish upon the whole of it, except where a few of the gems were formerly broken out by the invading Maharhattas.

The interior consists of nine separate apartments, the principal of which is that in the centre, of the same figure as the exterior plan. It rises to an immense height, terminating in the concavity of the dome, still of the same beautiful material, and inlaid in the same exquisite manner as the exterior, perhaps with even greater profusion; and herein is contained the real object of the building, the sarcophagus of Shah Jehan's favourite and most beautiful wife, Neur Jehan (Light of the World), a work intended by that prince, who built it, to immortalize her name, and to give posterity an idea of his unbounded affection for her. The block of marble which records her name and many brilliant virtues and graces, occupies the centre of the apartment, and is most extravagantly inlaid and bedecked with gems, in the fashion of the rest of the pile; and upon the upper face, and on parts of the uprights, it bears a long and beautifully wrought Arabic inscription, inlaid in jet characters, expressive of all the charms and divine gifts, which a fond devoted husband could discover in a wife, young and eminently lovely, even to a proverb. A minute description of this tomb-stone is quite out of the question; I am sure the reader will pardon me for substituting the accompanying little figures, which are fac-similes.

No. 1. represents the upper surface of the block.

No 1

No 2

FAC SIMILE OF A FLOWER ON THE HEAD OF THE TOMB

London W.H. Allen & Co 7 Leadenhall St.

MARBLE SCREEN IN THE CENTRE OF THE TAJ MAHAL

Let it be remembered, that every different tint in the pourtraying of a flower, is represented by a separate gem, so that many of them, which here appear as mere dots, are in reality composed of many hundreds of stones. No. 2. may give an idea of what I mean. The centre flower of this figure consists of three hundred different stones; the workmanship is so very exquisite, that the finest instrument can find no crevices, and scarcely can the eye detect where the two gems are joined; and now some conception may be received of the infinite labour bestowed upon the whole edifice, when I mention, that not this slab only, but the whole pile, is thus exquisitely wrought.

The sarcophagus just described, is inclosed within a screen, which many people admire more than all the rest; for not only is it equally finely inlaid, but it is carved into the most delicate lattice-work, similar to that described at Nizam-ud-deen's shrine at Dehli. This is also octangular; the accompanying figure, No. 3, represents one side, the tomb itself being visible through the arched door-way. The second moulding above the arch is in bold relief, and is inlaid with a brilliant stone of gold colour, of great price, and very rare, being esteemed, therefore, the emblem of royalty. The space within this screen is somewhat encumbered with a second tomb-stone, that of the Emperor Shah Jehan himself, placed beside the former, a position it was evidently never intended to occupy in the original design of the building, it being placed over the rich mosaic borders of the pavement.

Above, below, and around, wherever the eye can rest, is wrought in the same wonderful manner, and that which is really looked upon, strikes the imagination as far beyond the ingenuity or accomplishment of mere mortals: magic, or something superhuman, appears at once to claim the work; and yet the whole pile was erected for the comparatively small sum of eighty *lahks* of rupees, or £800,000, and not more than twenty years were occupied in its construction.

But, as I have before hinted, it is not the nicety of the handiwork, or the richness and beauty of the materials, which constitute its chief attraction; there is an air of grand and sublime majesty in the whole design, which irresistibly impresses the mind of the spectator with awe and veneration; and the effect of this becomes intensely heightened by the solemn stillness of the place, and the supernatural reverberations which echo to the gentlest stir. So wonderfully do the vibrations multiply, that the slightest whisper, or the fall of the unshod foot, is carried in expanding eddies higher and higher, until the whole edifice is filled with a confused, but most imposing and super-natural, music.

There is another casual circumstance, which very greatly enhances the thrill of these sensations; while a tropical sun is smiting with its vertical rays upon the glaring white without, so as almost to inflict blindness, yet the moment the person is placed within this sacred mausoleum, a sudden chill is shed through the system; and, blinded at first by the sudden transition from scorching light to comparative though only partial darkness, it is only by a slow process, almost magical in its effect, that all the grandeur of the interior is gradually developed to the eye.

All this must be seen and felt, again and again, before the mind is able to endure, without a painful sensation of its own inadequate powers, the train of combined emotions with which it is assailed. Day after day, in long succession, may be spent in the sacred precincts of this imposing place, and yet the beholder cannot shake off the overwhelming influence of something very near akin to the supernatural, nor can he readily bring his mind to a full comprehension of all the varied beauties spread before it.

This superb cemetery is now the property of the British Government, and is kept in repair at their expense. In 1814, the Company, ever distinguished for their open-handed generosity, and the princely style in which every boon is granted, sanctioned the expenditure of a *lahk* of rupees (£10,000) for these repairs. The gardens are extensive and most tastefully laid out; they are let to natives at a large rent, for the sake of the fruit trees, more particularly the oranges, which are wonderfully abundant: some of the gateways, ornamented with tessellated mosaic-work, are very handsome buildings.

It is strange that in a work like "The Picture of India," esteemed to be very correct, and generally authentic throughout its historical matter, we should find so egregious a blunder as that of an assertion that Neur Jehan was the wife of Jehanghir, while any child in Agra could have corrected the author with the assurance that she was the wife of Shah Jehan, the son of Jehanghir, reputed to have been the most beautiful and accomplished woman of her age in Asia, and in reverence for whose illustrious beauty, virtues, and accomplishments, Shah Jehan erected this most elegant mausoleum over her remains.

It is stated by tradition (but I am not aware that mention is anywhere to be found of it in ancient history) that Shah Jehan, before his death, commenced a building upon a similar model, but of larger dimensions, on the opposite side of the Jumna; intending it as a cemetery for his own remains, which was to be connected with the Tajh Mahal by a bridge over the Jumna, but that he died soon after the task was commenced. It is difficult to conceive wherein this story had its rise, except in caprice or ignorance; for the fragments of foundation, pointed out in support of the assertion, have not on close inspection the remotest affinity to that of the Tajh Mahal; still stranger it is, that the tale should have gained such universal credence, and should have been confirmed in the works of many able writers.

A few years since, a wealthy native, relying for success upon Lord William Bentinck's notorious gleaning system, made overtures to Government for the purchase of the Tajh Mahal, for the sake of its materials, offering three *lakhs* of rupees (£30,000) for it; but, for once, his lordship's propensity to convert every thing into tangible treasure, yielded to his better judgment, and the offer was rejected.

Until I was about to quit Agra, I had been so engrossed by the Tajh Mahal, that I devoted every spare moment to wandering about it; for it gains more strongly upon the admiration the more it is studied; and it is an universal remark with all persons who have seen it, that they have been more and more delighted on each successive visit. Thus, when on the eve of departure, I found there were other relics also of great interest, which I had neglected, and a hasty inspection was all I could find time for. Among these, it will be sufficient to mention the tomb of Etimaun-ud-dowla, Shah Jehan's prime minister, situated in some beautiful old gardens upon the opposite bank of the Jumna. The exceeding beauties of this tomb, as described by other travellers, I was unable to discover; it is certainly very elaborately and most gorgeously ornamented with tessellated enamels of all colours, but the design of the building is altogether without grace, its proportions are clumsy, and the towers at each corner appear to have been surmounted with their cupolas, before they were carried to their proper height. Over the centre apartment is a square attic story, anything but elegant, roofed with a dome of white marble, more like a dish-cover than anything else to which I can compare it. Some of the screens in the windows and door-ways are very beautifully carved, and the sarcophagus within is also elegant; but these are its only attractions.

The Jumma Musjid should be mentioned, but it is now only deserving of notice on account of its picturesque beauty. It stands on the north-west side of the fort, and is now in a ruinous condition, broken, black, and overgrown with weeds and creeping plants. It has evidently been a handsome building, but could never have rivalled that of Dehli, either in size or beauty: it has long been disused for purposes of devotion.

I was occupied in the examination of all these magnificent monuments of the glory of Akburabad, about eighteen days, and sincerely did I lament the necessity of so speedy a departure; but I was constrained to go, and as a last farewell to the lovely Tajh Mahal, I visited it by moonlight, and spent two or three hours in wandering about its holy precincts. If so grand and imposing, as I have described it, in the broad daylight, let the reader conceive how thrilling is the solemnity by moonlight. It was Sunday night when I thus saw it, and on this day only, the fountains are kept playing, it being a favourite lounge of the society at Agra, when propriety forbids more open indulgence in amusements or parties of pleasure: the only disagreeables which intruded on my solemn delight, were glittering lights, and bursts of merriment, issuing from the Jummaut Kanu, on the south side.

CHAPTER XII.

THE JUMNA, FROM AGRA TO ALLAHABAD.

Below Agra, the banks of the Jumna are even more strikingly picturesque than they are to the westward of that place. In parts they are well-wooded and cultivated, but they more generally consist of high rugged land intersected with abrupt ravines and watercourses, the overhanging brows of which are clothed with shrubs and thorny jungul, seldom without a ruined tomb or temple to adorn them. But all this, which so greatly adds to the pleasure of the traveller, is also the chief source of his uneasiness.

On my route from Cawnpore to Merat, I had occasion to remark upon the impudent depredations of the thieves in the district of Ettaia; but I then believed the mischief to be confined only to the *choars*, a comparatively harmless race of robbers. Now, in approaching the ancient capital of that district, although not more than thirty-five miles distant from my former track, I found my boats beset nightly by a very different and much more troublesome enemy, the *dukhaits,* a race of marauders whose exploits, not in cunning, but in violence, far outshine those of the sheet-stealers. The ravines and broken ground of this district offer a temporary hiding-place to these villains, and, when pressed by pursuit, they easily escape unseen, into the neighbouring independent states. Gwalior, and the other territories still under native control, on that side of the river Chumbul, seem to be peopled almost entirely by these lawless tribes, and nothing short of the most vigorous measures on the part of our Government, and the establishment of a more efficient police, can protect our navigation on this part of the Jumna.

Night after night I was pestered with these wretches, and having but a small force, I thought it very probable that a more numerous body of assailants would attempt to force my boat. The plan of attack adopted by these men is truly ingenious, and, until discovered, was continually successful. A party of about six or seven, having fixed upon a particular boat, seek the shore, one by one, at different points, keeping themselves carefully concealed, if the night be light, beneath the underwood or behind the points of the rock. One or other of them, within hearing of the boat, then begins imitating either the cry of certain birds, or the noises of the deer, wild hog, jackals, wolves, leopards, or of any other animal they may think most likely to entice the occupant of the boat from his castle, in search of the supposed game. Should this be successful, the decoy then leads his dupe further from the intended spoil, retreating from point to point, as the pursuer advances, but at the same time keeping carefully out of sight; in the mean time, some of the party, acting as musicians or in some other character equally well adapted to the purpose, engage the attention of the domestics, while other accomplices slip into the boat unseen, and hastily do the work of spoliation.

This is their quietest way of working; but when hard pushed by want or inordinate covetousness, or tempted by an unusually rich booty, they do not hesitate to use more terrible means. It is a very common practice among them to set a boat on fire, when determined upon rifling it, and then, amid the alarm and confusion of the inmates, they seldom fail to reap a rich harvest. Notwithstanding the most careful watch, too, they frequently manage, after the manner of the *choars*, to find an entry to the boat or tent, without being perceived; but if engaged, they will be found a more formidable enemy than the former, being not only more dangerously armed, but also much more athletic in person, and more expert in the use of their weapons. I was tormented nightly by the cries of jackals and other beasts about my boat, which I have no hesitation in ascribing to the agency just mentioned, as in more than one instance, a man broke cover at the very spot whence the cries proceeded, upon my firing balls into the jungul or bushes.

I arrived at Ettaia, the old capital of the district so called, without any particular adventure, and I must certainly admit that my indemnity was most likely owing to the exertions and activity of the civil authorities along the banks, who had evidently made the most of their inefficient police; and this I more than once experienced, for my boat being small, and my retinue still smaller, I was constantly a lure to the *dukhaits*, who probably expected to find me an easy prey.

Ettaia is a populous town, standing on the east bank of the river, about seventy miles below Agra. The banks are here very high and precipitous, and the town, being built over several separate hillocks, has a picturesque effect, independent of its *ghâts* and temples. These, by-the-bye, which have chiefly an aspect towards the water, form a strange contrast among themselves; many of them are in complete ruin, and the rest appear to be still unfinished, there being none in the intermediate stages of their existence: shewing that the place, if neglected of late years, enjoys again the advantage of some public-spirited individuals, or at least such as are anxious to gain themselves a name by building new ones. A few of these temples and *serais* are worth visiting; in one of the latter, an old Brahmin amused me greatly by his assurance. I put a question to him relating to one of the temples; his reply was, "Give me a rupee."

"That is a modest request, my son," said I; "what more would you wish to have?"

"Modest! of course, it is modest," replied the Brahmin; "if I asked for a gold mohur, it would be very modest. Have not you, *Compni-ki noukur lōg* (servants of the Company), reduced me and all my family to beggary? Have you not filled your money-bags by shaking ours into them? and do you grudge me a rupee? My forefathers were worth hundreds of *lakhs* annually, and I am starving. Do you call it robbery that I should ask alms?"

"Why," said I, "you are the first black man I have ever heard cry out against the Company or the Company's servants; we are generally lauded to the skies, and are said to have enriched all who were formerly starving, by taking away from the superabundant hoards of the princes of the land, and distributing among the indigent."

"What, among the Brahmins? No. The priesthood are thrust out of their power. They were once the wealthiest in the country, and now they are all beggars. Will you give me a rupee or not?"

"No; most certainly not, you impudent fellow," replied I, as I walked away; and the man, calling after me, said, in derision; "here, you poverty-stricken *feringhi sahib*, come back, and I will make you a present of a thousand rupees. Do you see yonder beautiful *ghát*, that I am now building? in my coffers are treasures sufficient to have built it of gold instead of stone."

This town possesses the finest jail in the Upper Provinces, doubtless for the accommodation of the most distinguished thieves in the whole country. It is not simply that the jail itself is spacious, and well-suited to its purpose; it enjoys a much greater advantage in excellent superintendance and strict management, such as might be with great benefit extended to other establishments of the kind.

Fifteen miles below Ettaia, the river Chumbul falls into the Jumna. This river forms the boundary between the provinces of Ajhmere and Gwalior. In some parts of its course it is of great breadth, though shallow; in other places, it is pent up in a narrow channel, between numerous undulations and broken cliffs, which alternately form the character of its banks: it has no great volume of water; but, from the peculiarity just mentioned, the stream forms a very beautiful feature in the landscape, aided by a low range of hills, which here intersect the plain, and appear, for several miles, to turn the course of the river, but through which it ultimately forces a passage. This forms a strange contrast to the scenery upon the opposite side of the Jumna, the Doáb, which is one vast extent of plain, broken only by the accidental ravines already mentioned, from its western extremity, Allahabad point, unto the Sivalic range, below the Himálas, a distance nothing less than five hundred miles.

Below the junction of this stream with the Jumna, there is a long reef of limestone rock, which very much impedes the navigation of the river, and renders the passage very dangerous even to small craft; the flood through it, at this season of the year, being only sixty feet in breadth. Through this narrow channel, the current rushes with great violence, boiling and foaming over the submerged shoals, with a roar like that of a cataract; and here it is impossible to pass, if the wind be at all high; even in calm weather, and when the water is clearest, the passage is not unattended with danger.

During the Marquis of Wellesley's administration, it was the intention of Government to remove this obstacle from the bed of the river, and a few pioneers have been picking and scraping at it ever since, without doing much good. A month's vigorous application, with a few barrels of powder, and a skilful engineer to direct the work, would exterminate this dangerous obstruction. When I passed it, there were half-a-dozen pioneers upon the reef; two of them raking up loose stones, two bathing, and two smoking their *goor-goorris*.*

* The *goor-goorri*, Anglicè *hubble-bubble*, is the small *hookka*, smoked by the poorer classes of natives; it is upon the same principle as the *hookka* and *kullian*, the smoke being inhaled through water; it consists simply of a cocoa-

The neighbourhood of this impediment appears to be a rendezvous for thieves, robbers, and rascals of all denominations; possibly in consequence of the frequency of wrecks, or of boats run aground, or, otherwise, of their being detained on either side of the reef by high winds. This latter was my own case, for neither threats nor bribery would induce my *manji* to hazard the flood, until the wind abated; so I was under the necessity of coming to a stand-still in most suspicious ground. I selected the bank upon the Doáb side, as possibly under a more strict surveillance of the police; and there being moreover an old bungalow, and the remains of the pioneers' lines, which, although deserted, I fancied might awe the *dukhaits* into some respect for an officer's boat. The civil powers of the district evidently strive, by vigilance and rigour, to do their best in the maintenance of subordination, with the inadequate means allowed them. I found the village officials particularly civil and attentive; and, immediately upon my application to them, I was furnished with a couple

nut-shell, in which the water is held, and a small *chillaum* stuck upon a reed, or hollow stick, the smoke being drawn through a small orifice in the side of the nut-shell, most inconvenient of access to the mouths of any but natives, who practice it from childhood. It is not uncommon to see a little urchin, whose hands can hardly grasp it, puffing away at the *goor-goorri*, quite proud of the accomplishment.

of *tchokedars*, and I observed that several larger boats, employed in the conveyance of cotton and other articles of commerce, were similarly provided.

About midnight, I took my customary perambulation, to see that my sentries were watchful, and to reconnoitre the neighbouring ground. All was quiet, with the exception of the melancholy yelling and screaming of the jackals within the ravines, to which I listened at first suspiciously; but, believing myself to be an adept, I became satisfied that jackals alone disturbed the silence, and that no *dukhaits*, however accomplished, could imitate the cry to such perfection. I then returned to my boat and lay down to rest, but I had probably not been asleep half-an-hour, when I was aroused by a terrible *hurri-burree* upon the shore, and vociferous lamentations, with cries of "*Aug! Aug! Choar! Dukhait! Dukhait!*" Springing from my bed, I seized my gun, and sallied forth to ascertain the cause of alarm. The cotton-boats were all in flames, and by the light of the conflagration I could see men engaged in rescuing the bales from destruction. I instantly suspected the nature of the case, and hurried to the rescue, with four or five of my crew, leaving the rest to guard my own boat. So rapidly did the flames spread in the combustible materials, that in a few seconds the whole scene became illuminated with a red flood of light, which rendered all that was passing as distinct as if seen by day-light. A shout of triumph from the owners of the boats greeted my appearance among them: "*Uchha! Uchha!* here is a sahib, with his gun!"

"Where are the *dukhaits?* which are they?" I eagerly demanded of those around me.

"There, sir, there," cried one of the *manjis;* "those two young men going up the bank are *dukhaits;* they are carrying off our cotton. Shoot them, sir, shoot the pigs.* They have fired our boats, and behold we are ruined men: take their blood, sir, or we shall lose our revenge."

Instead of firing at the men, who were about two hundred yards distant, I gave chase, and speedily came up with the hindermost of them. He was perfectly naked and besmeared all over with oil, and not knowing exactly where to seize him, I ran stealthily behind him, which, being unshod, I effected without his being conscious of my presence. I heard the rascal tittering with

* *Soor-lōg,* "pig people," a term of inveterate hatred and contempt among the natives, both Hindus and Mussulmans.

inward merriment and delight at the success of their enterprize. At that moment, coming close up to him, my shadow crossed his path, and turning his fear-stricken countenance full upon me, he drop this bundle; and the next moment, before he had time to recover his surprise, I stuck my foot between his legs, and, by a vigorous thrust, cast him headlong over the bank into the hands of the boat's crew, who followed. The drop was about fifteen feet, sufficient to have broken his neck had he fallen with his head undermost; but the other end proving the heavier of the two, he came to the ground with no other injury than a sprained wrist.

Having seen him secured, I hastened in pursuit of the second; but he, having heard the shout of delight which followed the overthrow of his accomplice, dropt his booty and fled. I again gave chase, but the ground was strewed with thorns, and not being quite so indifferent to such trifles as are all black men, I was unwillingly compelled to halt. I then shouted to the fugitive to stand also, or that I would shoot at him, but he heeded me not, and having once again warned him with as little effect, I brought my gun to the present. He was at this moment about fifty yards distant, and taking a careful aim at his legs, I discharged an ounce of No. 4. at him: he dropt as though he had been shot through the head with a bullet, and my mind misgave me lest, by mistake, I had used the wrong barrel; for the second was charged with a ball. I ran to the spot where the man had fallen, but there being a deep crop of cotton, I was at first unable to see him; the moment I descried him, the villain sprung to his feet and fled again. My feet were much lacerated, but being determined not to let him escape, and unwilling to run the risk of killing him outright with the ball, I dashed after him at my best speed, and quickly overtaking him, I struck him with my fist a blow upon the ear, which rolled him over and over. He cried my mercy, and demanding his knife, I took him prisoner. This weapon was stuck through the knot of hair upon the top of his head, which, had it not been thus armed, would have been the only part about his person upon which a fair grasp could have been fixed. One of my servants, a fine spirited young Mussulman, by name Sahaduk, coming up at this moment, I bound the hands of the *dukhait*, and led him to my boat.

My shot had done no material damage to the

fellow; the greater part having lodged in his thighs, and where a few corns of shot were of little consequence. He had happened to look round, however, at the moment that I fired, and had received three of the shots in his face, two near the eye and the other in the end of his nose, which gave him great pain: these I extracted with a lancet, but for the others, I contented myself by prescribing cold water, and, if the man thought fit, an application of butter.

Our best efforts were unavailing in reducing the fire, and the only property saved besides that which was conveyed on shore, was by an act which I had great difficulty in persuading the *manji* to sanction. Jumping in at one end of the barge, while the other was enveloped in flame, I succeeded, with much labour, in chopping, with an axe, a hole in the bottom, so that the whole quickly sunk. I think I never saw anything more effective than this disappearance; it was the last boat burning, and as the waters closed over it, hissing and gurgling as they came in contact with their opposite element, the light was suddenly extinguished, and we stood in darkness; except such faint reflection as was cast by the embers of the other barges. Including this, which was damaged with the water, about one-fourth of the property might have been preserved.

The prisoners told us that their gang had consisted of ten men and three women, the latter being used in the conveyance of the booty from place to place, as the least liable to suspicion, and because, as women, they were gifted with more tact and a readier invention of subterfuge (I quote the man's words). The men were very tractable and wonderfully communicative, in the hope of impunity; and I heard from them many interesting anecdotes of their life and adventures. Neither of them, albeit they had practised their profession from childhood, had been in custody before, though their escapes had frequently been very narrow. I asked the man whom I had wounded, why he carried the knife in his hair?

"To protect it from the grasp of my pursuers," he replied.

"But, are you not fearful that, if you fall, it may cut you?"

"We do not fall;" said he.

"No? Why how was it when I struck you?"

"You knocked me down."

"Well, then, may not the knife cut you, when you are knocked down?"

"Oh, that comes but once or twice in a man's life," retorted the *dukhait,* "and, if it be his fate to die such a death, certainly the knife may stab him; but might it not do the same in his hand? Why do you shoot? your gun may burst. Whether a man walks, or rides, or sits in a boat, he will always find a danger peculiar to his situation. We are not gods; we shall die as our fate is cast for us."

Now, putting a little of the fatality aside, is there not some display of philosophy in the *dukhait's* argument?

The two captives begged hard for a release; but such was not my will. On the morrow, finding that the wind had abated, and being anxious not to lose the opportunity of getting through the bar, I was obliged to confide the prisoners to the charge of a *jemmadar,* to be taken to the magistrate of the district, sending with them a succinct detail in writing of the circumstances of the case.

These *dukhaits* are by no means the worst tenants of the junguls and ravines upon the banks of the Jumna; the whole country upon the west side is infested with bands of *thugs,* a race of robbers who, in the execution of their trade, seldom omit to make away with those whom they plunder;

indeed, murder forms a part of their religious ceremonies, or rather of their superstition, and every life taken they consider as a holy sacrifice to their goddess Kalli, who is the goddess of evil throughout all India, being esteemed the female image of Mahadeo or Siva. She is also known as Devi, and as Subhadra, and to her name may be imputed at least one half of the cold deliberate bloodshedding, so frequent among all classes of the Hindus. The *thugs* profess to worship no other deities, though they believe in their existence, and also in the existence of many forms and modifications of their favourite goddess, and in the being of inferior agents, such as ghosts and administering demons.

It is only within the last few years that the systematic annihilation of human life practised by these men has become known to us; much less were we prepared to believe that thousands of the native population in many districts were in the league, and in secret deliberation of means and opportunities for destroying their fellow-creatures.

I must here premise, lest I should lead the reader into error, that, with one or two exceptions, where the *thugs* were constrained for their own safety's sake to depart from the by-laws of their fraternity, the English have ever been exempt from their merciless practices, either because they are unfit for their religious offering, or because Europeans would be more surely missed, and more likely to bring the vengeance of the British power upon them.

The *thugs* dwell together in villages by gangs, or otherwise, having no fixed place of abode, they travel in companies from place to place in the execution of their bloody employment. Fifteen years since, the whole of the provinces on the western bank of the Jumna, including Agra, Ajhmere, and Gwalior, were so infested with these wretches, that they could not be passed in safety even by parties, who, for security sake, travelled in large bodies. Scores of human beings have, ere now, been swept off by this insidious mischief, when they believed themselves protected by their numbers from such violence; but, however careful the travellers, however exclusive the original projectors of the expedition may have been in the admittance of their members, the chances are, that one-third who set forth are themselves *thugs*, acting as decoys; and these being in secret communication with the rest of their gang, find it easy to appoint a fitting time and place for the execution of their damnable design, and the travellers fall an unsuspicious prey to the deep-laid scheme. Instances are mentioned in the annals of *thuggi*, wherein eighty and a hundred lives (I think I remember even a greater number being stated) have been thus, in a moment, extinguished, while the victims were yet relying for security upon their murderers.

There are two classes among these *thugs*; those who allure, and those who consummate the deed. The former are chosen from among the younger and less hardened of the band, and even women play a part in this act not unfrequently, possibly for the same reason which the *dukhait* avowed in the employment of them; the perpetrators of the murder are selected from the best experienced, and such as, by their acquired hardihood and savage inhumanity, will be likely to perform their office without flinching, and be prepared to defend themselves or lead a retreat in case of their being disturbed in the execution of their work.

The wide influence exerted by these wholesale destroyers of human life, through all classes of the natives of India, will not be credited until more fully and more indisputably published to the world. Those who were situated in the very centre of the scene, where this secret diabolical agency was in full play, were ignorant of the fact; and were, moreover, incredulous of it, even when brought to their notice. It does not exist merely in the provinces above mentioned, but in every corner and division of the land: numbers of all classes among the Hindus take part in it; and even Mussulmans, who have no plea of religious devotion to the evil goddess, have been known to connive at, and even assist in the inveiglement of the victims, though the sacrifice is never intrusted to their hands. It has lately been discovered, that the *thugs* have a code of signs or words, by which they recognize one another as masons are supposed to do; and it is probable, though of this I have no proof, that they are bound to assist one another in emergency: that they do so, we have evidence, in instances where the parties were strangers to each other, but that any obligation exists, I believe, has not been ascertained.

They have distinct ranks and stations among themselves, to which officers are appointed according to the proficiency and tact displayed; and these honours are avowedly sought by the junior members as a post of distinction, and for the sake of an increased share in the booty. A certain number of the candidates for these offices accompany the most skilful, to gain instruction; and when an opportunity offers, without danger to the gang, a subject is intrusted to their operation. Timidity or misgiving having been once noticed in any individual, he is at once debarred all chance of advancement, and thenceforth he is only permitted to perform the part of a decoy.

We shall doubtless be soon made familiar with all the habits and practices of these men, for the government have taken most vigorous measures for exterminating the evil, and a highly judicious selection of instruments has been made. Jubbulpore has been constituted the head quarters of an establishment for the suppression of the system, and the superintendance of it has been entrusted to the Honourable F. Shore, who by his intrepidity and love of enterprize, and his intimate knowledge of the habits and manners and customs of all classes of the natives, is, perhaps, (I do not wish to draw an invidious distinction) the most fitting individual for such a service, who could have been chosen; and from his able pen it is not unreasonable to expect disclosures which others are unable to afford. These active steps of the government have already intimidated the *thugs* into a show of disruption, and, in a very few years, the system must be altogether abolished.

Thousands have been apprehended and hundreds have been executed, besides almost as many who have turned king's evidence; and, from the confessions of these, facts and deeds of horror have been elicited, which surpass our most exaggerated romances of the bloodthirsty cabals of monsters and demons. From time immemorial, from the earliest traditions of the *thugs* themselves, human blood has not ceased to flow over the altars of the insatiate Kalli.

Their methods of entrapping the victims are various; but the operation of despatching them is, with few exceptions, that of strangling, and both are performed with wonderful artifice and unerring certainty. No time or pains are spared in first gaining the confidence and esteem of the parties devoted to destruction. Months are frequently expended in this, which being at last fully and unreservedly accomplished, an opportunity is waited for, when the victim, being about to travel with treasure, is glad to accept of the escort and protection, not only of his devoted friend, but also of third parties, introduced by the latter as tried worthies, travelling the same road: and thus, of those who constitute the expedition, one half will very possibly be *thugs*. All things being prepared, a scout is sent forward to the rest of the gang, with information of the route, the strength of the traveller's party, and possibly with notice of the amount of booty. Immediately on receipt of this intelligence, the chiefs and directors of the ceremonies perform certain rites and incantations by which the will of Kalli is ascertained, her commands being signified by certain signs and omens, in which long experience only can make them expert. These prognostications are drawn principally from the winds and the habits of birds and beasts; certain accidents and irregularities in these being considered as ominous of evil; whereas, if there be no departure from the usual course of their observations, a favourable result is anticipated for their undertaking. Besides these, the cries of certain birds or animals at particular times, or the appearance and disappearance of them, are also received as signs portending good or evil; and by these they are decided in the execution or abandonment of their purpose. Should the omen be inauspicious, there is nothing which would prevail upon them, and no treasure which would tempt them, to undertake the deed; and on the other hand, if favourable deductions be drawn from the prognostics, they would suffer no difficulties to deter them from the attempt, unless, indeed, their numbers be less than double those of the party to be sacrificed; for, in such a case, they will on no account essay an attack: unless two of their own party can be mustered for every one of their intended victims, they invariably forego their intentions until the requisite number can be collected.

A rendezvous having been appointed in the most retired spot along the road, either in a dense jungul remote from towns, or at the ford of some stream, a pretext for delay is readily found by the betraying *thugs*, and while the travellers are probably resting themselves, or eating their *suttoo*,* they are suddenly seized by their hands; at the same moment a noose, formed of the *kummurbund* (waist-cloth), is cast about their necks, and before they have recovered their surprise, they are at the last gasp. If more than a few are thus given over

* *Suttoo*, a hasty meal taken by the Hindus, consisting of coarse flour kneaded to a dough, and in that state eaten without being cooked. Having wrought it to the proper consistency, they roll it into lumps about the size and shape of a sausage, and one of these delicate morsels forms a mouthful. Pure water, or water even if it be not very pure, forms the beverage to this dainty fare.

to destruction, a signal from the chief ensures a simultaneous attack upon the whole, so that resistance is out of the question, the assailants being two to one upon the surprised travellers. The moment life is extinct, the persons are searched and their treasure and baggage secured; after which, the bodies are carefully buried at a great depth below the surface of the earth, in order that the effluvia from decomposition may not betray them. If only one or two have been sacrificed, it is deemed sufficient to cast them into a well, and ere they may be discovered, the perpetrators will probably be many miles from the scene, or else so disguised as to cut off all clue to their identity.

It was a general opinion throughout India, for many years, that the *thugs* never deviated from the plan of strangling here described; but latterly, several instances of the contrary have been brought to light. It is not uncommon for them to allure their victim, if he be a solitary one, to the brink of a well, and suddenly to cast him headlong into it; in other cases, they have been known to strike with a dagger or some sharp-edged weapon, particularly when the traveller has been sleeping; at other times, they have had recourse to a more clumsy method, that of hurling their dupes over precipices, or throwing them from a boat to drown them in the river. These departures from their usual *modus operandi*, are I believe unwillingly entered upon, or only when necessity urges them for their own safety sake; they are at all times considered indicative of evil fortune. The chief care of the gang, after the consummation of their enterprise, is to share the booty and disperse, without loss of time, into districts where they may be free from pursuit, or protected if discovered; this they do, even if no investigation or suspicion should be moved.

The whole of these facts related of the existence and manners and customs of the *thugs*, including the lowest prostration of humanity which they exhibit, are subjects affording ample scope for the investigations of the metaphysician and the philosopher; here is more filth from the sink of superstition than we can find in any other record of savage depravity; even cannibalism falls short of the diabolical influence which in *thuggi* has spread over thousands of square miles, and among all ranks and sects. But the moral deductions and analysis of the case I leave to the more profound,

while I hasten to escape out of these regions of murder and rapine.*

A few miles from this barrier stands the town of Butteesa, chiefly remarkable for the exceeding beauty of the scenery around it, and the broad lake-like appearance of the river, as it meanders quietly through its precipitous banks. I can recal no spot more beautiful than this in my wanderings through India: it has none of the grandeur of the Himálas, but it has a homely charm in its stillness and repose, which is more fascinating, though less striking.

About a hundred and sixty miles below Agra, I arrived at the town of Kalpi, a place of considerable commerce, more especially as a mart for cotton. The town is prettily situated upon the eminences left by a number of ravines, which are yearly washed deeper and deeper by the floods

* Since writing the above, a long article has appeared in the Edinburgh Review (No. CXXX.) Jan. 1837, consisting principally of extracts from official reports, which give a much more detailed and perfect account of all the various habits and religious ceremonies, &c. of the *thugs*, than has ever before been published; indeed, the facts therein displayed are for the most part perfectly new to me, and are equally unknown to the majority of Anglo-Indian society. Of the authenticity of these papers there can be no doubt; they are official documents printed by the Government in Calcutta, for the information of their officers. In consequence of the article here referred to, I have thought it advisable to expunge from my work many passages which, if printed, would have been deemed a piracy, though written many months before the appearance of the review.

during the monsoon. Upon the principal height, is an imperfect attempt at something like a fortress; but although the position is naturally a strong one, the fortifications are so badly designed, that a handful of British soldiers would take it with little difficulty. In a ravine below this fort, or rather upon the side of the cliff, is a beautiful little temple, dedicated to Krishna, which by its own form, and the romantic beauty of its position, must catch the eye and admiration of all passengers up and down the Jumna. From the old *jogi* whom I found within this temple, I obtained two or three idols, which he assured me had been consecrated by the god himself, at the time of his sojourn upon earth; but unfortunately, the brass bears evidence of the file and graver certainly within twenty years.

It was at Kalpi, in 1765, that a memorable action was fought between the English, under General Carnac, and a large army of the Maharhattas, mercenaries in the pay of Suja-ud-dowla. This was the first time that our troops had encountered the Maharhattas, and their complete success did honour to their arms, and to the general who conducted them. After an obstinate resistance, and a bloody loss on the part of the

Maharhattas, the English put the enemy to the rout, and drove them in precipitation across the Jumna into the Doáb.

The next place at which I stopped was Hummiapore, a small civil station on the west bank; but here I found no inducement to remain longer than to take in a fresh stock of provisions. I had only got a day's journey beyond this place, however, when I met with an adventure which detained me several days upon a sand bank, in rather an uncomfortable condition, so that I have cause to remember the locality with little affection.

On the evening in question, I had secured my boat beside a low flat of sand, overlooked by high projecting cliffs; which, owing to their ravines, and the jungul about them, I looked upon as a suspicious neighbourhood, as cover for *duk-haits, choars, thugs*, and others, from some of whom I anticipated molestation. I had been shooting all day, and arrived at my boats very much fatigued. After dinner, I retired early to rest, having given my gun to a servant to clean and to reload; with directions for having it put in its usual place, so that I might lay my hand upon it in case of necessity. I then cautioned my watchmen to be especially guarded, and ordering two or three of my servants to sleep in the head of the boat, I went to my bed, with a comfortable assurance of being continually awoke throughout the night, either by false alarms or by an attack.

Shortly before midnight, I was awoke by a strong sense of suffocation and a smell of fire, and instinctively guessing the cause, almost before my eyes were open, I became aware that my boat was burning. I started from my bed in great alarm, and found the front and one side of the grass-hut in which I lay, completely enveloped in flames: the heat was intense, and the smoke so thick that I could scarcely breathe. I saw my peril; my clothes were of the most readily inflammable materials, and the only egress was already occupied by the flames. The coils of black blankets, in which the servants slept, lay in the fore-part of the boat, and I rushed to awaken the men, but found the blankets empty; the servants were not there; and yet there was no alarm, no confusion outside; the distant sounds of song and music were the only signs of life to be heard. My thoughts reverted at once to the *dukhaits*, and I could only conceive that the servants had gone in pursuit of them without having awoke me: my gun lay on the deck, the barrels here, the stock there, and the locks in different places. I seized my pistols, and then stripping myself of my most combustible garments, I wrapped the upper part of my person in a blanket, and pulling a fur-cap over my head, I rushed against the burning mat which served for the door; it instantly gave way, and with scarcely any injury from the fire, I sprung a-shore. Not a creature was to be seen but the two goats picketted to a stake, looking upon the blazing boat with wonderful resignation. The reflection from a fire in a *tōp* of trees near, from whence the sounds of music and revelry proceeded, explained the absence of my slaves.

Not a moment was to be lost; in a very few minutes, my little property would have been all consumed. I shouted at the top of my voice, "*Aug! Aug!*" "Fire! Fire!" the music ceased for a moment, and then recommenced. I now resorted to my pistol to recall my servants, and just as I was about to fire, I caught sight of the large *gumla* (earthen jar, containing about eighteen gallons) filled with water, and which was upon the roof, lashed to the mast. I levelled my pistol at it and fired; but the ball, instead of smashing it, passed clean through it, and only allowed the water to escape by two small orifices in useless quantities: I therefore seized a bamboo and broke the jar in pieces, and this checked the flames for a few seconds; but the boat was of too combustible materials to be thus easily extinguished.

My servants now came running to my assistance, though at first they were so petrified with alarm that they could render me no service. They found me standing up to my elbows in the cold river, throwing the water upon the flames with a large piece of the broken jar. I directed the servants to pull down as much of the burning roof and sides of the boat as they could, but finding them backward in facing the flames, I was obliged to set them the example myself; still they did not go earnestly to work, and I was obliged to suspend my own operations in order to quicken theirs by compulsion. A small bamboo about the thickness of my thumb quickly brought them to an active exercise of their duties, and before the flames had reached the property in the hold, they were arrested and extinguished. One man only exerted himself with spirit; this was

Sahaduk, the young Mussulman before mentioned.

The exertion, the excitement, and the alarm, to which I had been subject, together with my exposure in the cold water, brought on a fit of shivering and exhaustion, which prevented my taking any part in the labour of restoring things to something like order. Everything was in a most uncomfortable state; my clothes and nearly all the contents of the boxes on deck being saturated with water, and begrimed with soot and ashes. After considerable delay, clean raiment was provided, and rolling myself up in a blanket, I lay down upon the ground to sleep, having a couple of mats put over me in the form of a roof to protect me from the night dews, which are highly injurious to the health, and are the cause of more agues and other diseases than the most trying exposure to the sun. Upon this sand-bank I was obliged to remain two or three days to refit; but the game being abundant, I had no lack of amusement.

Three days' sail below Hummiapore I came to a little village, called Mháo, the sixth or seventh of its name within the district of Allahabad. It is remarkable for two isolated hills upon the

Doáb side of the river jutting into the middle of the stream. These hills are of red sand-stone, which is quarried by some European who has a house here; they abound in deep caverns and curious recesses, many of which I explored, but without making any discoveries, and without being able to gain access to that which particularly excited my curiosity. In the face of an abrupt rocky precipice, a little arched window like a pigeon hole was cut, within which there was apparently an apartment of some kind; its height from the nearest flat below it, was about forty feet, and it was some ten or twelve feet from the brow of the steep above it. I sought on all sides for an entrance to this place, but without success, and being determined to explore it if possible, I sent off a servant to the boat for a rope, with the intention of lowering myself from the crest of the precipice to the window. From this foolish risk I was, however, deterred by the approach of a terrible storm, which drove me for shelter to the house already mentioned; and in my scramble over the summit of the second hill, I fell in with the remains of an old Brahminical temple, which by the massive and rude proportions of the materials strewed about, and the barbarous

ISOLATED ROCK OF BARAUL.

attempts at sculpture, were apparently of great antiquity. I put one of the young gods in my shooting coat pocket, and ultimately carried him captive with me into England.

Another day's sail brought me to a village called Daraol, opposite to which, in the very centre of the river, is a curious tower of rocks, crowned with a cupola of free-stone in perfect repair. This conical island is a very picturesque feature in the landscape, more particularly on the east-side, the rocks being piled one above the other, with a regularity which looks more like the work of man than of nature, though in reality they are too stupendous to have been raised by his arm. It has either been washed away from the main land by the force of the current, or else quarried away by the stone diggers, who are still at work upon the banks.

Landing in my little wherry on the rocks at the bottom of the island, I fell in with an old friend whom I had known in the Himálas, he also being on his way to the Presidency; I proposed that we should attempt an ascent of the rock, though there was no staircase visible, neither did the steep rocks at first appear practicable. A closer inspection, however, discovered to us a rough sort of stair hewn out of the solid rock, here and there assisted by the natural projections, and up this we had little difficulty in making our way until within a few feet of the summit; here the ascent became very difficult, requiring a quick eye, a steady head, and a sure foot, and therefore my friend preferred remaining where he was, until I should discover something worthy of the risk. This, however, I did not fall in with ; there was nothing in the cupola to reward me ; it was of recent date, and had a small marble inscription in Persian, recording the name of him who built it ; nor was there anything particularly romantic in the scenery.

While I was trying to decipher the inscription, I was startled by the discharge of a gun immediately below me, and the shot entering the vaulted roof of the cupola fell all around me, the report awaking echoes which reverberated until the whole place shook again. The discharge was from Sahaduk's match-lock in the boat below ; but instead of bringing down the pigeon it brought down an immense mass of rock, tumbling and bounding from the summit, which dashed into the water, not an oar's length from my boat, half filling her with the splash it created. The whole place continued to vibrate so long and so forcibly, that I really thought it would have come headlong down, and I hastened to get me fairly out of so awkward a chance : the descent, however, I found much more difficult, and I was all the happier when I found myself safely at the bottom.

My next halting place was Allahabad, which stands at the confluence of the Jumna and Ganges, and which the reader will remember, that we visited in our route up the country ; and now as my voyage all the way to Calcutta will be over precisely the same course which I then pursued, I will make no apology to the reader for hastening forward.

CHAPTER XIII.

THE GANGES.—DINAPORE.

RETURN TO CALCUTTA.

I FELL in with no adventure worthy of notice until my arrival at Dinapore.

Having been detained by contrary winds after quitting Ghazipore, I did not reach this place until reduced to my last egg, and the only remaining pint of flour; and for the purpose of laying in a fresh supply, I found myself compelled to put in for a few hours. This was unfortunate, for in the interim a foul wind sprung up, and blew so violently as to prevent me from getting away. To this I impatiently submitted, for, alas! there was no remedy. Instead of moderating towards evening, as I had hoped it might, the fury of the wind increased, and the appearance of the weather was so suspicious that I thought it advisable to haul my little wherry high and dry upon the shore.

At nine o'clock, it blew a heavy gale from the south-west, which in the course of an hour or two had wrecked every boat upon the leeward side, within sight of Dinapore; but I was not alarmed about my own boat, believing it to be protected from Eolus' utmost fury by a high projecting cliff, under which I had brought-to: the water, however, was running very high, and in my little nut-shell of a boat I was tossed about with a violence ten times worse than any thing which I remember to have experienced at sea; but quieting myself with the most philosophic maxim, that a soldier should never be discomfited by the ups and downs of life, I contented myself with a frugal cold meal, (cooking was out of the question,) and lay down to rest.

At ēleven o'clock, I was awoke by the violent pitching and tossing of the boat, which was rendered the more disagreeable by a nasty short cross kind of jerk, making it by no means an easy matter for me to keep my position in bed. Every now and then, moreover, the boat came thump against the bank, with a shock which carried every thing away, and which I saw would inevitably knock her to pieces very quickly. I jumped out of bed, and ran on deck to look to her fastening, and if possible to concert measures with the *manji* for her greater safety. The wind was roaring tremendously, exceeding in violence any hurricane which I can remember to have witnessed; the lightning, too, was fearful, and the waves had risen to a height which I could not have deemed possible upon a body of water so small, when compared to the ocean. I found my crew all busily engaged, notwithstanding the deluge of rain which poured down upon them, in endeavours to secure the boat, which threatened every moment to carry away the hawsers. Two of the upper planks of the hull had been stove in, and the *luggis* (bamboos thrust out to ease the boat off the bank) had all been smashed, so that she was knocked about completely at the tender mercy of the winds and waves.

The storm continued still to increase, and seeing that there was little chance of saving the boat, I determined to remove as much of my property as possible on shore. My first labour was to fix a strong warp to the boat's timber-head, and having had that well secured on shore, so as to keep her bows towards the bank on which she was continually striking, in defiance of our most strenuous effort to keep her off, I then called to the *manji* and four of the *dandis*, and ordered them to open the deck and take out my baggage, box by box. The *manji* remonstrated strongly against this, declaring that the boat was not in the least danger; and it was only with great difficulty and the application of personal chastisement, that I at last effected my object: the fact was, that the man wanted my valuable cargo to act as ballast in keeping his boat steady; so that even after I had forced the men to their work, they did it with an ill grace, and once purposely dropt a box into the water. But a repetition of this I effectually checked, by awarding as a punishment to the next who should be guilty of such an offence, that he should be lashed to the boat, and run the chance of sinking or swimming with it.

The boat had repeatedly struck upon a point of rock, with great force, and I saw that she must inevitably be a wreck in a very few minutes; the greater part of my property had been conveyed on shore, and I was hastily collecting a few small articles of value, which being in daily use were lying about in all directions; when, suddenly, a lurch more violent than the rest, threw the boat broadside-on upon the rocks: she instantly stove in, and I heard the waters gurgling through her bottom. I rushed on deck, and was about to spring ashore, when a flash of lightning showed me that the boat had recoiled, and that the leap was too much for me. She was now settling fast, but being checked by the warp, she again most fortunately neared the bank; I watched my opportunity, and with a vigorous leap, undertaken in right good earnest, I cleared the gulf and alighted on the bank; but as ill luck would have it, the lightning being too fitful to allow me any certain choice of ground, I jumped upon a greasy, slippery, sloping spot, and thus cheated of my expected footing, my heels flew up and I fell backward into the rushing waters; just as th boat settled down by the head, as a sailor would say, and disappeared, leaving only her mast above water to note the spot.

The current was running violently, and swept me away down the stream; but I ran no risk, being a strong swimmer, if I could make the shore before rounding the projection before-mentioned; this I succeeded in, though not till I was almost benumbed by the intense coldness of the water. When I returned to the place where the boat had been, I found no trace of her, the waves were dashing over her late position, and here and there were cast aloft a few old planks, the only remnants of my habitation. The *dandis* and servants who saw my exit from the scene, were too well accustomed to see me in the water to be under any apprehension on my account; but had I not been an expert swimmer, there would have been little risk of life, for the *dandis* being almost amphibious, would have plunged in to the rescue: as it was, they contented themselves by deputing one servant to walk down and meet me when I landed, to ask if I wanted assistance. I came suddenly upon the whole posse, as they squatted on the bank, smoking their *goor-goorris:* it was too dark for them to see me, until I was revealed to them by a flash of lightning, and I overheard one of them saying, (as nearly as English will come to the Hindostani idiom,) "*Wa! wa!* the Sahib is in for a wet jacket and a supper of cold water to-night; but what does it signify? the *sahib lōg* don't care either for fire or water, and would submit to be either burnt or drowned, if they can have a good reason given them why it should be so."

All my goods and chattels which had been saved from the wreck, I found upon the bank, exposed to the deluge which was falling; by paying a small sum, I managed to obtain cover for them in a carpenter's hut; but the man being a Brahmin, and having his family in the only apartment, I could not myself have shelter beneath his roof. The officers of my own corps were absent from the station during the practice-season, and I was unwilling to seek the hospitality of strangers at that late hour, and in such pitiable trim; moreover, I was at a considerable distance from the officers' quarters, and I therefore decided upon seeking shelter in the bazaar. A small house, built in the European style, but in great disrepair and neglect, had attracted my notice the previous evening, while I for a moment considered the chance of such a position as the present. To this hovel I now directed my steps, and commenced thundering hand and foot at the door, being impatient for admittance, for I was benumbed with the wet and wind, and under such circumstances my cheroot was but cold comfort. While I was yet weighing in my mind the expedience or impropriety of forcing an entrance, an European, with a lantern in his hand, passed along the road; and to him I applied for a lodging. He was particularly civil and attentive, regretted that he could not take me under his own roof, in consequence of repairs and a very large family; but he informed me that the little house before me was the habitation of the bazaar serjeant, an old pensioner, who would be happy to give me a room.

The man in question now made his appearance at the door, in answer to my continued summons. I made little apology for my intrusion; indeed, none was necessary, for the old soldier became at once almost too anxious to befriend me, offering me his own bed and all sorts of like comforts. But the friend whom I had picked up without came to my assistance, and declined all these delights in my name, assuring me that I should have every convenience sent me from his house, including a bed, dry raiment and a supper. This kindness I declined, except the offer of a change of apparel, and a dry blanket. The man took his leave, and having selected the room least open to the elements without, I employed myself in making a blazing fire upon the plaister floor, without a thought upon the inconvenience of smoke, *minus* a chimney. Here I was occupied drying and warming myself, when a *khidmutgar* made his appearance with a covered tray, containing tea, bread and butter, eggs, ham and the like, with all the necessary condiments and appurtenances for a comfortable meal, not forgetting a flask of *Vieux*

Cognac, and a bundle of cigars: these came with the *Mem-sahib-ki salâam;* and in rear came a bearer, ushering in a bed complete with clean sheets, clean blankets, clean quilt, clean dressing gown, clean shoes, clean nightcap, and clean everything, kept dry by an oil-skin pall spread over them. The white table cloth was spread upon the floor, and, having no chair, I sat upon my pistol-case to enjoy this most comfortable meal. I quickly cleared the board, well stocked as it was, and then lighting my cigar, I lay down to rest, delighting myself with reflection upon the good fortune which had turned up in my favour since the loss of my boat; and here I listened with no small degree of pleasure to the roaring of the blast, and the pelting of the rain without.

The next morning, I went forth to enquire for another boat, but there was little chance of my obtaining one, for all the small boats within sight of Dinapore, amounting in all to about forty, had shared the fate of my own; the remains of wrecks cast upon the sand were visible on all sides, and the weather was by no means moderating. The little iron steamer, the "George Swinton," anchored off the town, was rolling so violently, that even old sailors, of whom there were several looking on, expected to see her *turn a turtle* (in nautical phraseology) every moment.

Three days was I weather-bound by the continuance of the gale; but, on the fourth day, the weather broke up, and then several small boats put in to refit, and one of these I secured, though it took me three days more to get fairly afloat; and during this time, I still continued the guest of the old pensioner, receiving from time to time very kind attention from my other friend, whom I found to be a Conductor of Ordnance. The services of both were warmly tendered and courteously received; and the contact with these my inferiors in station, to which I had been subjected at first by accident, and afterwards voluntarily, I had no cause to regret; on the contrary, I shall always remember their kindness with gratitude.

Before quitting Dinapore I went on board the "George Swinton," one of the little iron steamboats built and sent from England by the Company, for the navigation of the Ganges. I could not but admire the beautiful finish of the works and machinery of these miniature engines: everything was fitted-up in excellent style, being kept free from flaw or stain, and carefully polished. The commander was particularly polite, and explained to me the use and application of the machinery, in a manner which shewed him to be well-acquainted with the subject and his duty. There are now four or five of these little boats upon the Ganges, plying between Calcutta and Allahabad. I forget their exact burden, but they are very small and being flats draw very little water, (if I remember right, only a few inches more than two feet,) and yet they are continually carrying away their paddles, and sticking upon the innumerable shoals and sand-banks which impede the navigation during the dry season. These boats are of very great advantage, both in convenience and economy, to the Government, for the conveyance of treasure and stores; a comparatively small guard of *Sipáhis* being sufficient, and there being of course no necessity for tents or marching establishments. They are also used as tugs to accommodation-barges fitted-up expressly for passengers; but unfortunately the fares are fixed at too high a rate to be serviceable to any, save the more wealthy or more extravagant of travellers. The same remark is equally applicable to the conveyance of baggage or parcels. A reduction of the rates would not only add very greatly to the convenience of the community, but it would also secure a larger emolument, by an increase of numbers. I was myself deterred, as were also three or four of my friends, from taking my passage on board the boat at Allahabad, in consequence of the heavy demand.

Some of my servants on board had never before seen such a thing as a steamer, and their wonder and admiration were infinite, as was their curiosity, to have explained to them the means by which the *augun-jehaz* (fire-ship) was made to go against the stream of the mighty *Gunga*, without sail or paddle. This I endeavoured, as well as I could, to explain; and I further told them of steam-carriages, and also of balloons.

"Nay, sir; now you are laughing at your slaves;" replied Sahaduk, "we are credulous; it is our nature; but we are not without reason. That the *augun-jehaz* goes by steam we have proof, and it is therefore easy to believe that a carriage may be moved in the same manner; but when you tell us of a boat flying in the air, we know that you do but make sport of our credulity."

Only a few days subsequently to this conversation, on my arrival in Calcutta, Sahaduk and his companions had an opportunity of witnessing the ascent of Mr. Robinson, the aeronaut. Sahaduk came to me and said; "Sir, you are right; the English are, indeed, gods; we have nothing in India which can be compared to this. Can your countrymen survive at the bottom of the sea?" I told him of the diving-bell, and his disbelief was again beginning to display itself when suddenly he exclaimed—"No; if you can fly in the heavens like an eagle, surely you may live in the sea. You are gods." When steamers first appeared in India, the inhabitants flocked in thousands to the bank of the river to worship them and implore mercy, believing them to be the engines of a supernatural creation. In how very few years will steamers and balloons be familiar to all classes of the natives, from the highest points of navigation on the Ganges and Jumna to Cape Comorin!

From Dinapore I made a rapid passage to Calcutta, meeting with no incident particularly worthy of record upon my route; and having now come back to the spot from whence I set forth upon my peregrinations through the Bengal Presidency, it is full time that I should make my *saláam.*

In looking back upon any lapsed portion of our existence, which has been spent in scenes foreign to our early culture, more particularly if any large tract of country has been travelled over, we cannot divest ourselves of the belief that we have met with a larger share both of good and evil, than would have fallen to our lot upon our native ground: the mind rests upon a scene of mingled pain and pleasure, which we persuade ourselves is more strongly chequered with light and shade than the same space could have been under other circumstances; and it is the bent of our nature to register in our hearts the occurrence of evil and misfortune, and to set too small store by the comforts and blessings which have been unceasingly dispensed to us. It is our disposition to look upon happiness as our right, and to feel that an infringement is committed upon our immunities, whenever, even by our own folly or imprudence, our gratifications may be suspended, or when any more positive calamities may beset us. Throughout the foregoing narrative I have endeavoured, as far as was consistent with the truth of my pictures, to turn the bright side of the mirror upon the subject.

On the 10th of April 1836, within a month of my return to the Presidency, the good ship Hibernia, in which I embarked for Old England, shook out her "Blue Peter," and in a few short hours, I was riding over a foaming sea, with a spanking fair wind, homeward-bound.

PLURIS EST OCULATUS TESTIS UNUS QUAM AURITI DECEM.

Plautus.

THE END.

Published by

Facsimile Publisher
Ashok Vihar, Delhi-110052 (India)
Website: www.facsimilepublisher.com

Distributed by

GYAN

Gyan Books Pvt. Ltd.
5, Ansari Road, Daryaganj, New Delhi-110002 (India)
E-mail: books@gyanbooks.com, Website: www.gyanbooks.com

2 222000 000608